Connecting The Wire

Texas Film and Media Studies Series
Thomas Schatz, Editor

{ STANLEY CORKIN }

Connecting The Wire

RACE, SPACE, AND POSTINDUSTRIAL BALTIMORE

University of Texas Press AUSTIN

For Jana, Roxie, and Jesse, who make all things possible

Printed in the United States of America
First edition, 2017

Requests for permission to reproduce material from this work should be sent to:

Permissions
University of Texas Press
P.O. Box 7819
Austin, TX 78713-7819
http://utpress.utexas.edu/index.php/rp-form

♾ The paper used in this book meets the minimum requirements of ANSI/NISO Z39.48-1992 (R1997) (Permanence of Paper).

LIBRARY OF CONGRESS CATALOGING-IN-PUBLICATION DATA

Names: Corkin, Stanley, author.
Title: Connecting The Wire : race, space, and postindustrial Baltimore / Stanley Corkin.
Series: Texas film and media studies series
Description: First edition. Austin : University of Texas Press, 2017. Includes bibliographical references and index.
Identifiers: LCCN 2016023739 (print) LCCN 2016024711 (ebook)
ISBN 9781477311769 (cloth : alk. paper)
ISBN 9781477311776 (pbk. : alk. paper)
ISBN 9781477311783 (library e-book)
ISBN 9781477311790 (non-library e-book)
Subjects: LCSH: Wire (Television program) | Television programs—United States—History and criticism. Baltimore (Md.)—Drama. Race relations on television. Social classes on television. Television programs—Social aspects.
Classification: LCC PN1992.77.W53 C665 2017 (print) LCC PN1992.77.W53 (ebook)
DDC 791.45/72—dc23
LC record available at https://lccn.loc.gov/2016023739

doi:10.7560/311769

Contents

Acknowledgments

This project began some years ago—who can say exactly what day, but likely in 2010—when my daughter, Roxanne, told me about this show that "she thought I would like." Being a thrifty sort, I ordered the disks from the library and made sure I maintained the correct sequence of seasons and episodes. As the disks came in, they resulted in late nights and darkened days of binge-watching.

As I finished my previous book, *Starring New York: Filming the Grime and Glamour of the Long 1970s* (Oxford, 2011), and thought of a related urban project, a book about *The Wire* came to mind. In what has been a far slower process (isn't it always?) than I might have anticipated, I have benefitted from the assistance and advice of many. Jonathan Auerbach read an early version and provided insights that aided the project in its development, as did my friend Patrick O'Keeffe, who provided encouragement and advice along the way. Trysh Travis, who founded and edited "Points: The Blog of the Alcohol & Drugs History Society" blog, devoted several guest posts to *The Wire*. My contribution to that blog, with her able critique, became a version of a portion of chapter 4. I would also like to thank my Cincinnati colleagues and students for their interest and support: the students in my graduate seminar in the English department and those who attended my various presentations. David Stradling and the late Zane Miller—fellow urbanists—read an early version of the prospectus and provided helpful comments. My cinema studies cohort, particularly Mark Shiel, Kirk Boyle, Erica Stein, and Josh Gleich were also instrumental in improving my study. Tom Schatz has been everything an author can wish for in a series editor, providing encouragement and editing acuity throughout the development and fruition of the project. Jim Burr at the University of Texas Press has also provided important support and advice.

I would also like to thank the Taft Research Center at the University of Cincinnati, and its current director, Adrian Parr for research leave and travel funds that made it possible to enhance and complete this project. My partners in the development of the Center for Film and Media Studies at the University Cincinnati, Michael Gott and Todd Herzog, have provided an institutional support system that I have missed for almost three decades. In addition I would like to thank Peter and Buck Niehoff for their support of my scholarship and the film studies program at Cincinnati. Peter, through his unflagging enthusiasm for film and historical scholarship has helped me maintain an (almost) youthful excitement for the often arduous task of revision and reminded me of many ideas and studies I thought I had forgotten.

Most importantly, I thank Jana Braziel, who has been a means of support, love, and inspiration in all phases of this project. I could not imagine a better collaboration or collaborator. Her gifts have significantly enhanced my more modest attributes.

Connecting The Wire

Introduction

The Wire has been widely acclaimed as one of the best television shows ever produced.[1] The HBO series, which ran from 2002 to 2008, provides a highly articulate vision of life among the underclass—poor African Americans, struggling working-class whites, the homeless—in a city, Baltimore, that is pictured as having seen better days. It also captures those groups' relationships with the police, the city bureaucracy, and a group of city real estate developers who benefit from their connections with the political class.

It constitutes something of a watershed in television history—along with its HBO predecessors *The Sopranos* (1999–2007), *Oz* (1997–2003), and even *Sex and the City* (1998–2004)—and in the history of mass culture. Its creator and showrunner, David Simon, employs five seasons and some sixty episodes to show the maze of relationships and forces that define urban social life, and the lives of those in the urban underclass in particular, in the first years of the twenty-first century. With *The Wire*'s very broad and deep canvas as my object, this study details and analyzes this distinctive view, paying particular attention to its picturing of a built environment and a relative geography in the era of neoliberalism. These emphases emerge from my discussion of the complex narratives presented. Indeed, *The Wire* is perhaps the most sustained and articulate exploration of urban life in contemporary popular culture.

Initially, *The Wire* asks to be approached as a series that employs the genre conventions of the crime drama and then as a subcategory of that type of presentation, the police procedural. Its initial season begins with a murder, and though that particular murder is not the topic of investigation that drives the season-long narrative, which is a departure in itself, the police inquiry into another murder and the efforts of law enforcement to control the reigning drug gang in Baltimore soon move to the center of the narrative. In each subsequent season there is likewise a central crime that needs to be solved and the presence of a police force that seeks to solve it. In season 1, as the central action becomes clear, it is the murder of a "civilian"—one who is not directly involved in the drug trade—who comes forward to testify against one of the Barksdale drug gang. In season 2, Officer McNulty discovers a woman's corpse floating in Baltimore harbor. In season 3, a drug dealer shoots Officer Dozerman, and his gun is stolen. In season 4, Bunk Moreland and Lester Freamon search for missing bodies in West Baltimore, specifically, the body of a young drug dealer—Lex. In season 5, McNulty leads the search for a nonexistent murderer of the homeless. Such plot devices define the show only in broad generic terms and tell us little about its emphases or scope.

Since its status as a crime series is only a surface feature, it develops—and emphatically so after season 1—as an exploration of how the social forces of the time affected a discrete section of Baltimore. Briefly, season 1 focuses on the absence of work in the African American neighborhood of West Baltimore and the resulting proliferation of the drug trade. Season 2 focuses on the decline of the shipping industry and the impact of that decline on unionized labor. Season 3 offers a return to the topic of drugs in the African American community and the attempt by certain members of the police force to legalize drug use and trafficking within a discrete area. Season 4 focuses on the vicissitudes of public education for the poor in a world where those children have little access to social capital, and where the public domain has been largely defunded. Season 5 talks about the decline of the daily newspaper as its business model proves insufficiently profitable for its corporate owners. The season dramatizes the result of the demise of this institution on the contemporary body politic and, more broadly, on perceptions of the public sphere.[2] But beyond these emphases and the very involved narratives that develop around them, the series is a compendium of people and relationships, individuals and their social world. Indeed, each season's narrative focus adds new complexity to existing characters and introduces new social networks.

The series invokes the specificity of Baltimore by emphasizing its locales and accents and history—including references to historical figures and events. For example, as Tommy Carcetti, who many say is based on the Baltimore political figure Martin O'Malley, runs for mayor in season 4, we see him meet an older politician, a one-term mayor, in a famous restaurant known to locals for its popularity with that group. The former mayor refers to the real-life one-term city executive Thomas L. J. D'Alesandro III, who is also famous as the son of another former mayor, Thomas L. J. D'Alesandro Jr., and as the brother of former House Speaker Nancy Pelosi. According to former mayor Kurt Schmoke, whose comments regarding drug decriminalization were the inspiration for season 3: "Longtime residents of the city could provide you with the names of people bearing great resemblance to the politicians, policemen, drug dealers, dock workers, teachers and preachers portrayed in this television drama."[3] But my goal is not, as has been the practice of some working in the social sciences, to mine the series for its "fact content." I look at the overarching contours of the narrative of each season and its means of formal presentation—its structure, emphases, and discrete visual elements—and develop an interpretive strategy that begins with the concepts of place, space, and time and focuses on the narrative as an interpretive response to a historical and social materiality.

If there is a "star" of the series, it is Jimmy McNulty, the first face we see in the first episode of season 1. McNulty is a police officer who moves from homicide to special investigations to the marine unit to a beat as a uniformed patrolman back to homicide and then back to special investigations. He is a deeply flawed character, a compulsive womanizer, an alcoholic, an officer of the law who has difficulty staying within the confines of legality. Though he is a rogue cop, he is not exactly corrupt. McNulty is emblematic of the moral complexity that the show ascribes to the early twenty-first century. He is a deeply fallible human being, one often mastered by his compulsions—women, alcohol, crime solving—yet our sympathies are frequently drawn to him, and he is the most effective crime solver in the series. Simon also introduces a complementary character named Omar Little, a bandit who robs only drug dealers. Like Jimmy, Omar appears in all five seasons, and like Jimmy, his often-questionable behavior is defined by an explicable and, in ways, admirable code. Such characters complicate Simon's use of genre and place the series more broadly within the moral ambiguities that define the neoliberal moment, which rewards a kind of theft and moral vacuity with riches and which treats a more honest kind of taking as a violation of the law.[4]

This complication of moral categories builds on the legacy of leftist films noir produced in the late 1940s, films that employed crime drama, and even procedurals—such as the notable "problem film" *Crossfire* (1947)—as a means of trenchant leftist social critique.[5] I am also thinking of the cycle of films called film gris, which exhibited a leftist pedigree and offered both direct and metaphoric critiques of midcentury capitalism, films such as Robert Rossen's *Body and Soul* (1947; written by Abraham Polonsky), Abraham Polonsky's *Force of Evil* (1948), and Jules Dassin's *Night and the City* (1950).[6] These films also define the murky line where law and morality become disjunctive. This is not to say that *The Wire* engages substantially in the formal strategies of noir, though there is an occasional high-angle shot, and at times those shots occur in black-and-white; however, more broadly, it offers a tone of despair, derived from the ineffectuality and corruption of key civic institutions.

Tracing *The Wire* back to its noir and film gris antecedents connects it to the breakthrough film *Naked City* (1948), also directed by Jules Dassin, which offered location shoots of New York and tried to integrate the city-as-place into its crime-procedural narrative. This film inspired the noirish police procedural television show *Naked City* (1958–1963), which is a direct antecedent of *The Wire* in its emphasis on place, its gritty urban situations, and its abiding realist aesthetic. (Each episode ends with the voice-over, as did the film, "There are eight million stories in the naked city. This has been one of them.") To further define the lineage of productions that led to Simon's series, it is notable that *Naked City* (the film) was shot with reference to contemporary Italian neorealist films such as Roberto Rossellini's *Rome, Open City* (1945) and *Paisan* (1946), and Vittorio De Sica's *Shoeshine* (1946), films that sought to integrate the texture of urban postwar Italy into naturalist narratives. Such emphases have appeared intermittently on television in shows to which Simon's *The Wire* can be connected, including *N.Y.P.D.* (1967 to 1969), starring Jack Warden and produced by David Susskind, which also featured noir-like effects and location shooting.

In more recent times, Simon owes much to Steven Bochco, most particularly his *Hill Street Blues* (1981–1987), as well as his later series *NYPD Blue* (1993–2005). *Hill Street* features urban textures but is not place-specific. The latter is explicitly set in New York. A realist aesthetic akin to that of *The Wire*'s is notable in both Bochco shows. Their dialogue features staccato cadences that create an edginess, language that is both notably colloquial and on the verge of the poetic. It pushed the edges of that which was allowable in broadcast television. Bochco's shows are like *The Wire* in that both marshal large casts of multidimensional, deeply flawed characters, and, perhaps most importantly, in how they introduce complex, intertwined narratives that are rarely, if ever, resolved in a single episode. *The Wire* draws on these innovations and extends them. Its language is scatological and obscene. It features nudity and some explicit sex as well as considerable and disturbing violence. It uses innovative dialogue, editing, characterization, and plotting as means of elaborating a complex and trenchant critique of the neoliberal moment. As an HBO show, *The Wire* extends the domain of the possible for cable television in the United States.

It is no accident that Bochco emerged as an adventurous showrunner in broadcast television just as cable television was becoming ensconced. Bochco's shows push the genre of the police drama to a new place, distending its formula in the interest of a kind of "realism." Simon's own earlier efforts, which are even more closely connected with the Bochco series, such as the Baltimore-based *Homicide: Life on the Street* (1993–1999) and, particularly, the miniseries *The Corner* (2000), are clearly steps on the way to *The Wire.*

Simon's dramas—including *The Wire*—ask for a referential reading, one in which significant attention is paid to their historical touchstones and their expressions of relative geography. By a "referential reading, I mean that the series makes explicit its connection with a discernible world and therefore asks to be read not as a document of that world but as an intervention, an interpretation of that historically specific entity. Such a reading strategy, following the insights of the critic and linguist Roman Jakobson, responds to a text's specific qualities, recurring elements that direct a reader toward its material-temporal context.[7] In the case of *The Wire,* its geographic and temporal specificity, its topical emphases, and even its use of dialogue and costume all direct us—to some extent—out of the show and toward its worldly commentary.

The series was possible only as a cable production for a decidedly niche market, even though it was not particularly commercially successful even by those standards. *The Wire* never garnered impressive ratings, nor did it ever win an Emmy, though it was nominated for writing awards in 2005 and 2008. It won a Peabody Award in 2003. These honors aside, the network at one point contemplated terminating the series. According to a 2009 story in the *Telegraph*: "In 2005, HBO almost cancelled *The Wire* because its modest viewing figures couldn't justify the $50 million it costs to make each series. The show was saved after Simon pitched the storylines for series four and five to Chris Albrecht, an HBO executive. Albrecht was so taken with Simon's script ideas that he signed HBO up for two further series, even though they were unlikely to attract many new subscribers. It is hard to imagine an executive at any other US network putting a compelling plot before profit."[8] HBO was aware of the distinctiveness of its particular audience and the way that the show's prestige enhanced its brand. This distinction was further shown by the nature of its ever-increasing audience, during its run and then after, which included significant numbers of educated and primarily politically liberal urban and suburban dwellers.[9] In addition, the show has made its way into college and university curricula in sociology, communications, film and television studies, American studies, African American studies, cultural anthropology, and urban history.[10] This academic and general interest seems to be continuing apace, even though the last episode of the show was produced in 2008. The show remains broadly watched and widely available via Netflix, cable reruns, HBO's streaming service, public libraries, and DVDs purchased privately.

This depth and scope can be attributed in large degree to the impact of David Simon. Simon was given far more creative control than most television executive producers. He writes of his ability to resist executive interference even as the first episodes of season 1 were awaiting production.[11] Simon's role in *The Wire* was central. While he was not responsible for every shot, scene, or word of dialogue, he was substantially responsible for the narrative arc of the seasons and the relationship of one season to another. He writes in the introduction to the compilation *The Wire: Truth Be Told*: "By the time we returned to shooting the first season, Ed Burns and I had drafts of the first six episodes in hand, as well as elaborate beatsheets that brought us all the way to the final episodes. Deliberate planning and overarching professionalism had nothing to do with it, but rather a sense of a story so intricate, with so many characters and so much plotting had to be considered a single entity."[12]

Naming Simon as the creative force behind the series recognizes his role in creating that "single entity," though the process of writing particular dialogue and developing the story lines for the show was clearly collaborative. Specific writers had more or less important roles in particular seasons: Simon and Burns in season 1; Rafael Alvarez in season 2; Simon and Burns—with an assist from Bill Zorzi, whose experience at the *Baltimore Sun* gave him insights into the politics of city hall—in season 3; Ed Burns in season 4; and Simon and Bill Zorzi in season 5. But Simon was the constant and the ultimate decider in this fairly open and clearly collaborative process. One of his cowriters, the crime novelist George Pelecanos, affirmed: "All the scripts are minutely mapped out . . . In the end, the final word is David's."[13]

In interviews and talks, Simon affirms that the general outline for *The Wire* came into focus as he finished work on the book and HBO show *The Corner* and felt he had taken that project as far as he possibly could. This illuminates the beginnings of *The Wire* and its particular emphases and innovations. *The Corner* derives from Simon and Burns's book about a particular sector of Baltimore's west side, which is also the area that *The Wire* depicts, and its role in the drug trade. In *The Corner*, the introduction of crack into the McCullough family results in the loss of virtually all the accoutrements of middle-class existence, and both Gary and Fran, husband and wife, find themselves addicts, like so many others. Life becomes a daily exercise of scrambling in the streets to get enough drug money. The focus of this series is not so much a matter of context but of the individual family. That is, it is distinctly about the failings of the McCulloughs and the vicissitudes that their bad choices cause. It also shows, though somewhat indirectly, how precarious middle-class solidity is in a world economy and a regional social system defined by neoliberalism and haunted by the residual and contemporary impact of racism. Simon's representational strategy and narrow sampling is affirmed by a case-study conceit and a quasi-documentary introduction to each episode. In contrast to the broad sociological approach of *The Wire*, *The Corner*'s point of view affirms that the McCullough family is being explored, not their historical situation—which, in a different framing, could be employed to explain their fate.

The Wire, as Simon affirms, picks up where *The Corner* left off. The earlier show is about individual choices, the road to and the power of addiction, and the implications of that condition for the addict and his or her nuclear family. *The Wire*, on the other hand, opens a discussion substantially focused on how urban despair is created and enabled by the institutional structures that articulate the terms and limits of ghetto life. Drugs are not so much the catalyst for misery as a symptom of the extremes of inequality and social isolation. And in developing a systemic view of drug use and its connection with race and class, Simon develops a place-specific narrative that delves into the social effects of isolation.

The Baltimore that Simon provides us with is substantially African American in its "civilian" population. Its police department is also one-half to two-thirds African American, and the preponderance of those involved in the drug trade share this racial identifier.[14] There are a few white addicts, including Bubbles's white friend Johnny, who we see in some detail, and we encounter the white Narcotics Anonymous leader Walon, played by the musician Steve Earle. In some views, the proportion of black criminals may point to a kind of uncritical racial determinism; however, this detail of inner-city life leads us to a backstory—sometimes explicitly noted, sometimes merely gestured toward, sometimes fully embedded in the narrative. This story is a broader historical recounting of black migration to the North and the lived experience of race in the urban United States. These factors point to the related impact of segregation in housing, as well as racial restrictions in labor and the way in which race exacerbates the impact of a declining industrial sector.

The representational power of a series like *The Wire* stems from its historical vision, and like all historical visions, this perspective is animated by a point of view, an interpretation of what makes a set of verifiable facts cohere. There is little or nothing materially represented in the course of this season, or any of the others, that is not socially and historically either verifiable or plausible. But such accuracy merely defines the undergirding of the show's worldview. *The Wire* dramatizes an urban environment that expresses, among other things, the wreckage and social chaos caused by historical racism, topics that are barely expressed explicitly but that, as a deep historical cause, can be found everywhere—work, housing, access to capital, and urban geography. In broad terms, *The Wire* focuses on the economic impact of the decline of the public sector, the effects of the globalization of finance, the far-flung production of all commodities, and the massive social inequality resulting from these policies and practices.[15]

BALTIMORE, THEN AND NOW

Simon affirms that his focus on Baltimore has added to the disposition toward referential reading as well as to the show's realist effect: "By choosing to tell our story in Baltimore and by showing fealty to the details of Baltimore, we reduce by some meaningful amount the artifice. We create an additional, though tacit argument on behalf of the stories themselves."[16] As a former *Baltimore Sun* reporter, Simon writes about what he knows, and this creates a series that is place-specific. His Baltimore is historically precise, but also similar to other cities of comparable size, employment structure, and demographics. It is like Pittsburgh, Cincinnati (where I live, a place I know well), and Buffalo: its post–World War II economy was mixed between the industrial and service sectors, and it benefited historically from its geography, including its proximity to a major shipping lane. Like those other cities, Baltimore was also the site of significant migration from the South, including a large African American contingent. But it is not like New York, Miami, Los Angeles, Chicago, or Houston in that it lacks a major financial services sector and does not draw appreciable population from regions outside the United States. Unlike those cities, it has little claim to world-city status and therefore lacks the economic dynamism that accompanies that designation.[17]

In the 1950s and 1960s cities such as Baltimore—those with significant industry and a role in international shipping—were a destination for those who had been displaced by the shrinking demand for labor in the agricultural sector. Ironically, while migrants continued to come to cities like Baltimore and Detroit, the jobs that had lured them were already moving elsewhere. By 1966, Baltimore was experiencing the beginnings of deindustrialization. Even in the 1950s, a period of national economic growth generally, the city's manufacturing base fell by 12 percent. This was a harbinger of things to come: between the early 1950s and 1990, employment in the manufacturing sector fell from 127,000 to only 40,000.[18] This loss of manufacturing jobs was largely part of a national trend, one that saw production increasingly moved to lower-wage locales in Asia and other places in the Americas.

And though Simon's Baltimore is far from a world city, it is by no means isolated. It at times looks out to the world beyond the local decay and connects with New York, Philadelphia, and even Europe, the Americas, and Asia. But primarily the Baltimore depicted is a city outside the central sweep of globalized trade. For example, contemporary gentrified Manhattan has more in common demographically and transactionally with the City of London, the financial district of that metropolis, than it does with elements of New York City's outer boroughs; this disjunction between conceptual and physical proximity is an aspect of the contemporary system of globalized commerce. A city like Baltimore is emblematic of a secondary or tertiary metropolis struggling to find a means to prosperity. According to Simon, "Baltimore is a postindustrial city, wedged between DC and Philadelphia and struggling to find its future and reconcile its past. In that sense it's like St. Louis and Cleveland and Philly and a lot of other rust-belt American places, and so stories from here have a chance of being about more than Baltimore per se. The storytelling here might be quite detailed in referencing local geography and culture, but it translates easily to elsewhere and therefore acquires additional relevance easily."[19] Baltimore is more regionally, rather than globally, connected, looking to the larger cities to the north: Philadelphia, New York (certainly), and nearby Washington, DC. Indeed, all these relationships find their way into the show.

Statistics also show, as Simon pictures here, that among African Americans, unemployment among women is relatively lower than among men. *The Wire* features any number of African American males, particularly younger men, aimlessly inhabiting the corners of Baltimore. Deindustrialization has disproportionately affected African American men, who have historically had a difficult time keeping pace with African American women in getting and keeping jobs. This long-standing condition is, to some degree, a matter of the racial politics of the employment market over the last seventy or so years. Since the primary mode of remunerative work for black people has been in the low end of the service sector—food service, cleaning, and other menial tasks—it has disproportionately been gendered as women's work. When African Americans were allowed into the industrial sector, mostly after the formation of the Congress of Industrial Organizations in the 1930s and then during World War II, men made strides both in numbers employed and in income. Deindustrialization has undone those gains. Indeed, for relatively uneducated black males, the financial possibilities of the drug trade seem particularly attractive.

Historically, Baltimore has long been home, as has Washington, to a significant African American elite. Figures such as Thurgood Marshall were products of this class. And while Simon does not differentiate among the full range of African American classes, the distinctions between the middle class and the class of people living in the projects is clear. The African American police officers—Lieutenant Daniels, Detectives Freamon, and Moreland—do not talk like Bodie and Poot, drug dealers from the projects, nor do they live among them. Initially at least, Daniels lives in a gentrified townhouse with his politically ambitious wife, and though we never see Moreland's residence, he states that he lives outside the city limits and is married with two boys. Also significant to the articulation of his class status and his self-definition is that he attended Edmondson High School with Omar Little, where Bunk was a star lacrosse player. This is one of his defining characteristics, revealing him as one who bought into the educational system far more deeply than a liminal character like Omar did, and that he involved himself in a "white" sport that had little prestige in the African American community.

To comprehend deeply the world as pictured, it is important to extend the show's represented chronology back toward an era of significant African American migration to the city. African Americans moved to the city incrementally in the first half of the twentieth century; the city's African American population grew from over 108,000 in 1920 to just over twice that in 1950. But between 1950 and 1980, the African American population doubled again, and by 1990 it constituted 60 percent of the city's population. Primarily, African Americans migrated on the assumption that the relatively plentiful industrial jobs of the 1940s would provide economic opportunity and that the relatively open social structures found in post–World War II northern cities would provide further avenues of mobility.

This migration, both during and after World War II, defined a significant shift in the nation's demographics, affecting virtually all northern cities. The ultimate outcome of this movement for many African Americans in the next generations would include social ills represented in *The Wire*—poverty, substandard housing, limited avenues to economic mobility. Some writers, such as Nicholas Lemann in *The Promised Land*, define the impetus for this wave as the industrialization of cotton picking; after 1944, International Harvester introduced machines to do the work that once employed numerous African American field hands, men, women, and children alike. Lemann provides details: "In 1940, 77 per cent of African Americans still lived in the South—49 per cent in the rural South. The invention of the cotton picker was crucial to the migration of blacks from the Southern countryside to the cities of the South, the West, and the North. . . . In 1970, when the migration ended, black America was only half Southern and less than a quarter rural" (6). And while Lemann's accounting for the role of the picker in this shift is significant, that technological development is far from the only cause. Also at play were the pull factors of better-paying industrial jobs, removal from a system of de jure segregation, and the relative persistence of the opportunities afforded to African Americans during the war. Further, in the general tradition of conservative analysis of African American urban poverty (Charles Murray and other critics), Lemann places the subsequent lack of social success substantially on the shoulders of the migrants, arguing that these later residents of urban environments brought with them self-defeating social practices—single-parent homes, child bearing in their midteens, questionable work habits. Such generalizations are problematic at best.[20]

The world we see in *The Wire* is distinct from the African American neighborhood of some four decades before, a space in which a variety of classes were represented. As an unintended consequence of the Civil Rights Act of 1964, class and space differentiation among African Americans became far more pronounced than before. What we see in *The Wire* is the flight of the more comfortable classes and the resulting disinvestment in the neighborhoods and houses where they had lived. Thus, our vision of West Baltimore contains an astounding number of vacant buildings. Indeed, the city of Baltimore, as of the filming of season 1, had 14,000 vacant houses and 12,000 vacant lots, giving it one of the highest ratios of vacant houses to population of any US city. Part of this was as a result of a loss of population from its peak of over 949,000 in 1950.[21]

As in many cities in the Northeast, Baltimore's public housing was built in the late 1930s as an extension of New Deal initiatives that began to address the conditions of urban poverty. Baltimore was a likely site for such improvements, since it possessed a substantial quantity of substandard housing, structures lacking central heat, indoor plumbing, and other amenities common in houses of the working and middle classes. From the beginning, public housing was segregated, reinforcing the patterns of segregation that were both a matter of law and white-mandated custom. In Baltimore, one of the primary considerations in decided-on sites for public housing was geography within a black-defined segregated zone. Thus, besides being built within the boundaries of segregation, this high-density housing, since it added units in the African American district, was seen as a buttress against further black encroachment on white areas. But this effort failed, and when African Americans began to live in areas around those projects, white flight increased. Further, local and federal authorities showed little respect for the role of small businesses in fragile, economically at-risk neighborhoods, razing viable businesses in order to build public housing.[22]

After World War II, in the US more broadly, public housing gradually lost its white component and eventually became almost uniformly inhabited by African Americans—a condition we see in *The Wire*. This occurred as a result of the migration of African Americans to the city, the decline in well-paid jobs in industry, and the massive flight of whites from the city. The impact of these factors caused applications for public housing among African Americans to rise substantially as available and affordable housing became scarce. Further, Federal Housing Administration lending policies made it virtually impossible for blacks to become homeowners, even if they could qualify for conventional home mortgages. Black neighborhoods were uniformly redlined by that agency, making federal loans unavailable for them, and black applicants were refused funding for properties in historically white neighborhoods, since the FHA professed a desire not to "destabilize' white areas. Public housing became one of the few viable options for lower-income African Americans.[23]

In the 1950s, as demand for subsidized housing burgeoned, the housing authority altered the means test for residency. This meant that better-off tenants were subject to not having their leases renewed. Thus, while the housing projects of Baltimore were already segregated by race, they increasingly became segregated by class.[24] Douglas Rae has written in his study of New Haven how public housing works to fix a population in place even when the original reason for moving to that place—jobs—has ceased to exist. Thus, public housing reduces geographic mobility and, in a declining regional economy, may be responsible for maintaining an urban underclass. This analysis assumes that there are jobs elsewhere for a given demographic, but his analysis also has significant validity. As Baltimore continued to lose jobs, particularly good-paying unionized industrial jobs, those recent migrants ensconced in public housing tended to stay in place.[25] It is, however, important to emphasize that not all of West Baltimore's African Americans lived in public housing. As the African American population of Baltimore grew, the real estate practice of "block busting" increasingly accelerated the momentum of white flight—and the riots of 1968 accelerated it further. According to a study of Baltimore's demography: "While in 1950, almost two-thirds of the region's white population lived in Baltimore, only 12.5% lived in the City by 1997."[26] In the period after 1990, the number of African Americans within the city limits began to decline as middle-class African Americans followed middle-class whites to the suburbs. The impact of both of these systems lingers on in the world of *The Wire*. When we see men without work, we can note that the historical impact of racist practices has important ramifications for contemporary economic conditions.

Perhaps as a result of the structural unemployment that particularly afflicts African Americans in *The Wire*, black characters from a variety of economic levels are engaged in a range of entrepreneurial efforts; Bubbles, the part-time informant and full-time drug addict, sells metal and T-shirts, and Bodie, the lower-level drug dealer, takes pride in the volume of his sales. By making enterprise a recurring motif, Simon seems to be directly rebutting notions of the "culture of poverty" thesis put forth by conservatives, who posit that habits originating from living as a oppressed minority in the South—such as lack of ambition, criminality, illegitimacy—have affixed themselves to African Americans intergenerationally and have resulted in a persistent inability to participate in the American dream.[27] Rather, Simon aligns himself with those who see the wave of African Americans migrating from the South during and after World War II as having no singular or fixed character; he shrewdly reads the historical record and rebuts the conservative view.

A GENERAL NOTE ON METHOD

When I began viewing the series, I found it immediately compelling and soon began binge-watching into the night. Beyond its narrative energy, the way in which it pictures lives proximate to mine, but not accessible as a matter of my experience, drew me in. As the seasons went on, I began to see how Simon employs the show as a means of developing a social vision of his historical moment, and as a device for critiquing many social givens. I wrote this book as a means of explicating the features of the series that lie below its narrative surface, including its embedded history of race and US race relations, and its related but less explicit attention to the category of class. My study contextualizes the series within urban history, sociology, and geography generally, and particularly in relation to the social history of Baltimore in the early twenty-first century.

One of the factors that attracted me to *The Wire* was Simon's emphasis on place and his representation of an articulate and discrete relative geography. This book follows my study *Starring New York: Filming the Grime and Glamour of the Long 1970s*. In that volume, I extended an earlier consideration of film and history to include a third feature: space. I considered a large group of films shot in New York City from 1969 to 1981, approaching them both for their narratives of urban life and for their visualization of urban geography. Every film narrative, since it is told with a substantial visual component, has a system of spatial relations. In films and television shows with a realist inclination, like *The Wire*, that vision of space is, in effect, a distinctive interpretive map of the world. As in the New York book, one of my analytical emphases here is the series' representation of distinctive relative geographies. Analysts and critics of the neoliberal regime, many of whom were trained as geographers, have come to see that what Edward Soja calls "the spatial turn" has an explanatory power that is a necessary complement to the temporal, and that this concern with relative space is particularly powerful when dealing with visual texts.[28] That is, representational visual texts provide viewers with a map of relational places and spaces. David Simon's Baltimore creates certain emphases that are lodged in his visual definitions of places and their connections with other places and spaces. On the other hand, certain places and spaces fall from his world completely.

Our intellectual and cognitive understanding of relative space is a vital determinant for defining the logic of a particular temporal moment. As Soja iterates, these concepts are mutually necessary: "Putting space first does not mean that spatial thinking should be practiced alone, divorced from life's social and historical realities. . . . [A] spatial perspective does not represent a rejection of historical and sociological reasoning but an effort to open them up to new ideas and approaches."[29] The spatial turn emerged from a group of Marxist geographers in the late 1970s who employed the precepts of postmodern thought to allow the concept of space to be decoupled from absolute empiricism. Space then became a relative term, one with significant implications for analyzing the post-Fordist regime of capital, a mode of production that employed the idea of space flexibly and conceptually. In *The Wire*, sometimes a precondition for a season's narrative, as in season 1, and sometimes a condition, as in season 2, commodity production is not place-dependent. It can occur anywhere. "German" automobiles may be assembled in Brazil from parts made in South Asia. And all those places involved in the production of such automobiles can be other places in a virtual wink of the eye. This is the domain of the postmodern, an era when the concept of place is subordinate to that of space. It is less a matter of where production occurs, than of how far in cost and time it occurs from targeted markets. Thus, place becomes a particular or lived locale, while space (or location) is general and tied to operative meanings of relative distances.[30]

In addition to Soja's seminal writings on time and space, I employ the considerable works of David Harvey and, to a lesser degree, Henri Lefebvre as aids to comprehending the role of space in defining a place and its broader meaning within a more expansive relative geography. Lefebvre's work is foundational in the conceptual recasting of space as a social construct, subject to the shifting definitions of its use by a broad undifferentiated public, as well as by elements of civic authority, including the state and its incarnations—the police, planners, housing inspectors, and so forth. When Lefebvre discusses "the production of space," he casts this conceptual process as being subject to the logic of a given historical situation and to the relative power of particular constituencies.

This recasting of space as other than reductively material and as broadly plastic allows for figures such as Soja to argue for its efficacy as an analytical category. In addition, George Lipsitz's *How Racism Takes Place* enhanced my understanding of the spatial dimension of race and class. Lipsitz discusses *The Wire* in a chapter focused on the series. He shows how segregation and ghettoization have become historically embedded practices defined by what he terms the "white spatial imaginary." He describes this means of conceiving of urban spaces as racialized and characterized by policies that "hoard amenities and resources." Such strategies, Lipsitz astutely shows, become a "nearly universal strategy for class advantage [that] follow a distinct racial pattern in the United States."[31]

The most prominent social theorist for my broader study is the geographer David Harvey. He has done nothing less than reimagine an integrated field of political economy with an important spatial dimension.[32] Harvey's evolving methodology increasingly provides a comprehensive means of seeing neoliberalism as a system of space relations that transform economic conditions and relations. This vision of an economic system with a prominent spatial component was invaluable for analyzing the range of assertions that may be gleaned from Simon's picturing of Baltimore. Harvey's discussion, connected with that of Neil Smith, of spaces being intentionally "left out"—and so not fully left out—of the circulation of neoliberal capital sheds light on the impoverished zones of Baltimore. Indeed, he allows us to see how such uneven development was both strategic and inevitable.[33]

My study follows the series in its presentation of an increasingly involved problematic. *The Wire* can be viewed as a developing representation or critique of the neoliberal city, one that takes on what is represented as fundamental aspects of public life. My goal is to explicate the deep frame of reference suggested by the components of the season's narrative. In chapter one, I follow *The Wire*'s portrayal of a community, paying particular attention to its represented spatial contours. The season provides a portrait of a group that is spatially segregated and economically self-contained. In addition, it pictures a world that is largely defined by the history of race relations in the city and nation, and by the ways in which race becomes definitional for certain spaces. The chapter employs work by the cultural geographers mentioned earlier to show the series emphasizing the spatial dimension of poverty. It also is prominently informed by the work of the sociologist William Julius Wilson, who has written extensively about the social and economic situation of the urban underclass in the postindustrial era. In particular, his landmark study *When Work Disappears* notes the impact of the prevalence of the drug trade and its centrality within these impoverished and isolated locales. Indeed, it reads like a template around which Simon developed his drama.

Season 2 focuses on the devaluation of labor, employing the waterfront of Baltimore and its embattled dockworkers' union as a case. To see how that example typifies the historical moment, I employ the social insights of David Harvey to show the dialectic between the local and the global at work. Harvey helps us see the space-specific contours of a particular labor market even as its workers are engaged in activities with global economic implications. Harvey employs Marx to show how the concept of "variable capital" allows capitalists to revalue the cost of labor within a world where technological change effectively can shrink relative space. I also employ work by the theorist of global social systems Arjun Appadurai for his vision of how the increasing volume of world trade and the search for low-wage production has produced a kind of resistance to those far-flung processes and a revaluation of the local, including beliefs, customs, and common affiliations.

Season 3 focuses on the decriminalization of drugs within a specified zone, called Hamsterdam in the series. This focus builds on the representation of relative space found in season 2, but rather than focusing on labor and capital in the production of space, season 3 goes back to a more refined concern with Baltimore itself, particular delineations of real estate, and the means by which those discrete zones are connected. Those lines of demarcation become a factor that informs how we look at class, race, comportment, and even the definitions of time. In this chapter, the dialectics of space become even more complex than in chapter two, as the relative relation among spaces and the contingencies affecting their value come into play. This broad emphasis leads to a discussion that employs Harvey's and Jason Hackworth's considerations of the meanings of relative urban space within the neoliberal regime.

Similarly, the vexed and complex issue of inner-city education in season 4 leads me to consider its representation of space-specific knowledge. I employ the sociologist Elijah Anderson to help show the relationship between race and space. The season develops a complex view of the idea of situated knowledge, and of education as the production of knowledge, an idea that I explicate through the work of the educational sociologists Edward Buendía and Nancy Ares. But beyond these commentators, I see in this season Simon and his fellow writers developing their most explicit analogy between the early twenty-first century and the early twentieth century. Developing this visual and thematic analogy allows us to see the similarities between contemporary neoliberalism and the doctrines of laissez-faire, which were dominant a century before—including the justifications of Herbert Spencer's social Darwinism.

In Season 5 I cite commentators on the media, including astute voices such as Michael Schudson and Daniel Hallin, to locate the terms and efficacy of Simon's critique of the contemporary urban newspaper. I also start "reading against" Simon's apparent pessimism and bring in the social theorists Michael Hardt and Antonio Negri to tease out a more hopeful strain embedded in Simon's series, emphasizing, as I do in the conclusion, how the gradual privatizing of civic institutions—schools, newspapers—may lead to a reevaluation of their role in public life and a generalized will to redefine them as part of what Hardt and Negri refer to as the "common." I develop this idea further in the conclusion, which emphatically reads *The Wire*'s often-dystopian urban landscape as symptomatic of its possible utopian alternatives.

This study of David Simon's series locates the spaces where urban geography meets Baltimore noir. I approach *The Wire* as a key expression of a period because of its depiction of the social logic of that time. But that social logic emerges from the complexities of the narrative of the series as a whole and the narratives of each season. Indeed, as I developed a more intimate and extensive knowledge of each season, I revised my prior vision of both the story arc and the emphases of its narrative. Events that I remembered as central remained important but were redefined by the extensive context in which they were lodged. Generally, the event that viewers generally think of as the key to a season, such as the public schools in season 4, do not occur for two or three episodes, so that by the time we get to Tilghman Elementary, a considerable geographic and social context has been elaborated, one that allows us to see the school in the context of a neighborhood and of the lives of the students we are tracking. But more broadly, as a realist text that derives both its power and authority from its connection with a palpable actuality, *The Wire* provides the perspicacious viewer with insights into the spatial logic of the neoliberal regime of a particular city, but one that is applicable to a number of others.

{ ONE }

Season 1

DRUGS, RACE, AND THE STRUCTURES OF SOCIAL IMMOBILITY

Season 1 is the most conventional of the five seasons in genre terms, but is nonetheless foundational for the four subsequent seasons. It elaborates on the underclass and its definition by space and race as well as by its involvement in the drug trade of West Baltimore. That business, then, frames a social world. Drugs are presented as a natural avenue of commerce for those motivated by economic ambition in an environment where conventional means of social mobility have ceased to exist. Violence and criminality, which are firmly situated within this well-articulated social context, become narrative features that, among other things, might make these behaviors comprehensible to an audience that otherwise might not have projected beyond its middle-class experience.

Season 1 was largely scripted by the collaborative team of Ed Burns and David Simon. Simon drew on his experience as a police reporter, and Burns on his background as a police detective. Rafael Alvarez makes this explicit: "Many plotlines from *The Wire*'s first year are rooted in a case from the 1980s, investigated by writer/producer Ed Burns when he was a city homicide detective."[1] This case featured the legendary Baltimore drug dealer Little Melvin Williams, who shows up in seasons 3 through 5 as the "Deacon." That case also turned on the decoding of numerical patterns sent to beepers. That noted, Simon receives individual writing credit on eight of the season's thirteen episodes.

Season 1 tells the story of the thriving drug trade in West Baltimore and the roles of its syndicate chiefs, Avon Barksdale and Stringer Bell, in the planning and execution of their enterprise. As the season opens, the dominance of that group is put in jeopardy by the murder of a man by Avon's nephew, D'Angelo Barksdale, in the high-rise projects. The case falls apart when a key witness recants her testimony. But the homicide detective Jimmy McNulty, watching the trial in the courtroom, becomes incensed by the apparent invulnerability of the drug gang and takes it upon himself to drive that group—and their means of commerce—out of the city. When another witness emerges and then is shot, the Baltimore Police Department assigns Lieutenant Cedric Daniels to the case. Daniels amasses a task force that includes McNulty, Lester Freamon, Kima Greggs, Roland Pryzbylewski, Ellis Carver, and Thomas "Herc" Hauk. All these characters are central to multiple seasons and appear in all five. The legal profession is represented by McNulty's lover—for now—Rhonda Pearlman, the assistant district attorney; Daniel Phelan, the prosecutor turned municipal judge; and the Barksdale syndicate's lawyer, Maurice Levy. These three, to varying degrees, also appear throughout the five seasons.

Barksdale and Bell respond to D'Angelo's bad judgment by moving him from the high-rise projects to the low-rise ones, where he oversees a crew of young drug runners including Wallace, Bodie, and Poot. Each set of characters—the criminals and the police—is complex and socially interesting. For example, we see Wallace's regard for his younger siblings, whom he raises in a vacant apartment in the housing project; Greggs's relationship with her upwardly mobile lesbian partner; McNulty's increasing estrangement from his ex-wife and children, and his failing relationship with Pearlman. In episode 4, the police detail decides it needs a wiretap, and in episode 5, it clones D'Angelo's pager. The wire becomes a recurring device and metaphor within the season and the series, elaborating both a necessary means of surveillance as well as a naming of the precarious link among disparate social entities.

The season features a nuanced and complicated narrative that sprawls over thirteen episodes. There are plots, subplots, and sub-subplots. We are introduced to two recurring secondary characters that are vital to all five seasons. In episode 3, Omar, a "rip and run" artist who steals from criminals, takes the Barksdale stash from under the noses of D'Angelo and his crew. Omar, a gay man who lives outside most social conventions, becomes an asset to the police after the Barksdales retaliate and brutally murder his partner, Brandon. Bubbles, another police informant, becomes motivated after his running mate, Johnny, is beaten by D'Angelo's crew for attempting to scam them with counterfeit bills.

The season intensifies its movement toward its culmination in episode 10, when Kima is wired and sent out with the Barksdale retainer and strip club owner Orlando, who is coerced by the police when he is apprehended while trying to purchase heroin. Kima and Orlando drive to a place in West Baltimore to buy drugs from the Barksdale syndicate. But Orlando is killed and Kima badly wounded when their scam is detected and shooting ensues. Once Kima has been shot, Daniels intensifies his efforts to apprehend Barksdale and Bell. A bug in Barksdale's strip club implicates Barksdale and D'Angelo, and they are arrested in episode 12. The culmination of the season is the murder of the low-level dope runner Wallace, who is suspected of snitching on D'Angelo, and then the trial of Avon, Wee-Bey, and D'Angelo. In episode 13, the Barksdales' lawyer, Maurice Levy, arranges a plea agreement in which Barksdale gets a limited sentence as a result of D'Angelo receiving a stiff twenty years for drug trafficking, and the Barksdale hit man Wee-Bey getting life for admitting to a number of murders, including some he did not commit. This conclusion emphasizes both the genre expectations of the season and the ways in which Simon and his collaborators shift them. Barksdale is necessary to the socially inscribed game of cops and criminals, so he cannot—either in narrative or system terms—vanish from the scene. But he is also indicative of the disparities faced by those charged with crimes, depending on their relative wealth.

In its emphasis on spatial isolation, this season is quite Baltimore-centric: its action is largely set in the Baltimore housing projects. A notable extratextual feature of this geographic focus is that the whole season was shot in the region represented. That is, contiguous west-side locations were used for the season's west-side orientation. In other seasons, the Baltimore represented results from suturing locations from around the city that have a kind of coherent look. The focus of season 1 is the elaboration of the realm of the drug trade and its attendant social networks within the spaces of the West Baltimore ghetto. It represents a world in which spatial segregation by class and race allows for a parallel system of commerce to take hold, one that is substantially outside the globalized economy of "legitimate" consumer products and "legal" financial exchanges. In this world, naked commerce is the rule, fully enforced by violence and the threat of violence. It is a world where enterprising, amoral, profit-driven suppliers have taken control of the single commodity purchased by a viable number of consumers within the discrete region. The Baltimore we come to understand is a city that coheres in its discrete regions but that is segmented into specific areas by factors connected with race, class, and wealth.

In 2002, African Americans accounted for only 28 percent of all business ownership in the city.[2] In *The Wire* of season 1, the only "legitimate" business owned by an African American is Stringer Bell's copying service, which is a money-laundering front for his drug business. The construction industry is white controlled, the convenience store from which Omar's lover is abducted is owned by the "Greek," and the downtown restaurant where D'Angelo and Donette, his girlfriend, dine is white owned and largely white operated.

Employment for African Americans seems to consist of working for the police, working for the city, or selling drugs. But even police work is relatively scarce, though the force is large (the eighth-largest municipal police department in the United States in 2000, with a total of 3,034 police officers). According to the 2000 US Census, Baltimore was the seventeenth-largest city in the United States, with a population of 651,154. And while African Americans constitute more than 64 percent of the city's populations, the police department was 43 percent African American in 2003. The police department we see in *The Wire* is blacker than the statistics indicate, but only relatively so. Perhaps this uneven distribution can be accounted for by the type of work portrayed, which is related to the sale and distribution of narcotics. We primarily see beat cops and those in the lower tiers of command, and African Americans are overrepresented there too. African Americans make up more than 64 percent of the people we see on the streets, but again, this is a matter of the region depicted and the emphasis on drugs and criminality. When characters venture to the Inner Harbor, the population appears fairly white. Such attention to the season's emphasis reveals the interpretive dimension of the show and the fact that it provides a reading of historical conditions that, while resonant and accurate, are not the only story that can be told about Baltimore or urban America.[3]

To complement its place-specific emphasis, the first season employs a visual style that allows viewers to devise a relatively clear sense of context. Frequently, a narrowly framed shot will lead to a wide pan that shows us more of the world that is around the dramatic action being emphasized. This method is confirmed in the voice-over to season 1: David Simon invokes the words of the late executive producer and supporting actor Bob Colesberry to "stay wide."[4] Simon defines this as a compositional motif, a desire not simply to film that which articulates the constrained action forming the plot of the episode but also to show more broadly the world in which it takes place. The meaning of this assertion becomes fairly clear as we look at the visual language of this season. *The Wire* is a character-driven drama, and as a result, it spends much time dwelling on close-ups and mid-close-ups of its central characters and their interactions with one another. Through such exchanges, we come to see individuals and their relationships with their close associates, in vivid detail. These many tightly framed two-shots show us major characters interacting: Bunk and McNulty, Greggs and Daniels, and Avon Barksdale and Stringer Bell. Often, as these conversations wind down, the camera pulls away slightly to reveal a wider, but only somewhat wider, context.

As Simon and Burns point out in *The Corner*, the drug trade burgeoned in the mid-1980s as work became increasingly scarce, white flight and middle-class black flight left the schools without a tax base and in disarray, and cheap cocaine, which became crack, pervaded the ghetto.[5] In *The Wire*, the first season starts to articulate the class system among African Americans, which became more pronounced as they urbanized and all the more significant after the 1970s. While the effects of the civil rights movement certainly played a role in creating the possibility of African Americans attaining relative wealth and relative freedom to live where they chose, it also marked a moment when economic disruption, and particularly the decline of the urban industrial economy, led to a constraining of opportunity for African Americans without an education beyond high school. *The Wire* chronicles the development of the intrarace class system in the black community, which had even more telling consequences than that among whites, since rates of unemployment and underemployment among African Americans dwarfed those for whites.

Like all first seasons of multiyear dramas, season 1 does a significant amount of work in elaborating the backstories of its recurring characters. The first episode begins with a trial, which is not entirely typical, since trials tend to come at the end of episodes. By starting here, Simon asserts the limits of the legal system and shows that its apparent conclusions are not usually conclusive. In the trial, D'Angelo Barksdale is acquitted of committing a murder at the high-rise housing projects after a corroborating witness, a security guard, recants her testimony under pressure—Bell, Wee-Bey, and others from the Barksdale gang look on menacingly as she testifies. This opening scene brings us into the season's plot, in which the investigators seek to build a case against the Barksdales. But like the series as a whole, season 1 by no means follows a simple narrative. The beginning is devoted to defining the police unit and its coming to knowledge of the extent and methods of the Barksdale gang. The futility of hands-on police work leads to a request for electronic surveillance, which Pearlman makes to Judge Phelan.

RACE, CLASS, AND THE "CULTURE OF POVERTY"

Regarding the series, Fredric Jameson writes: "Initially we approach *The Wire* as a crime story; that is, a struggle between two collectivities: the police and the crime gangs (for the most part, the crime is drug trafficking)."[6] But as Jameson acknowledges and discusses, *The Wire* is about much more than that. In the DVD commentary for episode 1, season 1, David Simon declares that *The Wire* is about the world of the city, and of those excluded from the America defined by material comfort, middle-class lifestyles, and predictable circumstances. This definition has significant implications for the emphases of the show. For Simon, the depth of the show emanates from a complex rendering of the "two Americas" thesis. That is, Simon informs the season with a vision of the United States as an intensely stratified society, a vision that goes back to the late nineteenth century and that was famously asserted by John Dos Passos in *The Big Money*, a novel of the mid-1930s.[7] This stratification is organized around definitions of race and class and is defined in a corollary manner by delineations of space.

Since the season's primary action depicts an underclass, the resulting definition of the city focuses on the ravages of economic blight. And indeed, the geography of *The Wire* in this season is always concerned with some aspect of some subsection of Baltimore. Much of the work done by the narrative and its visual elements in this season is formative for all five seasons, and the world depicted is largely that of the West Baltimore ghetto. But the definition of that region would be diminished if it were not defined relatively, so some of the season's emphasis depends on its picturing the places and people that define the middle- and upper-class city.

In the pre-credit scene of the season's first episode, we see Jimmy McNulty and a young African American man, who tells the officer the tale of Snot Boogie and his demise. The scene is shot tightly; the camera locates the men in a two-shot skewed from the left. The young man explains that although Snot attempted to steal the craps pot every time he played the game, he still was allowed to participate. When McNulty asks incredulously why this was so, the young man replies, "This is Amer-

Season 1, episode 1, McNulty learns of Snot Boogie.

ica, man. You've got to let him play." In this scene, Simon delineates the realm of the ideological, a system of belief impervious to empirical facts. Even for this young man, who has been provided few benefits by the United States, the illusion of opportunity still resonates. But for a character like the one who talks with McNulty, this context is largely inoperative, since the spaces of West Baltimore clash profoundly with the rhetoric of opportunity. The scene is punctuated by the flash of police lights, and it eventually opens up a little to bring in the street. This method circumscribes its characters within a place and a situation, showing the audience the degree to which context is everything—there would be no conversation without the murder—and that context is a limited set of circumstances. As the shot widens, we see that those circumstances take place in a slice of urban life that is West Baltimore.

Simon shows us this urban region as a vital social environment, but one where norms of behavior are decidedly different from those that a middle-class audience may conceive as usual, and where the conventional notion of opportunity is made absurd. This environment is driven by a culture of economic need and scarcity. The world that Simon portrays considers how commerce occurs when conventional forms of economic development cease to exist. There are no factories here, no McDonald's, and no Walmarts. Multinational concerns have abandoned

Season 1, episode 1, Bell and McNulty in the courtroom.

this world. We can see the drug trade as a form of business activity that emerges when conditions for a particular group and a particular place seem beyond redemption and therefore require a kind of energy and ingenuity that, though indeed nefarious in the end, fosters a resolve that viewers may find fascinating as the quintessence of entrepreneurialism. This tension between socially constrained space and the desire for wealth catalyzes the season's narrative.

The strategy of isolating a scene by constraining its visual field and then widening that context to provide a more nuanced interpretive frame shows itself in the next scene, in which D'Angelo Barksdale is being tried for murder. The courtroom is shot as a self-contained, very small space. We see two witnesses, both in tight close-ups and then in two-shots with their lawyers, and then a reverse-angle shot reveals the proximity of the judge and the onlookers. Key among these onlookers are McNulty and Stringer Bell, who we meet for the first time. The camera often pans between Bell and McNulty, asserting their closeness, both physically and thematically. Theirs is a cat-and-mouse game in which both enthusiastically participate. We also see, with accentuated closeness, the lack of distance between the witnesses and the thugs who are part of the Barksdale group and who are there to menace those on the stand, showing the danger of coming forward against these men. Unlike the street shown in the opening scene, the courtroom is a self-contained arena, and context must come from without.

Then, in the midst of this courtroom drama, the scene cuts to a stakeout in the West Baltimore ghetto. We see an SUV framed in a medium long shot against the fronts of largely boarded-up, mostly small apartment buildings. The lack of transition between these scenes is jarring, making them less causal than they might otherwise be; yet they ask the viewer to define a connection. The scene on the street cuts to inside the vehicle. An informant identifies a drug deal as we watch from a short distance. Greggs calls her support team, and its members apprehend the drug dealers and confiscate their guns. These street scenes accentuate the world where they occur as self-contained. The camera largely remains at street level, and the natural borders of the shots—buildings, cars—limit our field of vision. Immediately after the dealers are arrested, the scene cuts abruptly to the acquittal of D'Angelo. The sum of these scenes asserts the futility of the arrest and mitigates the apparent authority of those involved in the legal system. After the acquittal, the arresting officer declaims, "You think I give a fuck?" and when summoned to Judge Phelan's office, McNulty responds to the judge's questioning of why he cares when the case was not his, by asserting, "Who says I do?" But McNulty does care, which defines one of the keys to his character.

This season introduces us not only to characters that are central to the five seasons of *The Wire* but also defines the show's emphasis on space as a vital indicator of urban life in the era of deindustrialization and neoliberal politics. Baltimore is defined by the complexities of race and class. That is, in this realistic depiction, not all African Americans are poor, and not all poor people use drugs. But if you are poor, then the chances are good that you will be black and use drugs. One of the brilliant aspects of this show is the way it navigates the intrarace class system. That is, we see African Americans in a variety of socioeconomic situations—from high-ranking city bureaucrats and politicians to the poorest and most disrupted drug user of West Baltimore. And the way into that system is through the spaces of Baltimore's geography that are usual for each discrete subsection of African American society, a geography with a significant social dimension, since those who are defined by and definitional for that space find themselves more prone to adhering to its distinctive ethos and economic system.

Officer Kima Greggs provides a window into the complexity of this social world. In this first season, she is the one woman who is represented as focally involved in the world of drug selling and interdiction. Kima is a lesbian who seamlessly takes her place among the "guys." Within the show, the mainstreaming of nonheterosexuals is part of its residual narrative. Kima is intermittently the object of male lust, which she deflects gracefully. She is also the partner of an upwardly mobile African American woman who works as a newscaster for a local station. Subsequently, we see her exhibit the commitment phobia common among male police officers, and take lessons in deceiving her partner from the always-on-the-prowl McNulty.

Her middle-class lifestyle is notable for the way it connects with that of her fellow officers and contrasts with the lifestyles of those in the drug trade, which tend to be either more basic or more luxurious. The connection between the worlds of drugs and law enforcement is a matter of mutual obligation. Wee-Bey Brice, D'Angelo Barksdale, not to mention Avon Barksdale and Stringer Bell, are all wealthier than Greggs and the other police officers, yet lower in class by some definitions. They operate an empire that relies on the exploitation of the truly down and out, frequent regions that other African Americans of their relative wealth rarely go, and exhibit behaviors that make them social pariahs—murder, intimidation, substance abuse. In a scene in the first episode of this season, D'Angelo and Wee-Bey cruise the streets of West Baltimore in a late-model SUV. The vehicle is not inexpensive, the driver and passenger are well dressed, and yet the discussion of witness intimidation and fear of police surveillance situates them outside the behaviors and mores that would conventionally fit their economic situation. Simon's broader point is about class and not wealth per se; the Barksdale gang is defined not by the copious amounts of cash it possesses, but by the ways it fits—or fails to fit—into the spaces and conventions of respectable middle-class life in a US city.

True to the opening story of Snot Boogie, season 1 is on some level an ironic celebration of the American entrepreneurial spirit. The major players in the drug trade are far from unambitious. They are highly organized and financially successful. The triumph of the Bell and Barksdale syndicate is one of ruthlessness and strategy. When Avon talks of controlling the towers, he speaks of the work that went into securing them for his empire. When Stringer Bell attends class at Baltimore Community College, he is trying to suture the world of the ghetto drug trade to the principles of classical economics.

Even at the lower tiers of the organization there is a clear ethos of work and enterprise. We see D'Angelo's disquiet when he is demoted to the less dynamic drug market of the low-rise projects; we see the jeal-

Season 2, episode 3, Omar steals from the Barksdale gang.

ousy among the lieutenants when Stinkum is given a franchise, allowing him to become a limited partner in the Bell and Barksdale enterprise. And below that level of enterprise, the intriguing character of Bubbles, a drug addict and police informant, is ever on the make to turn a small profit. We see him involved in all kinds of schemes: trying to use bills made on a copying machine to purchase drugs, selling hats, and trading in scrap metal; he is the definition of a hardworking drug addict—even if he remains an addict. Similarly, Omar's occupation is to steal money and drugs from drug dealers, particularly the Barksdale syndicate. But despite his obvious criminality, Omar not only exhibits a code of ethics but is also a model of planning and discipline, the very qualities that those with access to the avenues of mobility define as the character traits that lead to success. We see Omar watching his targets at length, planning with precision, and executing his plan with care. Indeed, in another life, he might have been an engineer or a financial planner.

By situating his characters in economic tiers within an entrepreneurial model that parallels the mainstream version, Simon seems to be directly rebutting notions of the "culture of poverty" and aligning himself with those who see the wave of African Americans migrating from the South during and after World War II as having no singular or fixed character. Rather, Simon shrewdly reads the historical record and rebuts the "culture of poverty" view. In keeping with an analysis by the historian Jacqueline Jones, the "underclass" in *The Wire* exhibits its pathology in relation to limits in economic opportunity—some historically defined, some structurally defined by the nature of the US economy in the 2000s, and some defined by the situation of urban spaces within those other two narratives. In contrast to Lemann's or Murray's view, Jones writes,

> No matter where or when they lived, most black folks would say, "I work. I work hard—you can ask anybody out here—but I don' seem to get nowhere.". . .
>
> These comments of Southern migrants suggest a link between the world of the nineteenth-century sharecropper and the late-twentieth-century Northern underclass. Both times and places were marked by . . . deep structural forces of economic marginalization . . . Trapped within the South's plantation economy or the Northern central city, they lacked access to education and to jobs that paid a living wage.[8]

Simon explained his intentions in creating *The Wire*: "I knew we had to bring the political element. I argued passionately for the political element . . . If we had anything right in the first four seasons as to the nature of the city, its problems, and why those problems seem so insolvable, why is it that we're not intensely aware of those problems?"[9]

Part of the work of season 1 is to refer to the legacy of historical racism in Baltimore, as well as to introduce a visual language that helps us experience the economic and social distances between different races and classes. The patterns of violence and commerce that we encounter in the housing projects suggest, in general, a population that never became solidified economically, so perhaps it is a group that has not been in the city for long. When Avon and D'Angelo visit Avon's older brother in the nursing home, it helps define a crime family that seems to extend back to at least the late 1980s, assuming that Avon is around thirty and that his brother is around forty, and that he was born between Avon and Brianna. That year would place him in the center of the drug boom generation, but nonetheless would make him a figure that likely faced the residual impact of limited access to education, segregation in the job market, and restricted access to capital. He would also have been in the midst of an era of burgeoning drug use, a rise that took in all classes and races.

Simon and Burns illustrate the forces that led to the demise of a vibrantly mixed population in West Baltimore in *The Corner*, a narra-

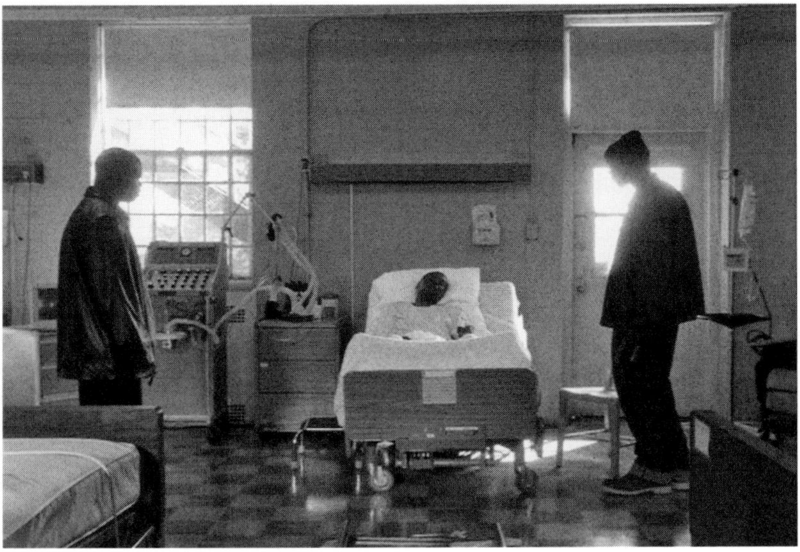

Season 1, episode 5, D'Angelo and Avon visit the nursing home.

tive that serves as a preamble to *The Wire*. The McCullough family's decline has at its center a tale of housing. Gary's father, William, labored persistently in a range of taxing physical jobs from the time of his arrival in Baltimore from North Carolina before World War II. Eventually, as a result of thrift and hard work, he was able to buy a small row house on racially mixed Fayette Street on the west side, one of the key streets in season 1. By the early to mid 1960s, the area had changed as a result of absentee landlords, the existence of housing projects—which changed both the density and class mix of the neighborhood—and the beginnings of the process of acquiring land for the construction of an interstate highway through the neighborhood. It was now all-black and almost all-poor. As deindustrialization continued, it became poorer and more dangerous.

The historian Edward Orser states that West Baltimore represents the legacy of segregated housing in the city. The west side had, since the 1930s and 1940s, when African Americans constituted a significant proportion of the city's population, been a place where a core black community resided; the racial dividing line was the east-west axis defined by Fulton Street. African Americans lived to the east of this line, and whites to the west. It is at Fulton and Lexington that the season begins with McNulty learning about the death of Snot Boogie. As African Americans moved to the city after World War II and whites left for the suburbs, the areas to the west of Fulton soon became integrated and then, as a result of white flight, became all-black. The ongoing demolition of black neighborhoods to build I-170 in the 1970s (a small stretch of the proposed road opened in 1976) and the relocation of their former residents, usually to already-congested racially defined districts, further decimated the neighborhood.[10]

This "slum" clearance further isolated the housing projects of West Baltimore even as they became more significant relative centers of population. And as the industrial economy declined, so did the living standards and relative wealth of those in the projects. It is not surprising, then, that in *The Wire* the housing projects form the center of illegal activity. Avon Barksdale and Stringer Bell, both astute businessmen, see them as the center of their enterprise. Their centrality invites an inquiry into their history and institutional status. How did buildings meant to provide adequate housing for a relatively poor population become an important aspect of that group's entrenched poverty?

By the late 1970s, Simon tells us, historical institutional anchors for Baltimore's African American community—Provident Hospital, Douglass High School, the commercial district on Baltimore Avenue—were failing. But the McCulloughs in *The Corner*, anchored by inertia, stayed, and as a result exposed their children increasingly to drugs and violence.[11] The area became a picture of a culture of disinvestment and despair; the drug trade remained about the only viable business around, forever burgeoning and offering the young and unskilled an opportunity to make money. Indeed, for young and unskilled African Americans in Baltimore, measurable unemployment hovers around 40 percent, and wages tend to be around the federal minimum.

COPS, CRIMINALS, AND THE FUTURE OF DEMOCRACY

Arguably, the entire apparatus of cops, administrators, judges, equipment, and so on exists because Barksdale and Bell predicate their fortune on providing illicit substances to a captive clientele—which exists because of the massive disinvestment in West Baltimore and its inhabitants. If these drugs were not illegal, then there would be no need for the gang. Its way of doing business would be utterly unnecessary. There would be no enforcers, no intergang battles for turf, no runners, no corner boys, and so forth. (Indeed, in season 3 we see dramatized the decriminalization of drugs.) But because the use and possession of heroin and cocaine are against the law, there is a need to insulate the trade from law enforcement officials, and the price of the drugs goes up even as their quality may go down. Because Barksdale and Bell exist, their capture obsesses people like Greggs, Daniels, and McNulty, and the city must hire more and more law enforcement officials to pursue them. Since drugs are illegal, they become not just a commodity like any other. They define a lifestyle. This is not to say that they articulate the process by which West Baltimore became devoid of lawful work and capital. Rather, they took root there and made that region captive as a result of the absence of other means of generating work and cash. William Julius Wilson, in his landmark study *When Work Disappears*, notes this connection:

> The decline of legitimate employment opportunities among inner-city residents increase the incentive to sell drugs . . .
>
> The presence of high levels of drug activity in a neighborhood is indicative of problems of social organization. High rates of joblessness trigger other problems in the neighborhood that adversely affect social organizations, including drug trafficking, crime, and gang violence.[12]

Wilson goes on to trace the types of drugs that were popular at a given moment, asserting that heroin, the drug of choice in *The Wire*, made a comeback in the mid-1990s. He also notes the impact of the prevalence of the drug trade on those not explicitly involved in it, since the associated lawlessness and increasing gun violence tend to weaken the social organization of these already-disrupted locales.

The Wire depicts the extended tendrils of the surveillance state. In some scene breaks, the realist visual emphasis of the series gives way to a bleached-out shot from the perspective of an omnipresent camera. This occurs mostly within institutional settings—the courthouse, the elevator in police headquarters. Such an emphasis asserts the use of technology to secure the boundaries of the spaces that define and contain the institutional structures of the state and its normative values. Simon talks about this emphasis, asserting that surveillance "is everywhere." But the visual emphasis of the season places it in particular places as a means of marking them as part of the post-9/11 environment. Further, as the discussion among Greggs, Carver, and Hauk (Herc) soon tells us, this sector is woefully underresourced, having not entered the age of computers even in the early 2000s. It is within this context that Carver tells us that the war on drugs cannot be called a war "because wars end." But this truism bears greater scrutiny.

As we behold this series in its post-9/11 context, perhaps the postmodern condition of war is that it is asymmetrical, of relatively low intensity, and perhaps perpetual. West Baltimore easily becomes analogous to a failed state. It is a lawless place where atavistic worldviews spawn random attacks on those with some affiliation to the West, such as Yemen.[13] So Carver's words become an ironic commentary on the mind-set of those who perpetuate the drug wars, and since they reveal a truism, they also direct us to the relative imprecision of the analogy. Somalia is not Baltimore: each has its own history, system of social practices, and so on. The application of the analogy, however, allows us to see that the drug war operates in the bureaucratic regime of the US government as a placeholder. Drugs disrupt our ideas of a "normal" social sphere and provide an issue that always inflames the public, which then allows an unelected bureaucracy to wield inordinate power. Empowering that unelected portion of municipal, state, and federal law enforcement increasingly imperils democratic rule. Controls on wiretaps lie within the discretion of judges, who may be more concerned with pleasing a narrow constituency than with broad constitutional safeguards.

After McNulty has informed Judge Phelan of the power and nefariousness of the Barksdale gang, the political impact of this knowledge resonates up through the Baltimore Police Department's chain of command. Late in episode 1, McNulty consults with a friend in the Baltimore field office of the FBI to discuss surveillance methods and equipment. The scene transition is again abrupt, moving from the office of deputy chief for operations Ervin Burrell to McNulty walking up the plaza to the FBI building. Security in this locale is more present and effective than at the city buildings we have encountered, and McNulty is denied admittance until his colleague Fitzhugh comes to bring him in. From the first we can see the superior resources of the federal agencies when Fitzhugh shows him a live surveillance shot of a drug-processing operation. But Fitzhugh, while willing to offer some material assistance, tells McNulty that his assistance will be limited because the emphasis of his office is shifting from drug cases to antiterrorism. Such an explicit marker of connection between these two enterprises asserts the analogy between them: from a law enforcement perspective, one endless war gives way to the next; but the process of surveillance goes on.

After we leave Judge Phelan's chambers, we move to a high-rise modernist rectangle, which we see from two low-angle shots. The door reads: "Narcotics Division." The cut is then to a pair of fingers pecking away at a typewriter keyboard. This general compositional strategy of defining Baltimore as a series of related but discontinuous spaces is one that is definitional for season 1. As we move forward in the season, we can see how this editing strategy not only highlights the relative physical isolation of the city's social spheres, but also shows the extent to which the goings-on in each sphere are comparable to, and yet distinct from, those in the other. As Greggs continues to peck away on her typewriter, the scene shifts abruptly, without transition, to a point-of-view shot from inside an SUV driven by Wee-Bey, who drives D'Angelo through the nighttime streets of West Baltimore. The inside-the-vehicle perspective makes the streets a context for, but not the subject of, the shot. Similarly, the relationship between Kima and these men is formed by the drug trade, but not as a matter of mere proximity—the building that houses the narcotics division and the vehicle in which these men drive are parts of distinct but related worlds. Wee-Bey, who supplies the violence for his gang, is to his system as Kima, who tracks and apprehends drug dealers, is to hers. Each is a competent, effective tool of his and her boss, but each is wedged into his and her position and cannot and would not choose to get out.

The relationship between cops and criminals is asymmetrical. *The Wire* asserts the hierarchical relationship between the institutions of the power structure and the underclass found in the ghetto. It is not as though the Barksdales survey the police; rather, the drug-dealing organization reacts to the surveillance set up by the law enforcement agencies. One of the conditions for the court order that allows for electronic surveillance to be put in place is that of exhaustion, meaning that other physical means of surveillance have failed. We see such exhaustion when Pryzbylewski, Carver, and Hauk, all drunk, invade the projects at two thirty one morning, expressing frustration at not being allowed to do any "real policing," they trigger a riot and end up retreating in the face of flying objects and gunfire. The scene is shot primarily from the point of view of the officers, showing us how the hunters soon become the hunted. Such a response reveals one way in which the projects are impregnable to the efforts of the police. (In season 3, we see the high rises succumb to forces from outside as they are demolished.) Indeed, that Omar can rob from the Barksdales, whereas the police cannot even record their illicit activities or, for that matter, find a picture of Avon Barksdale, shows the degree to which the ghetto is outside police control. Omar can reach into the projects because he is of their world.

Season 1, episode 2, A late-night visit to the high-rise projects.

The low-rise projects, the physical focus of the surveillance, are typically filmed as a self-contained space, but one that is contiguous with other ghetto spaces. The dealers sit on an orange couch in the middle of the courtyard, allowing D'Angelo, Bodie, and Poot a full perspective of their environs. The camera accentuates both their centrality and the way in which that courtyard stands for the relative insularity of policed and redlined African American neighborhoods, even if not of the projects in particular. Yet unlike most Baltimore locations we see in this season, the projects lead somewhere else. The principals of the drug trade stroll in and out of the courtyard, leaving for food or other errands. Such forays are some of the few in the season that allow the regular activities of urban life to take place on foot. In one instance, we even see D'Angelo taking a bus to work! The projects occur as part of a network of urban spaces defined by and frequented by the underclass; as the population center of that region, the projects are the site of the drug supermarket.

Generally, the establishing shot in the low-rise courtyard features a mobile camera that sweeps the field of vision in a semicircle. It is revealing that a clear exception to this practice occurs when Stringer Bell comes to talk to D'Angelo after Omar has robbed the stash. In that shot, the framing is classic—Stringer and D'Angelo stand framed against the brick buildings of the project: they are centered and at mid-distance.

Season 1, episode 12, Stringer visits the courtyard.

Omar's action triggers a specific reaction, one resulting from a sense of discomfort in this world that the Barksdales have largely defined. Stringer assumes that there is a security leak in the organization, but that surmise is as far as his imagination allows him to go. In this image, the courtyard becomes not the self-contained image of ghetto life; rather, it stands for the institutional apparatus and hierarchical structure of the Barksdale's drug organization. In this shot, Stringer is a CEO instructing a middle manager.

The relative equivalent of the ghetto for the police team is the bunker where the special investigative unit resides, a space in the basement of the old police headquarters, where the only exposure to daylight is through the high windows at street level. Those in the office can just make out a pair of shoes walking above them on the sidewalk. But the major distinction between this enclave and that of the projects is the investigative unit's access to means of technological intrusion. Through electronics, spatial distinctions can be breached and an alien culture can be investigated. Through their electronic pagers, the unit reconstitutes the geometry of the Barksdale gang, as we see by the chart on the bulletin board in the unit's office. It is telling that no form of face-to-face coercion is effective. This suggests the limits of proximity when there exists this gap in class and social function, and when one entity is absolutely estranged from the other. Such estrangement well defines a vision of urban life in which borders are rarely crossed and never really breached.

Just after the wiretap begins and an interrogation of the lower-level drug dealer Bodie by Herc and Carver yields nothing, we see D'Angelo and the mother of his child, Donette, entering a downtown restaurant, thereby moving outside their usual social and geographic circumstances. (A similar scene is in season 4 that involves adolescent school children.) Their palpable discomfort is accentuated by the visual composition of the scene. Here we see articulately the impact of shooting wide even as the world articulated by drugs and spatial segregation is narrow. In this scene, however, the context for the scene is the world that exists outside those spaces.

In the opening shot in the restaurant, Donette and D'Angelo are located in a long shot from a skewed angle; we see them diminished and out of place as they address the maître d'. In the foreground, sitting at a dark wooden bar are two middle-aged white men in suits and a younger white bartender wearing a gray server's jacket. When the black couple is approached by the maître d', it is with condescension, and D'Angelo catches it. He stammers and looks at Donette rather than the man, and the sound of his voice marks him further as out of place. That is, his vocabulary and vocal inflections mark him as a member of the African American underclass. Our sense of D'Angelo's discomfort is accentuated by his physical posture and the off-center angles of the shots. We also get frequent pans around the room, showing us well-dressed middle-class people, both black and white, who are smiling and moving about with ease. This further highlights the stiffness and discomfort of our young couple. To put a point on it, D'Angelo, ever sensitive, comments on his own feelings, asking, "Do they know? Do they know what I'm about. . . . Acting like we belong down here." In a close-up from an off-center angle, Donette says, "So? Your money good, right? We ain't the only black people in here." Responds D'Angelo, "It ain't about that. It ain't what I'm talking about." We see Donette react even as we hear D'Angelo expand on his feelings: "You know, I just feel some shit stay with you. Hard as you try, you still can't go nowhere." And indeed, not going anywhere is the key to this season. All roads lead back to West Baltimore, wherever its denizens wander. It is home, a place that is inescapable, akin to prison for the happy recidivist who cannot wait to get back to the familiarity of being behind bars. D'Angelo is comfortable and in command on his orange couch, but feels none of that security while sitting on a banquette

Season 1, episode 5, D'Angelo and Donette dine out.

in a downtown restaurant. Such is Simon's means of decoupling social class and wealth.

In one of the ensuing scenes, we see the aforementioned visit of Avon and D'Angelo to the state acute care facility, to see Avon's brother. The scene is profoundly institutional, and the camera work is mostly unobtrusive. A wide shot shows us the extent of the building as they enter. Avon tells of D'Angelo's mother "ragging at me to put him in a private nursing home." But Avon explains that he is unable to do that because he cannot show that kind of income: the use of his wealth is severely circumscribed by the means by which it has been acquired. As they walk down the charmless cinder-block hall, we see the facility "objectively," finding the two men together and proceeding through the hall. These shots allow us to view D'Angelo's extreme disquiet at the dreariness of the place and what it means for its inhabitants. Periodically, the shot shifts perspective to show us the scene through D'Angelo's point of view so that we can feel the basis of his despair.

When they come to Avon's brother, he is lying in a bed in a ward, completely immobile and comatose. Avon declaims on his gangster past and the fact that some happenstance led to his being in this state. The camera shows the brothers together, and Avon reveals his deep understanding of this state as a possible outcome of his professional life. It is suggested that the brother lies there because of some error in the execution of a plan, and that he was wounded in the course of his gangster life. The scene cuts to a close-up of Avon, to one of D'Angelo, and then to a wider shot to show both men, the ward, and one other bed. Again, this scene relativizes the gangster life temporally and metaphysically, showing us the limits of its rewards and its possible outcomes. Such views show us the desperation involved in such a lifestyle choice, robbing it of its promise of wealth and the allure of its excitement.

When the investigative unit finally identifies and makes contact with Avon, it is as a result of the wiretap, and it takes place amid the empty row houses on the west side, though to little effect. Avon has coached a neighborhood basketball game, and word of the game reaches the investigative team. Spying him on the sideline, they track him in order to do the thing that the listening devices cannot—provide an image of their target so they he can be physically tracked while committing his nefarious deeds. The tracking of Barksdale takes place on the west side, and our perspective allows us to see him on his home turf, a turf not impregnable to the police but clearly outside their element. We track through a variety of points of view as police cars become eyes on the streets.

The ultimate index of the geographic wonders of the ghetto on the west side of Baltimore is illustrated in one of the culminating events of season 1, when Kima goes undercover and is shot in an alley on "Warwick, near Longwood." She is accompanied by Orlando, whose car, a vintage early-1970s green Lincoln Town Car with a brown vinyl roof, is lost by the police cars tracking it. Kima and her fellow officers are disoriented by the terrain, and even after she is shot, it takes some minutes before her exact location can be deduced.

The camera work in this portion of the episode is suitably disorienting. We get frequent cuts between the tracking police cars, one with Daniels and McNulty, and one with Sydnor and Carver, who seek to remain in contact with Kima and Orlando. When Orlando is directed to stop in a dark alley of deserted buildings and trash, Kima tries to inform the tracking cars of her whereabouts but is unable to do so, offering only an approximation. Says Orlando, "Hoppers be turning the signpost to fuck with you all." Indeed, they are clearly off the grid of areas protected by police services, literally in between charted districts. We see a midshot of the car in the alley and it appears to be nowhere. As Kima strains with her head out the window to see both her locale and situation, she seems to be nowhere but in the car. This strategy also informs the frequent cuts to the two tracking vehicles. We cut to a tight shot of Daniels

Season 1, episode 10, Kima is shot.

in his car, then to a tight two-shot of McNulty and Daniels. The other police car is defined in the same visual manner, offering a disorienting sense of geography. We next get a quick cut to shadows of men creeping through the overgrowth of vacant lots and then a very tight shot of Kima, beleaguered and looking intently out the car window. We see the men jump from the shadows and shoot, but concurrently we see Daniels and McNulty hearing the shots as they race to where they hope they will find Kima. Kima's shooting is staged with a brief instant of temporal overlap—we both see it and then see others hearing it.

Such a compositional strategy has its roots in the early cinema, going as far back as Edwin S. Porter's short, highly influential film *The Great Train Robbery* (1903). It suggests the power of the technological medium to alter viewers' perceptions by reordering time. This assertion of the power of a viewing apparatus provides another index of the power of surveillance and the law-and-order apparatus that controls this means of intrusion; yet Kima is shot, the drugs still flow, and, ultimately, Bell remains free and Barksdale serves a limited prison sentence. Clearly, there is some reordering of social power at work here.

For the first time in the series, we see the world through the surveillance devices mounted on a helicopter as that device sweeps the streets in search of Orlando's car. This represents a step up in viewing technology: we are provided highly mobile point-of-view shots from this fast-moving vehicle. Yet finding Kima in the maze of streets and alleys is difficult. Though the eye in the sky eventually finds the immobile car with Kima and Orlando, McNulty, driving those same streets, finds it at the same time. Such a result finds us questioning the advantages of technology in such terrain. Perhaps this urban zone is impregnable to outsiders? Or perhaps efforts to regulate a natural market, both physically and economically, are futile?

STRINGER BELL AND ADAM SMITH

In episode 8 of this season, McNulty tails Bell to Baltimore County Community College and finds him in an economics class. As the officer, who knows nothing of such things, strains to listen at the door of this light but clearly institutional classroom, we hear a young woman instructing her class in macroeconomic theory, explaining the changes in markets arising from product supply and consumer demand. She explains that some products are subject to inelastic demand, based on the needs and desires of the buyers. Bell chimes in to answer her question, clearly having heroin in mind. To see heroin not as the provenance of gangsters but as just another product of the international marketplace implicates the ghetto in a global network of exchange. It also subjugates morality and class to simple, apparently natural principles of trade. In economic theory, heroin is neither bad nor good; it simply *is*. And seeing how money has the capacity to create more money is the furtherance of a basic principle of capitalism.

As Bell learns about capitalism, Carver and Hauk (Herc) in a parallel cut, study for the police exam. As Bell aces economics, the police officers learn the arcane and self-referential rules of the Baltimore law-and-order bureaucracy. Bell inhabits a classroom of light and expertise, while the police officers labor in the shadows of their cellar offices. We next see Bell in his newly opened copying shop, lecturing his staff, which consists of his drug workers, in running a business and in the necessity of doing so competently and professionally. This signals the application of his knowledge on a small scale. It also shows how he is diversifying, suggesting that he is plotting his path out of the criminal life, echoing Michael Corleone's assertion in *The Godfather: Part II* that the business of the mob will soon be legitimate. Though it turned out not to be true in that case, such a vision of diversification also informs Bell's

Season 1, episode 8, Stringer Bell and Adam Smith.

thinking. And as we see the copy shop in the business sector of Baltimore, and see Bell among the other students at the community college, it appears that ghettoization can be ameliorated, in certain conditions. That, as Donette says, money is money, and no one cares how you make it. Indeed, Joseph Kennedy was quite likely a bootlegger, and his son became president. Bell seeks to transform his cash into a place in the legitimate economy of neoliberalism, shrewdly seeing that the growth area for him to access is real estate and business support services. Indeed, in the ensuing seasons, the distinctiveness of drug money, or its relative lack of distinction, is one of the issues that recur.

Further, Simon places this broad query into contexts that show how wealth is produced—political graft, by which politicians make money, and buying influence, by which the buyers create their own road to wealth. We also see the scale of power that creates conditions in which the rich get richer as a direct result of the poor getting poorer. Indeed, this logic extends to the state; Simon develops an embedded narrative of neoliberalism in which the state, because of its inability to tax sufficiently, gradually loses its capacity to function effectively. In this regard, season 1, despite the failure of the state's prosecutors to put Avon in prison for an extended period, stands as a moment of relative triumph for the "system." But that system is that of capitalism and individual financial gain at the expense of those lower on the food chain. Though Avon, because of his place in the drug hierarchy, is given a relatively short sentence, D'Angelo and Wee-Bey suffer far harsher treatment. Inequality, then, seems built into the system in all its incarnations, including that of the "justice" system. Season 1 provides the preamble to the next four seasons as it segues from its genre basis to a more focalized examination of key urban institutions in the age of neoliberalism.

{ TWO }

Season 2

THE WIRE, THE WATERFRONT, AND THE RAVAGES OF NEOLIBERALISM

The season begins with a scene that includes near-perfect visual and verbal suggestions of the thematic range of the story ahead. Because of his insubordination in season 1, Officer James McNulty has been moved to the place he said he would never want to work: on a boat in Baltimore harbor as a member of the harbor patrol. This pre-credit scene provides a shot of a previously unseen Baltimore: the harbor, a location with a specific history that calls up the city's past—indeed, its reason for existing and relatively prospering. We encounter a locale—piers, warehouses, abandoned factories—that suggests Baltimore's day as a busy industrial port, but that time has clearly passed. In a point-of-view shot, we see McNulty and his new partner, Diggins, motoring past cranes and industrial plants. Says McNulty, "My dad used to work there." "Beth Steel?" asks Diggsie. "Shipyards there," says McNulty. "Had an uncle who was a supervisor there, got laid off in '78," responds Diggins, "'73 for my dad." This brief and laconic exchange defines as typical the experience of workers displaced in the economic restructuring that defined the 1970s, the historical moment when the system of increasingly globalized exchange was being put into place. This was the moment when the Bretton Woods system of monetary policy, a set of agreements put in place after World War II, was altered and national currencies ceased to be backed by gold. As a result, national currencies floated in a world market, a market in which the relative value of a means of exchange defined by a nation floated in relation to the value of other types of money. Such fluidity in the world financial system allowed multinational companies to invest in far-flung regions. It also enabled the circulation of goods throughout a world system, since currency could be exchanged freely. For Bethlehem Steel, which had not made

Season 2, episode 1, McNulty, Diggs, and the postindustrial harbor.

sufficient capital investments to modernize its facilities in the 1950s and 1960s, competition from Japanese steel makers resulted in losses, plant consolidations, and closings.

The means of making this larger point about the cascading effects of deindustrialization is a story of the waterfront union, its leader (Frank Sobotka), and his efforts to save his local. Sobotka is the secretary-treasurer of the Baltimore chapter of the International Brotherhood of Stevedores (IBS). His goal is to make the members of his union prosper and, more generally, to preserve the longshoreman's way of life in an economic environment that degrades blue-collar work, unionized labor in particular. It is likely that the stevedore's union was named with some sense of irony, since the job of stevedore—the word refers to the loading and unloading of ship's cargo by human labor—has ceased to exist in an age of mechanization. To make money for his local, Frank involves himself with international smugglers, the Greek and his subordinate Stavros, and makes himself a conduit for their importing of illegal commodities into Baltimore: primarily, drugs and women. His plan is to take the proceeds of his illegal activities and buy votes in the state legislature—through lavish campaign contributions—and thereby produce the political will to fund needed improvements in the port. But given the history of petty theft on the docks, and the dire situation of the workers, who barely receive sufficient work to support themselves, Frank's corrupt practices catalyze other corrupt practices—theft, further smuggling—and the formerly clean port of Baltimore becomes increasingly lawless. The result is both an economic and family tragedy: Frank is killed by his smuggling partners, his son Ziggy is incarcerated for murdering one of the smugglers, his nephew Nick is implicated in heroin smuggling, and the projects that Frank sought to fund remain unfunded.

The narrative momentum of the season is provided by two events that trigger the plot action. Both Sobotka and police commander Stan Valchek donate stained-glass windows to their church, but only Sobotka's, the larger one, was installed. Valchek responds with a vendetta against Sobotka, which includes an investigation of the union. In the second incident, McNulty, as part of the harbor patrol, finds a woman's body in the water and traces it to a shipping container on Sobotka's dock. Later, another dozen dead young women are found in a shipping container. The investigations into these two occurrences eventually merge, and we come to see that Sobotka has been involved with international criminals.

The opening scene introduces the major spatial emphases of the season. It begins with the image of McNulty riding a police boat in the harbor, moves immediately to Bodie—a young, lower-level figure in the corner drug trade—heading to Philadelphia to pick up drugs that have been shipped from outside the country, and then shifts to shots of the Patapsco River shipping terminal in Baltimore harbor. These points of reference connect this season with the preceding one; the drug trade is referred to through Bodie, a member of D'Angelo Barksdale's crew at the low-rise housing projects. He becomes a device to link that trafficking with its source—the harbor—and thereby to a network of higher-ups and enablers such as Sobotka and the international smuggling concern headed by the Greek. The juxtaposition of these scenes involves the city in a complexly plotted network of spaces where, ultimately, relational definitions reconnect what, in other historical contexts, might seem remote locales. Nevertheless, this season elaborates the nature of those links, which give the season its thematic heft. We see Baltimore both as a historically significant shipping point *and* as a deindustrialized urban space largely left behind in the post-1980s restructuring of the US economy. Simon makes this connection explicit:

> If there's anything polemical about this second season, it's an argument about what happened in this country when we stopped making

> shit and building shit, what happened to all the people who were doing that. If you look at what the Port of Baltimore once brought in and out of this city and you look at what was made here and shipped overseas, and you look at what we do now, it's a very different world. Just as in the first season, where the institutions are not particularly sympathetic to those people who serve them once they have less use—once they're of less use to the institution, I should say—the same thing happens in the second season.[1]

This focus provides a narrative emphasis that explores the fate of unionized work in the era of neoliberalism, and the underside of globalized trade. Although shipping is a natural area of growth within the economic regime of globalization, the situation of Baltimore and its longshoremen suggests how trade becomes centralized and labor perpetually degraded.

The competence and relative lack of corruption that marked the Baltimore waterfront in the World War II era are largely matters of retrospection and, therefore, nostalgia in this season. In the series, the local, as Valchek tells us, consists of no more than one hundred dues-paying members. This may indeed seem paradoxical, since with the coming of enhanced global trade in the 1980s and 1990s, it would seem to follow that ports would be busier and therefore would be one of the few unionized sites where labor demand exceeded supply. But Baltimore was one of the ports left behind, because of its geography and partly as a matter of its particular economic situation. Baltimore's shipping channel is relatively shallow, which was a limiting factor throughout the twentieth century. In the container ship era, this feature has been particularly restrictive, constraining the efficiency with which cargo could move into the docks. For reasons also connected with geography, shipping to Baltimore requires traveling an extra distance from the Atlantic shipping lanes. Historically, Baltimore was far more important as an exporting port than as an importing one. Initially, Baltimore was a major shipper of grain and, later, textiles, and, later still, steel. In the last decades of the twentieth century and the beginning of the twenty-first, Baltimore's docks could not compete with Hampton Roads, Virginia, or Newark/Port Elizabeth, New Jersey. In 2004, at about the time this season was shot, it was twelfth in imports and around twentieth in exports among US ports.[2]

In season 2, we see a conscious effort by Simon to broaden the scope of the show. He explains:

> If we hadn't gone somewhere else in Baltimore, we couldn't have said to anyone we were trying to write about the city. Ed and myself and Bob Colesberry—who inspired the visual look of the show, and who sadly passed away—the three of us said, we want to build a city. If we get on a run, we want people to say, "That is an American city, those are its problems, and that's why they can't solve its problems." If we had just gone back to the ghetto and continued to plumb the Barksdale story, it would have been a much smaller show, and it would have claimed a much smaller canvas.[3]

Though the season was broadly conceived by Simon and Burns, in order to develop a working knowledge of the Baltimore waterfront, Simon leaned on Rafael Alvarez, a former reporter for the *Baltimore Sun* and a contributor to season 1. Simon explains why: "When it came to longshoremen, we added Rafael Alvarez, a former reporter and short-story writer who had quit to join the seamen's union and whose family was three generations in the maritime industry. And the rest of us, myself included, spent weeks getting to know longshoremen and the operations of the port and the port unions, just hanging around the shipping terminals for days on end, so as to credibly achieve those voices."[4]

This season alters the specific emphasis on constrained spaces that marked season 1, in order to characterize a city that projects out into the world. On the other hand, it offers a world of even smaller spaces than the ghetto as a kind of complement to this larger vision of networked Baltimore: small offices, the shipping container where the dead woman are found, a booth at a diner where smuggling is transacted, the prison cells where Avon, Wee-Bey, and D'Angelo currently reside. As the larger geography suggests, those waterfront settings and the prominence of the shipping industry provide a means of dramatizing international commerce and the related fate of unionized labor. But each scale, the large and the small, is presented as related to the other. The season develops a strategy that emphasizes how the distended geographic networks of globalized commerce create their own terms of opposition: narrow networks defined by proximity and specific affiliations: Polish American dockworkers; Greek, Ukrainian, and Israeli smugglers; and African American drug dealers (some incarcerated). Such connected groups suggest the prospect of a counterforce to the dogma of neoliberalism even as that force fails to coalesce.

As the season ends, the devices of regnant globalized commerce seem triumphant, since we see that further gentrification of the port is on the table. This poses the question whether the improvement of the port, which will create many ongoing union jobs, will take precedence over building condos for yuppies. (We see in season 5 that it doesn't.) This issue of the use of urban spaces is fundamentally a political one: who has the political wherewithal to affect policy, the real estate lobby or the unions?

In keeping with season 1, central to the investigation of international smuggling is the use of electronic surveillance. In the first two seasons, the thread connecting season to season is organized around the detail led by Lieutenant Daniels to investigate drug dealing. In season 1, it was the impenetrability of the Barksdale gang, which led to the need for the wire. In this season, the dead woman's body floating on the river causes a panic among politicians and police bureaucrats, and Daniels is detailed to lead the investigation into her death and those of the smuggled women found dead in a shipping container, an inquiry that quickly leads to the union local and to its role in the drug trade. As in season 1, the ethos of the local culture makes it almost impenetrable to outsiders. As a result, electronic surveillance is instituted. But this investigation is far more complex than that of the previous season, which merely tried to pick up telephone conversations from drug dealers. Further, in episode 7 we find that evidence of prostitution is, by law, not sufficient for requesting a wiretap. So this season focuses on other forms of electronic surveillance, particularly tracking the electronic means that routs and manages cargo on the docks. This is a system of tagging and sequencing loads, which is vital to expediting the movement of cargo. This movement of goods is central to globalized trade. While focusing on unionized work, Simon also provides a window into the highly rationalized system of modern shipping and shows how technology makes labor redundant. This technology also enables both corruption and a means of detecting that corruption—with the right tools. The wire of last season expands into the world of cloned computers, which allow the tracking of cargo in real time. The docks of Baltimore become part of an international network, but the drugs, prostitutes, and other contraband that pass through them are commodities with important local implications.

When we see the Barksdale gang in this season, we are able to understand its role as a local aspect of an international network of drug dealing and distribution. The shadowy figure in charge of this operation, and many other organized-crime ventures, is known as the Greek, but he admits that he isn't Greek at all.

Simon and his cowriters develop a narrative of globalization and deindustrialization, providing a story that accesses the classic film *On the Waterfront* (1954) but updates that tale in moral complexity for the age of neoliberalism. Frank's union is called the International Brotherhood of Stevedores. The real-world analogue of this union seems to be the International Longshoremen's Association (ILA). The ILA was the subject of that classic film, written by Budd Schulberg, directed by Elia Kazan, and starring Marlon Brando. Not incidentally, that film was deeply involved in Cold War politics; it emerged soon after the writer and director were subpoenaed by the House Un-American Activities Committee.[5] Following the film's narrative, the East Coast incarnation of the ILA is one of the most notoriously corrupt unions in US labor history, with long-standing ties to organized crime, ties that remain today.[6] Yet Baltimore's waterfront was relatively clean, and at one time was cited as a model for all ports. Whereas Kazan and Schulberg operated in a moral universe of black and white, Simon and the Sobotkas clearly reside in a world of grays. Explains Simon of his desire to update the Kazan and Schulberg portrayal of dockworkers, "*On the Waterfront*, which is a great movie, but it's certainly about half a century old."[7]

Frank's corruption is at least motivated by a means-ends conundrum: he can engage in smuggling for the greater good of preserving a way of life with which he strongly identifies and which Simon asserts as worthy. One of the recurring questions posed by the plotline of *On the Waterfront* is whether the dockworkers will testify to the crime commission or remain "deaf and dumb" ("d and d" in the vernacular of the film). This ethos of not talking to outsiders and remaining particularly uncommunicative if they represent the powers of law enforcement is also portrayed prominently in season 2 of *The Wire*. In the end, we see that this narrative employs a contemporary rewriting of that film's central moral question and repositions the idea of "corruption," and even of crime, as a relative concept in an age when market concepts of profit and loss make notions of "the good" seem decidedly old-fashioned.

THE DIALECTICS OF SPACE

Season 1 was driven by an articulate sense of the definitions of the spaces of ghetto life, and particularly by a vision of the insularity of the extreme underclass's urban experience. It employed the drug trade as a device for understanding the early twenty-first century's deindustrialized city. The conditions of that city, to some degree, explain the terms and dimensions of that class, revealing the degree to which capital flight results in a paucity of services and opportunities for those left behind. Season 2 shifts the series' focus to the world of dignified and adequately compensated work, and its erosion in the era of globalization and regnant neoliberalism. It is about the dialectics of space, emphasizing how the expanse of a globalized system of trade and communication creates and relies on its other, a local and parochial system of affiliations and associations.[8]

It is as though the more expansive a relational network of commerce becomes, the more it creates resistance and narrow bonding on the local level. In contemporary international terms, such resistance is the stuff of the upsurge of religious zealotry and criminal syndicates throughout the world as globalization spawns and catalyzes oppositional modes of community. Such a vision of the dialectic between the macro perspective of the globalist and the micro perspective of those concerned with the local and with the bonds of narrow affiliation lies at the heart of the writings of the cultural theorist Arjun Appadurai.

Appadurai elaborates on, among other things, the ways in which the extensive and distended systems of cultural and economic exchange that are definitional in this age of the global produce a need among those less comfortably situated within those structures to produce and cling to the local—as do characters like Frank Sobotka and Stan Valchek. And while Appadurai focuses substantially on how ethnic minorities in particular corners of the underdeveloped world are moved to violence, applying the definitions that typically affix to those groups to our waterfront workers and their associates is illuminating, since it allows for a vision of affiliation within a category that is the direct target of neoliberal reorganization: unionized workers. Appadurai's discussion of the dialectics of space within an era of globalized trade and neoliberal economics allows us to see how these systems create their other. According to Appadurai, "Put simply, the task of producing locality (as a structure of feeling, a property of social life, and an ideology of situated community) is increasingly a struggle."[9] Such difficulty of coalescence and persistence results in the privileging of what Appadurai describes as the "neighborhood," an actual physical place within this season, one that houses the dockworkers and, to an extent, the Greeks. Physically coherent, it has been defined, though not unproblematically so, by ethnicity, class, and occupation—but it is being eroded by gentrification.

Appadurai goes on to consider the definitions and norms that characterize the articulation of these discrete spaces within the epoch of the modern nation-state and how these residual forms persist in the era of the global. He comments on the historical production of "modes of localization most congenial to the modern nation-state," which "have a disciplinary quality about them." While Appadurai carefully avoids an excessive valorization of the moment of the nation-state, he notes that its disruption produces "new instabilities that cause further social unrest."[10] He calls the response to these disruptions the "new patriotism," an extreme localism characterized by its varied and at times unproductive resistance to the global; and indeed, this resistance has included such barbaric acts as the flying of airplanes into tall office buildings. Such localism, then, constitutes the alternative structures of globalization and includes both the progressive and atavistic strains of social and political organizing. In our example, it includes both the solidarity of the dockworkers and the ways in which they can become affiliated with criminal enterprises that rely on their silence and that reach out to them through personal entreaties.

The local also includes an emphasis on the body and the personal. This season shows how the local may also be characterized by the absence of progressive ideas and by effective resistance to the regime of multinational corporations. This regressive type of localism becomes a visually emphasized motif within the season as we are tantalized by unrealized possibilities. The small spaces that suggest the antithesis of the global instead become corrupted into spaces controlled by petty narcissists. This emphasis on the power of those who command small spaces and particular constituencies is suggested in the opening shot after the credits in episode 1, which takes place in Stan Valchek's office. That shot accentuates both the smallness of the office and Valchek's pettiness. Yet it is Valchek's petty vendetta against Sobotka that triggers the investigation that creates the core plot for the season. It is his patronage of his son-in-law Pryzbylewski that creates the contours of the detail. When Valchek is annoyed with the fact that the church will not accept his gift, he tickets stevedores' cars parked near the pier. But it is in the first face-to-face confrontation between Valchek and Sobotka that we see the depth of their antipathy and the fact that it is based on no more than a personality clash and long-standing family antipathies.

Thirty or so minutes into the first episode, our second plot motivator appears, a narrative device that actuates the conventional police drama that defines the surface of the many-layered tale of the season. The shot cuts to a helicopter framed against the sky, and then cuts away to a point-

Season 2, episode 2, Valchek and Sobotka face-to-face.

of-view shot of a floating corpse in the harbor. The helicopter reminds us of the expanse that is policed by the officers of the city of Baltimore: that the urban space includes not only the landmass that defines that entity. It also harks back to the shooting of Kima in season 1, when helicopters were called in to find her assailants. As in the case of the harbor, these eyes in the sky provided a means of policing areas off the usual grid of areas where police can readily patrol. The view of the harbor also shows us how the city conjoins with other areas—and that those areas reach toward the space beyond the city, out into the world beyond.

The shot cuts to the corpse alone in the water, framed against a bridge, and McNulty and Diggins appear in their boat to claim the body. Their waterside policing is a vital adjunct to the helicopter patrol and defines a more hands-on engagement. In keeping with the season's constant moving back and forth between close views and distant views of the action, the very shifts that define the dialectics of globalization, the corpse is both an objectified statistic and a former living, breathing human. McNulty and his perverse conscience define her humanness with his obsessive quest to find out who she is and who "her people" are so that he can keep her from the anonymous fate of being a medical school cadaver. On the other hand, we see her reduced to a statistic as we see

Season 2, episode 1, A helicopter patrols the harbor.

local officials try to avoid the bureaucratic burden of having to investigate this death, by claiming it is a suicide.

Brief cuts to Frank's nephew Nick awakening in his parent's house, a small structure within walking distance of the port, and to the drug lord of season 1, Stringer Bell, visiting his partner, Avon Barksdale, in prison interrupt these causally related scenes. In prison, Bell and Barksdale talk about ways to strategically cope with their lack of good heroin while continuing to maintain their selling locations. Both scenes reinforce the dialectic between centripetal and centrifugal forces, the contrast that marks this season. We see Nick moving from the warren by the piers to the ship where the girls will be found. This juxtaposition contrasts the small and insular spaces of dockworkers with the ways in which their labor reaches into a world beyond the piers. Similarly, the spaces of prison are related to the larger world of drug commerce (a subject I return to in the next chapter). We soon learn that the paucity of product is due to the Drug Enforcement Association's arresting an importer from the Dominican Republic. That Avon Barksdale performs a small, adjunct role in a type of world trade suggests that local markets and decisions are involved in far more extensive systems of commerce.

Soon after, Beatrice Russell, an officer with the port authority, dis-

Season 2, episode 1, Barksdale and Bell confer in prison.

covers thirteen corpses inside a shipping container. The initial discovery is shot to accentuate the confines of the box. We see Russell in the doorway, flashlight in hand.

Though most shots of the containers on the docks emphasize their size and the ease with which these full boxes can be hitched to a truck, once we see the dead girls filling the shipping device, it immediately shrinks in proportion. That is, we can see that size is a relative measure. The containers are bigger than boxes and taller than a person; but as a home, however temporary, for many women, they are potentially lethal and certainly very uncomfortable. These women reveal another dimension of international trafficking: drugs, women, and guns comprise the largest categories of commodities shipped throughout the world.[11] They have, in effect, been executed by one of the sailors, making a largely peripheral character both the key to the season and the key to the fate of these women.

That these are white women from eastern Europe and that the drug importers are also white throws a wrinkle into pat racial assumptions that were too easily verified in season 1. Indeed, their whiteness is only a matter of situation, since the term specifically refers to a US-based system of racial classification. In eastern Europe, such a classification would be relatively meaningless: noting this allows us to focus more clearly on

Season 2, episode 1, Russell at the container.

their economic situation. We are able to see Baltimore as a space of trade that depends on the persistence of uneven development, both regionally and internationally. That disparity in wealth is the device that creates illicit traffic. Compared to the Dominican Republic and Belarus, Baltimore is relatively prosperous. Compared to the downtown lawyers, the dockworkers are relatively impoverished. Compared to the denizens of the ghetto, the dockworkers are princes of the city, and the police officers are kings. In this world, petty politics become a means by which the small become large: we see Valchek tormenting Sobotka, and the prison guard Tillman tormenting the Bell-Barksdale family hit man, Wee-Bey, who serves in the same prison as Avon.

In a related action, D'Angelo Barksdale, Avon's nephew, is strangled in prison by a man hired by Stringer. Again, the fact of small spaces and the ways in which the body is increasingly vulnerable in such spaces is further confirmed by the inevitability of this murder. Petty dictators who seek to maintain power within discrete spaces fill the season; but these characters' claims to authority are ultimately outside the world's flow of lucrative trade. It is only within such small spaces that local punishments can be exacted.

In a macro-spatial frame, what we are viewing in these spaces is redundant labor. This excess of workers is a product of neoliberal policies

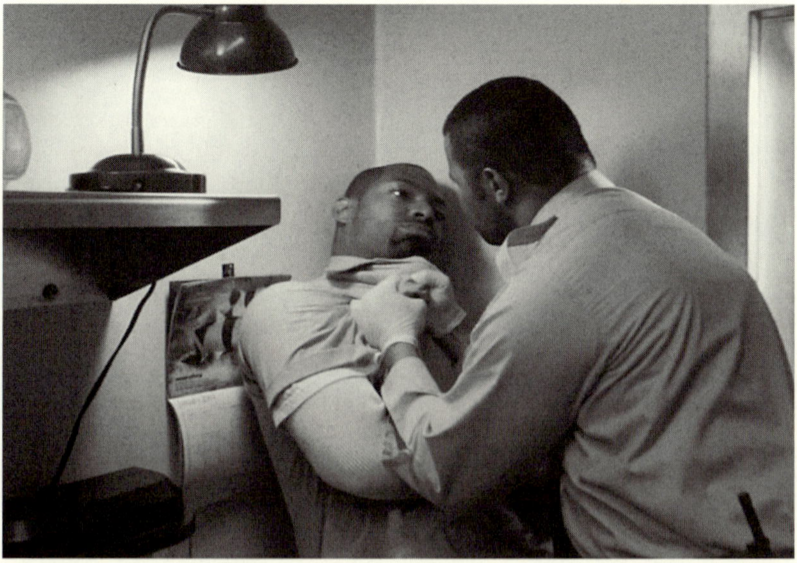

Season 2, episode 2, Tillman torments Wee-Bey.

and the related mechanization of work. The fate of these women and of D'Angelo has a direct connection with that of the idled waterfront workers. This view allows us to see the body as a form of variable capital. That is, within the current configurations of world exchange, a body attains value according to the demand for its services. David Harvey cites any number of contemporary practices, including the creation of unemployment, the revaluing of particular skills, and devices that "increase productivity" as creating an excess in the world market of labor, which can be exploited to keep wages down and workers powerless.[12] Thus, what we see in the container box and in prison are those who can readily be extracted from the sum of labor available and who therefore are allowed to fall from the marketplace. In such spaces, then, their fate is left to those who capriciously exercise authority over their small spaces. In prison, it is guards and those who exploit their corruption. On ships, it is stewards, low-level officers, and the criminal syndicates that exploit low-wage workers to do their bidding.

Such an emphasis asks us to look at the wreckage of Baltimore's local economy within a far larger dynamic of world commerce. As Harvey, a former Baltimore resident, explains in *Spaces of Hope*, Baltimore in the 1960s underwent a significant restructuring of its local and regional economy. Shifts in the "circulation of variable capital" resulted in a massive movement of jobs from industry to the service sector, particularly the hospitality sector. By variable capital, Harvey, after Marx, refers to a downward recalibrating of the value of labor in a particular time and place.[13] In global economic terms, this perspective allows us to see deindustrialization as part of a movement in world capitalism that saw investment in labor as a highly plastic cost and one that was judged to be important in determining overall profit. In the 1960s, '70s, and '80s, such a view relatively privileged labor costs above proximity to markets, raw materials, and managerial apparatus. With this focus, industries such as steel, shipbuilding, electronics production, and textiles, among others, moved out of the United States to lower-wage markets. Thus, Baltimore saw its market position as a relative center of production diminish, which required, within the logic of capitalist economics, its labor to be devalued. Since the structure of industrial work and its unions made such devaluation difficult within that sector, that type of work ceased to exist in Baltimore and was moved to locales where productive technology were more current *and* labor less expensive.[14] Factors of spatial proximity to resources and markets diminished in importance because of improvements in technologies of transportation and communication that, as capitalists had long sought, allowed the relative significance of space to be diminished.

Such larger perspectives allow us to see Baltimore within a far more expansive geographic and economic context, a view vital for defining the emphases of this season. When we look at the unused capacity of the docks and their proximate economic assets—the dry dock, the steel mill, and the grain pier—we are witnessing not just the deindustrializing of Baltimore but also the industrializing of China, Vietnam, and Malaysia. As Harvey explains: "What we now call 'globalization' has been in the sights of the capitalist class all along . . . In spite of the massive unintended consequences in the relation to nature that are increasingly felt, the belief still prevails that the conquest of space and time . . . is still within our reach. The result has been an inexorable trend for the world of capital to produce 'time-space compression'—a world in which capital moves faster and faster and where distances of interaction are compressed."[15]

Deindustrialization then becomes a way in which capital addresses a condition of uneven development. If labor costs are significantly less expensive in China, then steel can be produced there and shipped back to the United States, creating a lower-priced product with which to build, for example, New York skyscrapers. Displaced by this strategy are not only steelworkers, but also dockworkers who were employed at the ports where steel was formerly made and exported—in this model, the quantity of imported materials is far less than the quantity formerly exported—and any number of workers who were involved in providing and moving the raw materials necessary for steel production. So as Bethlehem Steel jettisons its Baltimore facility, those who work on the docks—like Frank Sobotka—see their wages suffer. Season 2 provides a human story that elaborates the costs for the US worker of this macro strategy. Characters such as Frank's nephew Nick, and even his son Ziggy, cannot get enough hours during the week to support themselves and have any hope for the future. Mechanization doesn't mean only less backbreaking work: it means less work in general. As a result, trafficking in drugs and women becomes too alluring to resist.

By seeing Frank's longshoremen's union within the context of globalized trade, we can understand that the costs of shipping are among those that industrialists seek to minimize. The longshoremen, like all elements of organized labor, are afflicted by capital's "race to the bottom." That is, industrialists constantly try to reduce the overall costs of commodities in order to maximize profits; but unlike workers in the early twentieth century, when Henry Ford's distinctly modern River Rouge Plant pioneered the assembly line, the workers in a discrete region need not also be significant consumers of a particular product. Since capital and consumers are increasingly mobile, it may not matter whether, to use the Ford example, those who make the Model T can afford to buy it. Those who make clothes for Banana Republic in Malaysia certainly cannot afford to buy them. If we follow this model, eventually the relative buying power of the US middle class may be less important than the capital available in the emerging markets in India and China, and therefore providing adequate wages to the US labor force in order for it to maintain its power to consume may not seem worth it. And so the compact in the United States between capital and labor that was definitional in the post–World War II expansion becomes increasingly irrelevant.[16]

The diminishing significance of unionized labor is a subtext throughout the season. Indeed, when the far more successful port of Newport News, Virginia, is cited by Frank Sobotka for its structural benefits—shipping into the Port of Baltimore involves sailing up the Patapsco River and therefore spending more time at sea—no mention is made of its nonunion employees in that right-to-work state. Perhaps this is a matter of not wanting to mitigate his point about geographic propinquity. In an economic landscape where technology allows for products and services to

Season 2, episode 7, "You can't get hurt if you ain't working."

migrate to low-wage locales, Frank's unionized dockworkers are at a decided disadvantage. Thus, in a cost-benefit analysis, Baltimore becomes a less desirable port, and therefore its workers suffer—just as its steel workers suffered as a result of the same analytical device. As Simon averred in an interview with Bill Moyers, "Unions and working people are completely abandoned by this economic culture and that's what Season Two was about. It was about one of the forces, one of the walls that basically make the corner culture."[17] By focusing on dockworkers, Simon draws implicit and explicit connections between these white, ethnic, unionized workers and those—African American and white—who sell drugs on the corners. All suffer from their status as redundant labor, and all are drawn into an alternative network of commerce defined by its marginal status.

Season 2 tells of the relationship between the local and the transnational in the historical moment of neoliberalism. Thus, the invisible hand that Adam Smith valorized has become a mercenary device that devalues work in the interest of abstracted financial profits. Simon chooses Frank Sobotka as his tragic hero, a fitting selection, since Frank signifies a type that is, as a matter of his situation, about to become extinct. Frank is a union man and a union boss, certainly a vanishing breed in the United States—even though he engages in an occupation that is vital to international commerce, and even though his local constitutes

Season 2, episode 1, Party boat.

one of the specific devices by which goods are moved from one nation to another. But even that occupation is under duress, and not only in Baltimore. In a telling scene in episode 7, Frank takes part in a seminar extolling the wonders of technology; it uses Rotterdam as an example. At this presentation, Frank and Nat Coxson, another union official, are part of group shown a video of the future of shipping. They sit in the dark as they watch the further terms of their own extinction. They learn that increasingly sophisticated technology—robotics, lasers, and so forth—will allow human employment to be severely reduced, even if shipping volume is increased. Frank and Nat are distinctive in the audience for their casual dress and their concern for workers. The slick presenter dodges Nat's questions about man-hours and instead tells them of reduced accidents—which are a direct result of employing fewer workers. We see Nat and Frank in close-up as the camera pans from one to the other. Frank affirms the obvious: "You can't get hurt if you ain't working."

Such a view affirms what was conveyed indirectly in episode 1. As the pre-credit scene develops, we see McNulty and Diggins continuing their cruise along the harbor. Following the initial reference to the decline of US heavy industry and its effect on unionized workers, we are provided a snapshot of the emerging two-class economic system in the contemporary United States. The two officers see a boat, not a working craft, ahead of them. "Party boat." "Pretty one, yeah." The boat, named *Capital Gains*, is registered in Washington, D.C. This name and location pun on the neoliberal conjoining of government and the financial sector to create great wealth for the few; and indeed, as they board the boat, it is clearly another world.

And, within the logic of the show, Frank Sobotka's smuggling is a device to generate cash to pay politicians to support his workers, which suggests that the degraded political process we see all through this season is one that makes politicians more like venture capitalists than they, or perhaps many others, would like to admit. Within the context of neoliberalism, the goal of personal economic gain becomes culturally pervasive; a figure like Frank Sobotka, whose illegal practices are substantially for the benefit of his constituents, is outside the reigning logical of the historical moment. The boat is filled with men in tuxedos and women wearing jewelry and cocktail dresses.

RACE, ETHNICITY, AND SPACE

This scene begins to define a key element of the season's emphasis. At first the harbor is largely a backdrop, employed more for its scenery than for its utility: a nice place for the wealthy to entertain. As the season proceeds, we will see that its primary value is to provide views of water for those, including many who have benefited from the service economy, moving into a district that is being gentrified. This emphasis on the redefinition of urban space is part of the season's exploration of contemporary configurations of class. The narrative depicts a world divided into distinct economic sectors—the wealthy, the eroding public service sector (containing a representation of the ebbing middle class), and the barely working or not working. Those with wealth include developers, corrupt politicians, drug dealers, and defense lawyers. Those with increasingly unstable incomes include public servants of all types—cops, public-sector lawyers—as well as some small-business owners. The lower class is made up of those collecting morsels from the drug trade, those with no obvious form of remuneration, and those who scrape together the crumbs left of the once relatively lucrative unionized work. Included in this category are the Russian women who are found dead in the shipping container: the demand for their skills has so diminished in the world of legitimate production that they are utterly objectified as bodies, and treated as cargo.

Representative of this last group are the longshoremen in the union led by Frank Sobotka. The union is a fraction of its former size. The decline of Baltimore's industrial base has resulted in far less material going out than before, and the decline of the port has lessened its ability to compete with other, more vital regions; such retrenchment is indicative of a general regional downturn, and a reduction in freight has reduced the capital available for necessary improvements. Frank attempts to use his illicit capital for two purposes: to restore the grain pier and to dredge the channel. To this end, he buys influence with state legislators to convince them to appropriate funds for these projects.

Sobotka is involved in smuggling of all sorts: prostitutes in containers (his participation here was unwitting), drugs, and chemicals for processing cocaine. Sobotka puts his declining port facility at the service of international smuggling, doing the bidding of the Greek. The link to Sobotka takes the viewer in a number of directions. In episode 2, we find out that the dead woman found floating in the river was part of a group of girls, all dead, who were smuggled into the United States through Sobotka's docks. As the season goes on we find that the girls were killed after a sailor aboard the smuggling ship, the *Atlantic Light*, killed the one who ended up in the channel. To make sure that no one can tell of this crime, the rest of the girls are suffocated by constricting further the limited air supply coming into the box. The women were sex slaves, brought in by an international syndicate; their fate is indicative of how the devaluation of labor internationally exploits those who are already reduced by their gender.[18]

The importation and inhumane treatment of human cargo recalls the slave trade of the eighteenth and nineteenth centuries. The historical narrative has been updated to reveal that uneven international development creates the conditions leading captive women from poor nations to sell their bodies in order to support themselves and their families. The analogy becomes further articulated if we compare the death of the thirteen women to cases like the infamous *Zong* massacre, a mass killing of slaves in 1781 that took place when the owners of an overcrowded slave ship decided that it would be more lucrative to destroy their human cargo and collect an insurance payment than to deliver those who survived. Indeed, season 2 is replete with embedded references to Baltimore's connection to the slave trade, including a recurring image of a neon sign advertising Domino Sugar, a combine that organized the most notorious slave-produced commodity of the nineteenth century.

That Sobotka connects with both Valchek and McNulty is only the

Season 2, episode 5, "They used to make steel there, no?"

tip of this season's iceberg. Simon develops a remarkable narrative: although sprawling and complex, it never seems distended. In fact, the more you think about it, the more it coheres. Contact with most of our focal characters from season 1 is maintained, however briefly, via the smuggled drugs, which are everywhere. We now see their point of entry, and are explicitly told of their importation from the South, whether from the Dominican Republic or Colombia.

In the realm of criminality, the connection between the geographically bound space of the ghetto and that of world commerce provides ample opportunity for irony and contrast. But even in exploring this relative distinction between importing and exporting, we lose the emphasis of the season, which is explicitly about the decline of productive industry. Indeed, this observation is made repeatedly: Diggins and McNulty comment on the demise of Bethlehem Steel, Spyros the Greek looks at the hull of the old plant and remarks, "They used to make steel there, no?" (episode 5); Sobotka notes that his brother was a casualty of the end the shipbuilding era in Baltimore. Although deindustrialization affects African Americans as a group far more profoundly than it does whites, its devastation is not confined to that ethnic group. There is also a significant class element. For whites who worked in unionized sectors of the economy and who were directly or secondarily involved in industrial production—like the dockworkers—deindustrialization has been a catastrophe.

For both groups, the absence of a bright future results in an excess of nostalgia; for example, longshoremen drink to excess and talk of the good old days when they shoveled grain with wooden shovels, to avoid creating sparks that would ignite the highly combustible grain dust. An older dockworker says, "Ain't ever gonna be what it was." Horseface, one of the key figures in the smuggling operation, replies, "We ain't ever gonna see another grain ship here in Baltimore, my friend." This is revealing, since it speaks to the known futility of Sobotka's efforts to refurbish the grain pier. And though the younger dockworkers mock their elders, the present reality clearly troubles the younger men: we hear Frank's son and nephew complain about the absence of work. As the narrow office of Frank and his union suggest, it is a large world out there, one with many forces that are ungovernable from that space.

That the city's relationships with other places and spaces lie at the core of this season become allusively evident in the succession of opening vignettes—for example, in the second scene of the season as Bodie drives to Philadelphia. As the Baltimore radio station fades, he is surprised when his partner explains that there are different stations in different cities. At this, Bodie asks, "Why would anyone want to leave Baltimore?" Further, the station he picks up is a public one, playing Garrison Keillor's *Prairie Home Companion*, a program that is the opposite of what Bodie listens to in Baltimore in almost every way—sound, concept, audience. Further, when we come back to Bodie later as he drives back to Baltimore by himself, he is still listening to the show. This is an odd throw-in, but it suggests the ways in which restricted experience robs an individual of the space to grow, to find situations and aesthetic pleasures that are not immediately available.

While the distinctiveness of the show is undeniable, it is not unique to a market. Rather, it can be heard in Baltimore, Philadelphia, New York, and Dallas, among the many places where it is syndicated. And it is primarily recorded in Minneapolis, but also in many other places. Further, Lake Woebegone is a nonplace. As we hear Keillor talking about the humid nights of tomato-growing season in the Midwest, we are left to ponder the placeless-ness of Keillor's description, and to wonder whether that is what appeals to the decidedly place-bound Bodie. In this arch example, we can see that the materiality of a place does not in any way define its affective range—an apt motif for a season focused

Season 2, episode 1, Nat and Frank disagree.

on Baltimore's relationship with a virtual world we never see, a world whose agents are shady "Greeks" who profess their non-Greekness, and who speak English, Turkish, Spanish, and Portuguese, and whose associates are Ukrainian, Israeli, and Colombian. The world beyond becomes merely a shipping site, a place to which things go and, much more importantly in this season and in this historically defined worldview, a place from which things come.

The vastness and the presence of this world are asserted when we first encounter the port terminal, which is framed visually by its bright sprawl: the bustle of technology defines its movements. The large frame is bright with sunlight and motion, and the shot is expansive and from a fairly high angle. The scene cuts directly to a close-up of a portly man sitting on a brown vinyl couch, framed against gray paneling that defines the interior of a trailer. The shot cuts to a longer one of four men sitting in a long narrow space; the only one standing is Nat Coxson, a large African American man at the depth of the shot, and his positioning suggests his distinction from the others and his individual significance. Sobotka argues that money must be put toward convincing legislators not only to renovate the grain pier but also to undertake the far more expensive project of dredging the harbor channel. Coxson argues that if the grain pier doesn't get fixed, then someone will build condominiums on the site, and he advocates profanely for the utility of focusing on the more modest project.

The scene contrasts the expanse of the pier with the smallness of the administrative office and its processes, suggesting how the device that defines the particularly Baltimore aspect of international trade comes down to two middle-aged men arguing about policy inside a trailer. The scene ends with Coxson walking out the door and the three other men musing about the exchange until Frank gets off the sofa and walks onto the piers, which are introduced by showing a seagull amid the trucks and shipping containers. Frank is dwarfed on the piers; the equipment literally surrounds him. But he seems content, drinking in the sea air and lighting a cigarette. This shot introduces Frank's romance with dock work as a way of life, a decidedly nostalgic perspective that fuels his desire to preserve, by any means necessary, the efficacy of the existence he has known. We can see that Frank is suffused with pseudomemories of an idealized past, which provides a further sense of the futility of Frank's quest. Yet the improbability of him achieving his goals in no way mitigates the nobility of his dream. We know historically that Poles dominated the longshoremen's trade in Baltimore in the twentieth century before World War II, and that Frank's desire to make the waterfront "what it once was" might include a gesture of ethnic pride and solidarity.

Soon, we are introduced to the means of smuggling. Frank is framed in an extreme close-up with his nephew Nick, whom he tells to go see the Greek and get a number, introducing the fact that Sobotka and his union are involved in illicit trafficking along the docks. But in following the visual assertion of the office scene, we can see that this trafficking is a narrow conspiracy with potentially far-reaching implications. We next see Frank's son Ziggy arguing with a truck driver over having lost his cargo in the container stacks, and the shot then cuts to Lieutenant Daniels, now working in a confining basement that is the city police's evidence room. These shifts in emphasis within a scene, and juxtapositions of one scene with another, reintroduce the motivated editing strategy of season 1. A stated intention of David Simon's in this season is to replace, not without complications, the more usual system of social sorting by race and ethnicity with that of class. In episode 7, Frank says to Nat in a close-up that leaves the African American man out of the frame, "Black, white, until that canal is dredged we're all niggers." Nat's rejoinder is "or all Polacks," which brings the ideas of interethnic and interracial division and solidarity to the surface. But Nat's response, which is

Season 2, episode 7, "First of all . . . you happen to be white."

not simply a quip and which also includes an expression that reveals impatience and some exasperation, recalls that the history of racial separation and exclusion does not easily dissipate into good feeling and cooperation. The dockworkers' power, which is already limited because of the gross power disparities between the other institutional players—government and corporate entities—and that of the reduced union's, is further weakened by this legacy of antipathy.

The degree of racial distinction that separates blacks and whites is at points called into question by white poseurs in the drug trade ("whiggers") who adopt the mannerisms of African Americans associated with inner-city life. And while a figure like Stringer Bell could be construed as "acting white," racializing his behavior would make all businesspeople white or white-aspiring. As for the white poseurs, like White Mike and Frog, the degree of affectation is notable and remarkable, and in both cases it is Nick Sobotka, who has involved himself in the retail drug trade, who does the noting. In one scene he reminds Frog that he is Polish and white, saying, "First of all, and I don't know how to tell you this without hurting you deeply, you happen to be white," and then lists his neighborhood, school affiliations, and parentage. After this declamation, Nick is briefly shown smirking on a door stoop, apparently appreciating his own wit. In another encounter with White Mike, a drug wholesaler, we see a degree of the same behavior, but this time Nick and Mike recognize each other from high school, each expressing a degree of surprise at their related pasts. In another scene, after Mike is apprehended, he asks for food by requesting that Kima "hook a brother up." The drug impresario Proposition Joe greets the Ukrainian gangster Sergei with a hug and the endearment "my nigga." And while all this suggests the porous terms of racial lines, it also asserts the fact of race and the necessity of authenticity. In this season, though blackness may be a multifarious thing and a social construct, its varieties of meaning do not remove it from association with phenotype.

Similarly, that the smugglers are known as the "Greeks" suggests the power of ethnocentrism. Sergei insists he is not Russian but Ukrainian, and that such distinctions matter. When White Mike gives up Etan, the drug conduit for the Greeks, he refers to him as a "Jew from that Jew country." There is clearly some point of interaction among ethnic and national-origin groups, but the lines of distinction remain bright. And as they were for Frank and Nat, these are means of separation, limiting affiliation and defining relationships that are substantially about business.

One of the recurring lines of the season is "stay close," a sentiment visually reiterated at key points. This phrase is uttered by Frank Sobotka to Nick, and to Nick by Stavros, the Greek's liaison to the dockworkers. Clearly, "close" here is the stuff of a secondary system of economic exchange, one that is enabled by the pathways of global trade but executed by those defined by narrow and personal affiliations. For Frank, asserting this after he finds that Nick and Ziggy have stolen cameras from a container, it means keeping the lines of communication open so that all smuggling is cleared through him. For Stavros, it means that Nick, who is on the docks, should tell his coconspirators of any apparent glitches in the system. But both assertions ask for a kind of proximity and intimacy that reduces a vast international network to one conduit who can be approached personally. All this suggests that the antithesis of the abstract and global is the corporeal and the local.

In a physical example of people staying close, many of the smuggling transactions are discussed and agreed upon in a small booth in a tiny waterfront diner tightly framed from the side. The framing of four men squeezed into the booth seems both a metaphor for the smuggling network and a means of locating each person corporeally. Indeed, that transactions largely take place in an undersized diner booth suggests a kind of enforced intimacy, a visual portrayal of what it means to "stay close." Such a visual portrayal marks a stark contrast between the ac-

Season 2, episode 8, Stay close.

tivities of the smuggling ring and the machinations of more legitimate international trade, in which the principals may never see each other or even hear each other's voices. These booth scenes and the emphasis on physical encounters are, to some degree, a matter of avoiding the electronic surveillance that may accompany communication by phone, e-mail, or texting. In another key scene, when the Greek intervenes in a drug transaction between Ziggy and Proposition Joe's nephew Cheese so that Ziggy can regain his cash and to some degree save face, the Greek's enforcer, Sergei, explains his interest in Ziggy's case simply: "Him we know. You? We don't know."

Besides being the antithesis of globalization, its shrinking of expanse, and its fetishizing of technology, the emphasis on bodily presence and definition is also a matter of the devaluing of work, particularly of the labor that results from the exertions of the body. In the port of the future, mechanization severely reduces the need for dockworkers, and the labor of those dockworkers is largely bureaucratized. They view incoming cargo on computer screens; they walk among the containers to locate them for the drivers. Humans interact mainly with and via electronic devices. The dockworkers' cooperative labor has passed, and only the nonwork residue of that practice persists—the men drinking at the Clement Street Café. And the decline of physical work and its cooperative nature is accompanied by a fetishizing of the past, an idealization of the greater ethnocentricity and physical exploitation that marked waterfront work in the pre–World War II era.

Indeed, this seems to be a version of Appadurai's "new patriotism," since the structures of feeling that derive from these memories create a kind of bonding among these men—there are no women in the club—that has no political consequence. In *Spaces of Hope*, Harvey writes of the political meaning of the body in this age of distended communication and abstracted work. Careful not to reduce the body to its physicality and not to assume that the bodily is commensurate with the political, he sees the engaged body as a vital site of struggle, since the corporeal selves of those who resist the logic of neoliberalism serve as a reiteration both of place-ness in this era of globalization, and of humanness. Nevertheless, he cautions that a body without a political direction is *not* an effective site of resistance.[19] In season 2, the absence of this direction is certainly part of what afflicts the dockworkers and the smugglers. As Harvey notes, "Abject submission to the dictates of capital, for example, may for some be a reasonable price to bear for adequate pleasures and fulfillment of desires in the realm of consumption."[20] And while none of the dockworkers have adequate capital to fulfill their desires, they are also not involved in any far-ranging political organizing. This is bread-and-butter unionism at its narrowest, since political action, for Frank, means not altering the system that oppresses them and that will leave them unemployed; rather, it means bribing the corrupt politicians who uphold the system that ships their jobs away. And Frank is the most forward-thinking character we meet, since the others are interested only in personal gain. It is revealing that when Nick is finally apprehended, his money is rolled deep into the rafters above his washing machine, in the very recesses of private and domestic space.

The posing of these issues of race, ethnicity, and class well follows the stated goal of Simon, who has said of this season that it is "a political tract masquerading as a cop show," and that he is "more interested in class than race."[21] This emphasis is textually emphasized, and the narrative suggests that in a world where the vast complex of media circulates the "common sense" of neoliberal rhetoric and practice, terms of resistance become very difficult to locate and articulate. But we can see that resistance at least begins as a kind of localism, since the logic of neoliberalism relies on the apparent openness and vastness of markets, and on applying the logic of the marketplace to all areas of life. Local bonds of affiliation may allow for the reinsertion of different terms of value, a fact we see repeatedly in this season. The dockworkers seem to live as

Season 2, episode 10, Ziggy steals cars and puts them back in a container.

a unit and largely to merge the workplace into a play space and living space, thus creating fraternity in a world where the usual intention that governs human interaction is that of fiduciary gain.

In one of the culminating scenes of the season, we see how business interactions that take on a personal dimension are subject to passions that trigger violence. Ziggy, whose life is a series of humiliations, small and large, decides that his entry into the world of criminal success will be to steal cars off of the docks and sell them back to one of the figures connected with the Greeks. George Gleikas (Double G) runs a retail appliance and electronics store on a commercial strip not far from the docks, and he serves as a fence for goods that come into the country illicitly. Ziggy's plan is to steal cars arriving from Germany and put them into containers that are headed to Greece, where Gleikas is from. But Gleikas refuses to pay Ziggy the agreed upon amount of money after Ziggy reroutes the cars. In fury, Ziggy executes Gleikas.

The scheme to send the cars to Greece presents a kind of genius. It sees all goods as infinitely mobile and all international transactions as fluid. Since the container offers a space for shipping, and since its contents are only a matter of a written description—the cars are listed as scrap aluminum, says Ziggy—then any dock may only be a way station to another. Indeed, in one of the recurring threads of the season, after

Valchek begins harassing the dockworkers, they steal his unit's security van and ship it by container all over the world. As it reaches a new destination, the workers in that port take a picture of it and send it to Valchek. Such an example points to extreme mobility as an end in itself. It also suggests the potential power of the workers at the point of loading and unloading—if they seize it. But the problem of system is one that mitigates that power, since, as Frank explains, if cargo is constantly getting lost at a particular shipping point, then that destination will be supplanted by another. Indeed, since transportation is relatively cheap, problems in that sector can be easily rectified. Ziggy knows this himself, so he steals the cars by cutting holes in the fence that contains them, even though they are only going back into containers. He explains this extra work as his desire to make it look like the thefts are not an inside job.

That these thefts end in murder is a by-product of the type of theft it is: the Greeks need liaisons in the United States, and Ziggy needs a liaison with a connection to a potential destination. This need for personal contact illustrates the degree to which such acts of piracy are outside the system, and since there can be no contracts involved, they also require a kind of honor among thieves. And if not honor, then they require that the parties be sufficiently fearful of each other to honor their end of the bargain. This vision of fear and power is antithetical to that of global traders, who use governments to pass laws favorable to their interests and to enforce contracts. In Ziggy's world, his lack of bodily stature is an ongoing limit. Ziggy's actions suggest that the world that has developed in response to the neoliberal regime also has significant problems, since its noncontractual and extralegal means of enforcement may mark a reversion to the law of the jungle. That the issue here is humiliation and not money is confirmed when Ziggy throws the envelope with the reduced sum at Gleikas's employee after he shoots him and as he walks out the door. Ziggy says, "You best not be doing me that way," and then in a tightly framed two-shot that makes clear his fury, he denounces him in as absolute a way as he knows.

Season 2 ends on a pessimistic note. The plot elements are tied up, but to little effect. The Greeks cut Frank's throat and throw him in the harbor; he is fished out by the police as his fellow dockworkers look on. And while under some circumstances he could be viewed as a martyr to the cause of preserving his union, his impact was extremely limited. Again, the lack of result that accompanies Frank's demise contrasts with the morally uplifting scene that ends *On the Waterfront* as the battered Terry Malloy leads his fellow workers into work, showing the end of the mob's influence on the docks. In our final scene at the docks, the union is under federal surveillance, and the response by the union, one of clear resistance, is to reelect the dead Frank Sobotka as secretary-treasurer of the local. But this gesture changes nothing within the big picture of work and global exchange. The Greeks move on to do business elsewhere; we see them boarding a plane. There is plenty of business elsewhere, and their transience is no more than a minor inconvenience. The case of the girls in the container is solved, but their murderer is long dead. Drug dealers continue to sell drugs for a profit.

The final scene is a montage emphasizing stasis. Nick peers through the fence at the docks, where he still cannot get work, and the song *I Feel Alright* by Steve Earle plays over the juxtaposition:

> I'll bring you precious contraband
> And ancient tales from distant lands . . .

As we see the world unfold, looking much as it has, we can muse on the machinations witnessed in the interest of attaining wealth and resisting the dominant forces of modern economic life. The steel mills and dry docks are still closed. There is still little work for the younger union members. The song's lyrics and refrain leave us only with a vision of entertainment and persistence. Simon's vision of futility is a matter of outcomes, but is not necessarily inevitable; rather, it is the absence of sustained analysis and a clear political project that consigns resistance to failure. Thus, the provocations of season 2 are worthy of thought and scrutiny, even though their narrative results are limited.

{ THREE }

Season 3

DRUGS, SPACE, AND REDEVELOPMENT

In season 3, following the dramatization of the role and cost of free trade in a second-tier US city in season 2, *The Wire* dramatically poses the question: what if the "victimless" crime of drug sales and use was limited geographically within a city and tolerated by the police within that zone? Simon explores the idea of drug amnesty and the arguments—civic, political, and ethical—for and against it by having the retiring police major "Bunny" Colvin, a sector commander, define a restricted space for the sale and use of controlled substances. Colvin intends to confine the drug trade to a particular place so that those in the rest of his district can live their lives outside the social chaos and violence that it causes. The implications of his decision are well defined throughout the range of political scales—local, state, and federal. But we see the most pronounced response on the local level as Mayor Royce considers allowing the drug zone to stand, but then comes to his political senses. On the other hand, the council member and future mayoral candidate Tommy Carcetti, who is also a major figure in season 4, and Erv Burrell, the ever-present institutional placeholder and chief of police, reveal their deep inclinations for political survival by responding with outrage, and never fully consider the policy possibilities.

In developing this central concern, the season more broadly focuses on distinct orders of real estate: housing projects; abandoned buildings, some of which are reconfigured as the police-sanctioned drug zone, called "Hamsterdam"; street corners in declining, substantially African American neighborhoods; gentrified buildings near and overlooking the harbor; and even the space of prison, a decidedly different type of real estate. Each of these types of property has its place in the extant economic and social order, and each affects the other. For example, at one extreme, both prison and Hamsterdam exist as administered zones that remove criminal elements from areas where private profit may be accrued, and that more generally limit the social impact of particular illegal behaviors. For drug dealers, the control of street corners by specific syndicates provides those groups with a competitive advantage, since the corners constitute a convenient and predictable locale for accessing drive-by purchasers, even though the presence of the dealers devalues abutting real estate and may ultimately lead to the abandonment of buildings. The gentrified zones near the harbor exist as a model of the free market and of the way in which private investment can build value. But the juxtaposition of these areas with other, less valuable zones reveals that private developers are dependent on public policy for creating the conditions of their market success: enhanced policing, tax abatements, and other development-enabling devices serve as means for those with capital to increase their wealth. Such development also has the effect of changing the city's demographic by providing inner-city housing for a wealthier clientele. In its focus on real estate and relative wealth and poverty, this season dramatizes the limits of free-market orthodoxy, bringing attention to the spatial ramifications of uneven economic development and its social consequences.

This emphasis on the relationship between property and policy occurs in the first, pre-credit scene of the first episode, which shows the demolition of a major high-rise public housing project. In broad policy terms, the projects must be torn down in order for gentrification to take hold in their vicinity. This is the building where some of the significant action of season 1 took place; for example, drug-market dominance in that locale defined the preeminence of the Barksdale family in the West Baltimore narcotics trade. In this scene, Mayor Clarence Royce stands at a podium framed in front of a high-rise housing project. Royce proclaims a new day for Baltimore, an era of reform, and with that, he announces the demise of the Franklin Terrace and the end of the misery it fostered; as the plunger goes down, the project crumbles. Simon affirms his intention in this season to explore the idea of "reform" in an urban setting more generally: "But the theme of reform is not just political. There are several characters who present themselves as potential reformers. Some of them actually will be reformist, and some of them will not. Part of the season, from the viewer's perspective, is figuring out who's who."[1]

The scene with the mayor standing before the exploding buildings does not occur in an uninterrupted take. We move in and out of his vi-

Season 3, episode 1, Royce declares a new day.

sual presence as we track the lower-level drug dealers Bodie and Poot as well as a friend of theirs. The very presence of Bodie and Poot and their continued status in the drug trade tells us that it is far from "a new day in Baltimore." Providing us with a different angle on this type of reform, Poot laments the demise of a place of fond memories. Bodie taunts him about having had his first sexual experiences there and shows no particular sentimentality himself while also chiding Poot about his taste in women and his frequent STDs, telling him that wherever and whenever he has sex, he will get the same result because he is "just doin' the same." In these conversations lies the antithesis of Royce's fatuous proclamations. The crumbling of the tower signifies neither change nor stasis. Without stable and substantial employment and the steps that precede it—education, drug rehab, job training—not much in Baltimore can change for the many; but the domain of the unemployed and the place for drug sales and use can be moved to other locations.

The Baltimore we see in season 3 is substantially like the Baltimore we saw in season 1: abandoned houses, drug wars, and unemployment. While gentrification creates a somewhat different demographic in some sectors, its benefits are not general. If anything, the razing of this public housing shows the city dispersing the building's former residents and redefining the spaces where they can dwell. That redefinition is a matter

Season 3, episode 1, Smoke overtakes the cheering crowd.

of a revised view of downtown real estate as a commodity.[2] Yet even if, as Bodie says, this is largely a different means of "just doin' the same," we see in this demolition a *desire* to break with history—the buildings are defined as remnants of an era now officially over—and to re-elaborate the space formerly occupied by housing stigmatized by its state ownership and the poverty it housed. Of course, the history of public housing in Baltimore and in the United States is not simply one of failure. Despite what Royce, a Democrat and an African American, says, public housing, when it was created in the 1930s as a New Deal initiative, was a valuable commodity for many of those who had been dispossessed by the Depression.[3] It was not until the late 1950's and early '60's that it became a place of poverty and crime.

With the demise of the buildings, smoke and dust suffuse the cheering crowd. There was clearly a need to contain the debris that inevitably resulted from the explosion. This unintended consequence in ways defines the event and, arguably, the season. The season provides a view of public officials developing institutional policies to contain the forces unleashed by the contemporary altering of social structure; in effect, it is a tale of the concept of the free market and its limits. Involved in this presentation of a neoliberal vision of the market is the related erasure of the memory of other possibilities, of alternative social and economic practices that might be or might have been considered effective. While Royce sees the projects as a failure of the administrative state, making necessary a shift to market-based forms of housing, for the former residents and denizens of those buildings, the rationale for destruction is not so clear, nor is the result of such a move quite so positive.

In this opening scene, we are for the first time introduced to the world of explicit politics. This is not to say that we had not encountered the shadows of such a world in season 1 and, to a lesser degree, in season 2. Those seasons represented the political class largely in its effects.[4] In this season, with the introduction of Royce and the related plotline of Councilman Carcetti involving himself in police business and then deciding to run for mayor, we are fully in the world of electoral contests and the means by which policy is made—or in this case, *barely* made. Since it is an election year, Royce puts pressure on the heads of his police department to reduce crime. But no one seems to have much of a sense of how to accomplish this or even how to measure crime and its reduction. Here Simon introduces a world of political expedience that stands where law enforcement should be. We are provided with a few weak strategies, but nothing that asks fundamental questions and develops methods around those resolutions.

The season introduces to policing the managerial method of defining crime called CompStat (computer statistics), a system used in many cities to map crime by time and space; it has the effect of reducing crime and its decline, if any, to its statistical representation.[5] With the political class's need to show such decline serving as a backdrop, we see Commissioner Burrell and his deputy director for operations, Bill Rawls, blasting their regional commanders for not producing the statistical indicators that will provide these leaders with the political narrative they seek. This type of pressure is part of Colvin's motivation for creating Hamsterdam. But the direct cause of the policy is the shooting of Officer Dozerman while stopping a drug suspect. Colvin, upset at the injury to his officer, looks at the waste of time, effort, and lives devoted to policies of drug interdiction and decides that rather than play a never-ending cat-and-mouse game with the network of drug dealers who frequent the corners of his sector, he will instead force them into distinct, narrow, virtually depopulated areas. In its recognition of the intractability of the drug problem, this strategy represents an innovation in policing.

In emphasis, then, this season is far more macro than season 1. It asks large questions about space and policy, including the phenomenon of gentrification, which we view by watching Stringer Bell attempt to move from the drug business to the real estate business. Bell believes that developed, market-based real estate can replace drugs in his economic portfolio. It is the post-project, gentrified urban space that Stringer Bell seeks to enhance. He sees its redevelopment as a means of personal profit: real estate becomes the heroin of the moneyed classes.

But his efforts are limited by his inability to deal effectively with bureaucracy, both local and federal. This inability allows him to be fleeced by state senator Clay Davis, who repeatedly makes him pay in cash for access to federal funds and officials, but who simply pockets the money. While development in Baltimore is encouraged by its government, the relative paucity of capital within the city, and Stringer's status as an inexperienced outsider in the world of development, make him something of a mark. This is not to say that there is not a market for his buildings, only that he is kept from full participation in this market by man-made obstructions, including rules and social circuits. But unlike the business of providing heroin to addicts and possible addicts, real estate is not nearly so compelling for its consumers, and many factors make its market more contingent. The value of Bell's real estate is a matter of the context in which it is elaborated, and the context here is clearly affected by the massive public investment in city improvement projects—such as the Inner Harbor and then, in the context of the show, the grain pier development that marks the end of season 2. Public investment that buttresses the property market also includes the emphasis on crime reduction and policing that is a large part of this season, since, as many have pointed out, public safety, or the *sense* of public safety, is a precondition of gentrification. Carcetti and Colvin both assist in creating this feeling, and though both talk about the service they do for all races and all classes, the effect within this political and economic environment is to create housing for the relatively well-to-do, and most of the well-to-do are white.

Nevertheless, Colvin is the figure in the entire police and city bureaucracy who stands out for his willingness to devise a strategy that is other than "doin' the same." He decides that for the average citizens in his district to be spared the violence and general antisocial behavior that accompanies the drug trade, he will induce those involved in that trade to move to one of the designated areas of his district, areas where the abandonment of housing has left no population. By allowing these vices in regions where there is no one to harm, he will free the rest of his citizens from the ravages of the drug trade. Colvin's notion of space reterritorializes certain sectors of Baltimore as areas where drug laws will not be enforced. In ways that relate to the contemporary regime of capital,

Season 3, episode 10, Colvin legalizes drugs.

he believes it is in his power to impose such a reconfiguration. In the end, he cannot enforce the borders he has configured. Crime and drug use, though largely contained, still spill out of his district, as do their political impacts. Space cannot be so neatly delineated and policed.

When Colvin's experiment is found out, as a matter of cost and of political will, it is abruptly stopped. As Colvin stands unapologetically before the command at a CompStat meeting, he declares that he has reduced crime by making drug enforcement a lower priority in three sectors. Rawls immediately catches on, exclaiming, "He's legalized drugs!!" In Burrell's office, Colvin offers a more involved explanation as he stands before Burrell, Rawls, and the crime consultant from the mayor's office. The arrangement of this scene is revealing: all three bureaucrats slouch on one side of Burrell's desk, while Colvin, shot in mid-close-up from the chest upward, gradually gets bigger as the scene progresses, whereas the other men's postures seem to show them shrinking and losing their spines. Though Colvin's initiative as conceived and executed clearly has problems, the political response from these men raises the question of how a leader might deal with the drug problem in the inner city more effectively. With this in mind, we see Burrell come before Royce, the "reform" mayor. The visual portrayal of Colvin emphasizes his failed heroism and his strength of character.

Though the crime in the Western District drops dramatically, we are not allowed to see Colvin's experiment as a success. Hamsterdam gradually takes on the identity of an urban hell; children run amid the chaos of drugs, prostitution, drug paraphernalia, bold theft, and violence. We can see this erosion occurring as what was once a relatively orderly place of drug use and sales becomes a site of general chaos. When a murder in Hamsterdam is investigated by detectives who are not part of Colvin's force, his plan begins to unravel. The requirement for secrecy suggests the limits of this social experiment. Within the restricted area of Baltimore, such a secret is unlikely to avoid general disclosure. Soon after the murder, Colvin comes clean at a CompStat meeting, to the horror and amazement of his superiors.

Colvin's gesture lacks the full courage of its convictions in its surreptitious and limited adoption. At the point of its discovery, we see political figures running for cover, though the strategy clearly produced results. Not least, by allowing health care workers to operate in Hamsterdam, at least some of the inherent problems of the drug trade—HIV, hepatitis, and similar illnesses—were ameliorated. More significantly, Colvin points out that this geographic restriction of the drug trade made the rest of his district more livable, confining the petty crime that goes along with drug addiction, along with the major violence that accompanies drug trafficking, to a place out of the way of ordinary people. In the end, the experiment fails and the site is razed.

Royce's assertion regarding the "failure" of public housing obscures its particular history, its initial role in the history of the city, and the reasons for its decline; similarly, the leveling of Hamsterdam eliminates the evidence of Colvin's civic intervention and its relative successes and failures. These demolitions constitute an erasure of the historical record, allowing for a political revision of the narrative of "what happened." Such a vision of the thinness of history is an element of postmodern thought as well as a feature of a conceptually related neoliberal orthodoxy. In postmodernity, the belief in the disjunction between the word and the thing it represents dematerializes history, giving fact-based historical narratives little more efficacy than any other narrative about the past. Since this skepticism is culturally definitional, the past as a body of material occurrences loses its significance. Similarly, neoliberalism dwells in the realm of the narrowly economic, making all equations a matter of cost-effectiveness and rewriting historical moments of market failure, such as the Great Depression, as episodes of misguided interventionist policy.[6] Following this logic, housing should not be created by the state because it then unfairly waters down the housing markets for private developers, who, in the view of adherents to neoliberal precepts, do the job better and more efficiently. With the funding of the public sector diminished and in disfavor, public housing becomes dirty and dangerous because of the absence of adequate funding for its security and maintenance, among other factors; which means only those who have few other choices will reside there. Within neoliberal thinking, the role of the state is primarily to ensure national defense and internal public safety.

In such a worldview, the drug war is either a legitimate issue of public safety or, in the place where liberalism meets libertarianism, a massive intrusion on individual choice. Simon, who is of the liberal persuasion, is on record as calling the war on drugs a failure: "It's a fraud. It's all over except for the tragedy and the shouting and the wasted lives. That'll continue. But the outcome has never been in doubt . . . Look. For 35 years, you've systematically deindustrialized these cities. You've rendered them inhospitable to the working class, economically. You have marginalized a certain percentage of your population, most of them minority, and placed them in a situation where the only viable economic engine in their hypersegregated neighborhoods is the drug trade."[7] This follows a speculative statement by Baltimore mayor Kurt Schmoke, who wondered whether legalizing and regulating drugs might be a viable alternative to the failed efforts to interdict them. Simon elaborated in an interview: "I remember having lunch with Peter Beilenson and Kurt Schmoke in the '90s. Schmoke had read *The Corner* and asked to have lunch with Ed Burns and me. Schmoke basically said, 'You guys get it. That's why I came out for decrimininalization."[8]

Unlike season 2, which largely looked outward, this season allows Simon to explore further the relationship among the social segments and geographic regions of Baltimore, as well as, but only secondarily, their connection with a world beyond. We meet developers and become more intimate with the world of politics. The experiment with the drug zone also poses questions of scale: Can a city and its population be redeemed by purely local solutions? What is the role of law and law enforcement in developing such solutions? In this season, geography is an explicit social dynamic. What takes place in the drug zone would be intolerable one block outside it. In this manner, we can see how the proximity of relative spaces is far less important than their de jure and de facto definitions.

This season puts the genre aspects of the show on a different footing. There is no wire to speak of, since this season moves from the world of rank-and-file law enforcement to that of police administration; solving crimes is less important than in any other season. We see the recurring police characters—McNulty, Daniels, Greggs, Herc, Carver, and Pryzbylewski, among others—but they are subordinated to politicians and to people like Major Rawls and, of course, Colvin, two police department bureaucrats. As Simon explores this idea of the relative legalization of heroin through the delineation of three kinds of drug-related spaces, he also plots the rise of a drug king even more vicious and amoral than Barksdale and Bell: Marlo Stanfield, who exhibits the coldness and bottom-line concern of a trader on Wall Street. The character of Stanfield and his burgeoning empire allows the viewer to juxtapose distinct types of commerce, questioning the apparently clear distinctions between the legal and the illegal, since Bell's foray into the "legal" world of real estate results in his separation from a large chunk of his ill-gotten wealth.

SPACE, REAL ESTATE, AND RELATIVE VALUE

Season 3 defines an urban world where neoliberal policies are fundamental for the re-elaboration of the value of particular types of real estate. Through the juxtaposition of these relative spaces, and the representational strategies for depicting them, the viewer can see the connections among them, and see how those connections constitute a broader program that reinforces both poverty and wealth. This broader program is created by a government-business partnership that masquerades as the "wisdom of the market." When Royce eliminates public housing as a physical entity, he demolishes one of the legacies of the welfare state and replaces it with the Nixon- and Reagan-era reforms that provide low-income people with vouchers to rent housing wherever they can secure it—though no landlord is required to accept the vouchers. This shift places the poor in the housing market and theoretically disperses the indigent population.

The public housing we see razed and the policies that created it were very much a feature of the modernist epoch. That is, they were redolent of the administrative state, an early-twentieth-century means of "reform" that attempted to regulate individuals and behavior defined as lying outside mainstream US culture, by using apparently rational measures to push those individuals and groups toward the cultural center. Public housing was one such measure; clean, new, high rises with modern amenities would, it was hoped, induce better behavior among the poor, make that group more a coherent mass, and subject it to effective oversight. The style of these developments was also within the modernist vein, offering uniform rectangular apartments in uniform rectangular buildings.

In the 1970s, as manufacturing declined, real estate became a commodity that cities possessed in surplus. They encouraged development through tax abatements, tax credits on investment, and access to low-interest federal loans. In this method of funding, all inducements are in the form of indirect subsidy; since neoliberal ideology focuses on market-based solutions, private corporations did all the development, a fact we see in this season. Also significant is the degree to which the cities found themselves receiving relatively little money from state and federal governments, a situation that required municipalities to employ the relatively few resources available to them.

The limits of such resources and the ways in which all forms of commentators emphasized (or overemphasized) the reduced role of government at the federal and state levels, and thus the centrality of local and individual decision making, take us back to the image of the elimination of public housing units. Yet the end of the Keynesian era of US governance and capital management, which these images mark, is very much a phenomenon with roots in world politics and economics. It represents nothing less than the accruing of political capital through the exponential gathering of material capital by major financial actors in the world economy. Jason Hackworth tells us: "With the decline in Keynesian economic redistribution, and social compensation, local institutions increasingly serve as filters for wider economic processes. Though the boundaries for acceptable policy action have narrowed, localities have been thrust into the position of determining how to address, contest, or embrace larger issues in the global economy."[9] Baltimore's decline resulted from its changing relationship to world commodity markets; those changes resulted in its increased reliance on its own abilities to generate revenue. This reliance focuses to some degree on the upward revaluation of the market value of its real estate.

In the postindustrial world, real estate, somewhat counterintuitively, becomes another fluid commodity on the global market. After 1960, and certainly after the mid-1970s, when inner cities declined in both wealth and population, their urban cores deteriorated, a highly visible condition in Simon's Baltimore. The shift in the reigning economic and governmental model that occurred in the last quarter of the twentieth century often produced conditions that were propitious for a limited reclamation of a city's housing stock. As capital circulated freely throughout the developed world, one of its objects was strategically located real estate, property that was desirable to those involved with the higher-revenue aspects of the international service economy—lawyers, doctors, people in the financial industries. Hackworth explains:

> Cities have continued their outward growth, but unlike the earlier period, the pattern is being joined by considerable inner city reinvestment and inner suburban disinvestment. But these parallel processes were relatively minor in extent until recently . . . No one dared speak of a spatial fix to mid-1970s economic travails, largely because processes like gentrification and inner city real estate development seemed both minor and unconnected to wider economic restructuring. But by the 1990s it started to become clear they were also connected to a wider reorganization that was occurring in a variety of industries. In particular, the inner city became restructured as niche real estate, service sector employment, tourism, and other replacements for waning heavy manufacturing. Capital had "switched" into finance, insurance, and real estate, and the urban fabric was morphing to accommodate these changes.[10]

The razing of the projects enhances the prospects of gentrification and reduces overall units, thus adding value to an existing commodity—urban housing. This occurs in a number of ways. Key among them is that moving the poor away from this gentrifying zone becomes economically important for development: the concentration of poverty near the downtown development zone depresses demand for renovated properties. The demolition of the projects, on one hand, moves us to the post-housing-project world of neo-laissez-faire; on another level, it returns us to the pre-housing-project era of urban life, before the 1930s. The rhetoric of the free market revalorizes important aspects of an earlier era of governance. The demise of the buildings disperses their former residents into situations where they are not physically circumscribed by the projects or caught up in their prevailing rhythms of life. By employing the visual metaphor of dispersal—through the spreading debris of the blast—this episode provides an image of the problems of assumed containment, a problem central to the depiction of Hamsterdam later in the season.

In a broader stroke, the architectural critic Charles Jencks dates the end of the modernist era and the beginning of the postmodern from the demise of the enormous Pruitt-Igoe projects in St. Louis beginning in March 1972 and continuing for four years. Though Jencks was hyperbolically discussing aesthetics, the change went far beyond that. As David Harvey explains: "The social conditions of Pruitt-Igoe were much more at the heart of the problem than pure architectural form."[11] But the architectural box that defined those projects represented the modernist administrative state, just as the playful and likewise historical Phillip Johnson–designed AT&T Building in Manhattan (1981–1984; currently called the Sony Tower), for example, represents, in a structural way, a turning away from the social problems recognized and wrestled with by the modernist state.[12] With the loss of belief in "grand narratives" and the viability of the regulatory state, the reified concept of the wisdom of markets becomes an ideological explanation for allowing the disadvantaged to fend for themselves. Reform becomes the destruction of the old and the absence of the better.

Though the market for drugs, like that for real estate, is also contingent, it is less so than that for property. In the first episodes of season 3, we are introduced to three competing drug operations, each operating by a particular market philosophy. The reigning syndicate—governed now primarily by Bell, as Avon languishes in jail—operates on his view that if you have the best heroin, the addicts will beat a path to your door. By contrast, his competitor Proposition Joe defines his idea of commerce by a simple, arithmetic model—buy for one, sell for two, and avoid ruinous competition. Marlo Stanfield, a cold-blooded killer devoted to the cause of his own dominance, sells drugs by even simpler standard: any means necessary. This competition stems, in part, from the disruptions caused by the shift in public housing practices. Until Hamsterdam comes into being, the dealers and the users are dispersed, allowing the best business model to emerge.

For drug entrepreneurs, the absence of the high-rise projects enhances the value of strategically located street corners in West Baltimore. This is brought home early in the season when Bodie and his crew set up in the middle of a block in Stanfield's territory. Competition for drug revenue becomes a battle for prime drug-sales real estate. A camera that juxtaposes the efforts of each crew shows this contest as well as the relative impact of having real estate that is not on a corner where cars can easily stop. Bell instructs Bodie not to physically engage with his competitors, just to sell the high-quality product from his midblock station. Both sides prosper to differing degrees for a time—until Stanfield

Season 3, episode 2, "It ain't about the real estate": Bodie deals from the middle of a block.

decides that he can regulate this zone and drive his competitors away. He does this by enlisting his followers to assault the Barksdale-Bell group with baseball bats.

In this case, market forces come to include physical coercion. This resorting to bats is, of course, a metaphoric reference to the ways in which the United States guarantees its economic centrality by maintaining and using a massive military force. The use of such a force is fundamentally in contradiction of the rhetoric of liberty, since force is the ultimate coercive. In the libertarian view of commerce, any behavior that is rational within the domain of buying and selling goods should be allowed by the state, which has a role only to allow the relations of the marketplace to prevail. Stanfield's behavior clearly fits within this definition. Yet his domain is protected by the elemental act of asserting one's right through might. He dominates because his empire is ascending and the Barksdale fortunes are diminishing. Thus, Stanfield controls his corners.

In turning away the violence of maintaining control over prime drug corners, Bell decides to use his capital to develop property. He recognizes that many of those who currently reside in the inner city are effectively unable to create wealth: they lack capital of all kinds and have little means of attaining much, if any. So he—rationally—moves toward real estate rather than a more productive enterprise that may employ those on the social margins. As we see the work crews on his buildings, he draws his labor from places beyond the site of construction. Bell is disadvantaged by his background but advantaged by his wealth. His junior college economics class will not prepare him to work at a brokerage house, but owning and developing property apparently requires only cash and some know-how.

This lack of know-how proves telling for Bell. The kind of naked assertion common in the West Baltimore drug trade is less effective in the real estate business. Factors influencing the value of property include the input of tax dollars and the return of a critical mass of upper-middle-class residents, not to mention a decline in federal subsidies for suburbanization in the form of improved roads and inexpensive fuel. In this regard, we can see that Bell might benefit from the unleashing of market forces; but unlike the drug trade, a business controlled by the bold and the unencumbered, the real estate business requires certain niceties. A real estate developer should not coerce his competitors at gunpoint. Stanfield can begin to dominate the drug trade through sheer violent will, but Bell is limited in his ability to become a major player in gentrified property.

Again, we can see that all opportunity is not created equally, and we encounter an increasingly beleaguered Bell trying to navigate a never-ending bureaucracy. His agent in this process is state senator Clay Davis, who exacts large cash payments from Bell. As Bell reaches his breaking point, he consults his drug lawyer, Maurice Levy, who informs him that he has been scammed. Levy's explanation that Davis has no special access and that everyone doing business with the city and the federal government has to navigate the same process is at least a little questionable. In this ambiguity, we find the area in which the legitimacy of Bell's legitimate enterprise is less certain. In Bell's real estate plans and his aspirations, we see that no local process is self-contained. Bell can be exploited because he requires permits and approvals, and more broadly because he seeks governmental support in the form of grants. Local governments may encourage development, but they are limited in their production of housing for the poor. They must seek assistance from state and federal agencies and then cooperate with private developers. This system of relationships applies to Hamsterdam too. Despite the apparent autonomy of Colvin, his imperative is nested in the authority of city gov-

Season 3, episode 8, Clay Davis takes Stringer's money.

ernment, which is nested in the authority of state government, which answers to federal government: and all are, to some extent, the captive of global capital.

Royce's ultimate response to the fact of Hamsterdam shows his awareness of the city's relative lack of autonomy, thus making the drug zone a purely local phenomenon in every way. Simon here is not only exploring the apparently insoluble dimensions of drug-related crime in the inner city, but also testing the language of freedom. We are left with the dichotomy between drug legalization, which clearly reduces crime and can, with the providing of sufficient social services, reduce related diseases, and the politics, and the resulting economics, of prohibition. When Royce considers modifying his initial negative response to Colvin's experiment, he searches for a politically feasible way to continue the drug zone. Public health administrators inform him of the remarkable results and prospects for such a social experiment. Ultimately, however, he lacks the political will. We see the wisdom of his choice politically when we view television news reports from Hamsterdam reducing the explanation of the zone to the graphic "City Legalizes Drugs." We also see his relative wisdom when he is visited by a bureaucrat from Washington who promises that if the zone is maintained, Baltimore will lose up to half a billion dollars in federal and state aid a year.

Such responses show how cities are not autonomous and, as stated earlier, the scale of the relationships between levels of government. This lack of independence is connected with the economics and politics of development in the postindustrial city. With no commodity to tax beyond real estate, and with new developments largely tax abated, cities exist mainly for the very poor and the wealthy, since they provide few services that are not privatized. The very poor have little choice regarding their housing, and the very rich pay for the services they desire. For expensive real estate to retain its value and for contiguous real estate to appreciate in value, a sense of law and order must prevail. Further, federal dollars may be a vital means of maintaining this sense. From the developers' point of view—and thereby in the view of local politicians—Hamsterdam is ultimately bad for business.

The existence of Hamsterdam becomes a recurring commentary on the efficacy of neoliberal assumptions. While it exists as a free-market zone for drugs, its status is a direct consequence of policies dictated by public authorities—however irregular the type and use of authority in this case. Further, its existence has ripple effects across the real estate markets of Baltimore, since it becomes a magnet for drug activities and therefore draws from other places those who seek to partake of those behaviors. But its existence is, ultimately, untenable in a world where development is king.

In employing varieties of property as a motif, the season explores the limits of neoliberal ideology as it addresses the significance of and relative connection among geographically bound spaces. In this dramatization, the tensions between local and larger scales of space are always calling into question how regimes of exchange affect general social welfare. We see that limited government, a model favored in neoliberal philosophy, fosters a kind of neo–social Darwinism that, in the end, valorizes a world where the powerful get richer. As the contingent relations among types of real estate reveal, competition seems not to be the primary motive here; rather, it is maximum gain for the few.

TIME-SPACE AND POWER: AVON BARKSDALE AND THE TWO DAYS OF PRISON

Besides providing the means to critique neoliberal theory and practice, the season's narrative develops a view of the relationship among bracketed spaces and shows how scales of space have significant implications for definitions of time. As we look at these depictions of time and space, and the ways in which those concepts are relative and contingent, the opening of the season takes on a somewhat different cast. We see a managed environment where the narrative of the historical city—the city's tale of its change over time—is actively being manipulated. Such attention to the stories that define the city in the present suggests that time is being managed in order to re-create space in terms that those who manage it would assert as a perpetual moment. We see this when the demise of the high-rise projects has the mayor triumphantly announcing a new era as a result of the city "having learned from its mistakes." The bad old days have passed and better days have arrived. History has ended, and we are in an era of new practices and meanings, an era detached from that preceded it.

One means of viewing this particular intervention is through the prism of the failure of the administrative state, its inability to make the temporality of the projects conform with that of the "normal" world. For example, in season 1, when Pryzbylewski, Carver, and Herc, drunkenly stir them up at two in the morning—an event briefly discussed in chapter 1—they find a ready and willing group of residents to engage them. That the high-rise buildings were the site of a twenty-four-hour-a-day drug supermarket made their trading cycles quite different from that of, say, a law office or a bank. With their demolition, the dispersed residents are more subject to the time discipline of the "normal" world, with its more conventional intervals of work, play, and sleep. Three of the forms of real estate that the season focuses on—the corners, Bell's downtown buildings, Hamsterdam—are defined by the variations of "normal" time that mark their relative distinctness as spaces. Each is also defined by the degree to which its time-space discipline can be enforced. Colvin sees the corners as places of drug sales, but he seeks to turn them into just street corners. Hamsterdam is his effort to do so. By driving all drug trafficking to empty areas, he seeks to re-create the corners as time-spaces that coincide with the desired life rhythms of ordinary Baltimoreans, a definition that is a matter of market norms. Bell's real estate was the ghetto but is now part of the sprawling downtown gentrification zone. It has therefore left the ragged rhythms of the under- and unemployed and taken on the respectable contours of the nine-to-five workday.

Bell seeks to belong to and thrive in the conventional world. We see his very businesslike copy shop and his apartment overlooking the Inner Harbor as indicative of his affiliations with the Baltimore business

Season 3, episode 11, Bell and Barksdale reminisce.

community. In this season, this central character is, surprisingly, murdered. On the night before he is shot, his breach with his partner Avon, who has recently returned from prison, becomes openly articulated. The death is foreshadowed by the two drug lords reminiscing nostalgically as they look down on the city from Barksdale's balcony—a recently gentrified space—where they are sipping cognac. Bell explains that he has to leave "because he has a meeting in the morning." Such a nod to his temporal life as a conventional businessman, as a real estate developer, points to his own vision of thin history. Since he has stopped dealing drugs, or is trying to subordinate that identity to his new one, it is as though the old Stringer Bell is gradually ceasing to exist. Like his revamped real estate, Bell's incarnation suppresses knowledge of his former state and status. Real estate is as people see it, as it presents itself. One of the defining aspects of a gentrified community is the absence of excessive street noise caused by the irregular living habits of the un- or unconventionally employed.

Those who have not found a place within this new Baltimore may find themselves further pushed to the margins of urban life. Within the world of neoliberal policy and its construction of urban entities that express its values, a space outside those urban zones becomes part of a system of relational spaces: that of the prison. As Loïc Waquant discusses,

US prisons serve "as the historic crucible of punitive containment as technique for the management of marginality and living laboratory of the neoliberal future."[13] As public housing ceases to exist, those who are either too bold or too timid in embracing the "freedoms" of the free market may find themselves fully outside the spaces of the neoliberal city, in prison. This institution represents a kind of real estate that is far from the urban grid but that, by its naked assertion of statist power, paradoxically enables neoliberal precepts of freedom.

A little more than halfway through episode 1, we return to prison to find the incarcerated Wee-Bey and Avon Barksdale, but now they stand with another man, called Cutty, whose real name is Dennis. (This nickname is a reference to the notoriously violent Jessup House of Correction, known as the "Cut.")[14] This scene is shot as the men stand by a prison softball game, the field defined by a chain-link fence. Within the prison yard, then, we have a regimented enclosure in which behavior and activities are defined by conventions of both the prison and the game. In effect, we are watching a game within a game, an enclosure within an enclosure. In this encounter, we can see an extended metaphor of the logic of the neoliberal world. While that system rhetorically defines rules of human interaction and existence that seem to coalesce around the apparently immutable laws of commerce, we can see that such strictures are far from natural or universal. The rules of softball are specific to that game and different from those of other games; the rules of commerce in the twenty-first century are likewise distinct from those of the nineteenth. Of course, the "Game" is a term frequently employed by the likes of Omar, Barksdale, Proposition Joe, and Stringer Bell. It refers to the drug trade as a volitional enterprise defined by its own set of unwritten rules, a game with winners and losers, whose participants cannot reasonably complain about outcomes when they have chosen to play.

As we look at the three men—two Barksdale family soldiers who have done or will do extensive time for their misdeeds and one who heads the organization and will do only about one of the seven years to which he is sentenced—we are reminded that justice is not equal, nor is the status of the inmates. Indeed, as in all social circumstances, situations are contingent on one's access to resources. In this shot, the camera emphasizes the fence as the three men discuss Cutty's impending release. A skewed-angle close-up of Cutty is shot through the fence, emphasizing that he is "penned" up, and then the view shifts to the three men standing in a line on the fence. Barksdale tells Cutty of the demise of the housing projects, adding that despite the shift in physical circum-

Season 3, episode 1, "I've been here fourteen years."

stances of their trade: "The Game is the game. I'll just have to take my thing into some new places."

This vision of change and stasis segues into a brief discussion regarding the nature of time and change, whether time is a natural or a perceptual category. Reiterating a line heard in each of the preceding seasons regarding the nature of prison life, Barksdale says: "If you got your mind right, you only do two days. The day you go in and the day you go out." To which Cutty replies, "I've been here fourteen years." This discussion poses the question whether the restriction of space—and indeed, this *particular* restriction of space—has implications for the meaning of time. Cutty reintroduces the issue of the world outside going on while that of the prisoner has virtually ceased to exist—prison defines the limiting of interaction and experience that people typically use to define change and time. As Avon talks about the demise of the housing projects and, by implication, a type of social life, Cutty comments, "A lot of changes."

This vision of the relationship between time and space re-elaborates their connection, but does so in a way that is distinct from our conventional understanding of the terms. This revision of the relationship between those two conceptual entities is not only a key one regarding the nature of prison life but also has significant implications for economic life beyond the guard towers and fences. Within the capitalist formulation of exchange, the imperative is always to shrink relative space in order to compress relative time. As many have pointed out, including Marx, one of the visions of technology in capitalism is that it can be used to alter the relationships between time and space, ever reducing the meaning of space by altering its temporal meaning.[15] Capitalists have traditionally attempted to redefine the historical and residual concept of space in order to bring areas involved in the production of goods for the market closer together in time, and thus to alter the meaning of space.[16]

In neoliberal ideology, time is fetishized, since it remains an impediment to the flow of capital. Since neoliberalism seeks a means of ordering the world that will give rise to a model of social life that ultimately enables the fluidity of markets, the time-space impediments to such transactions are a focal obstacle. On the other hand, with the embedded belief in the efficacy of subordinating all processes to those of exchange, the goal is to render space less meaningful by reducing its temporal meaning. To do this, an individual must have access to technological means of apparently transcending space, along with the power to employ those means toward a specific economic end. Though Barksdale is penned in, he takes control of his situation and shrinks the apparently "fixed" time of his sentence. He does so by mutually dependent material and conceptual devices. He is able to smuggle in contraband of all kind—food, drugs, and so forth—as well as to communicate by cell phone, also a disallowed device in prison.

Prison presents the opposite of the ideal time-space relationship central to neoliberal theory. Whereas the object of neoliberalism is to shrink open-ended space, prisoners attempt to maximize theirs. They are intentionally placed very closely together by devices—bars and rules—beyond their control. Their closeness is an index of their relative lack of power. In response to that condition, their restricted range of movement becomes an inducement to shrink time. Unlike technology in the world of capital, in prison it is used to enforce restricted space—cameras, electrical fences, body scans—rather than to transcend it. As Avon asserts, within the domain of the penitentiary, prisoners, who have little control over their daily schedule, may be able to assert some control over their *sense* of the larger passing of time. The goal of the system is to disrupt that internal discipline with petty annoyances—harassing guards, limited opportunities for education and recreation, enforced uniformity of spartan quarters, mandated proximity to other inmates within enclosed spaces. Such features of prison life constrain space in order to *extend* a sense of time through boredom and discomfort—the sentence that never ends—and to render an ex-convict unable to function outside the penal system, since he or she will emerge no more skilled but much more psychically damaged than before he went in. Avon, through his strategic use of capital, exists simultaneously as both a prisoner in the cell and, through his means of participating in the world outside the institution, a man of the larger world.

In her study of the history of the time concept and its variable applications, Barbara Adams talks about colonization *with* time, a means by which primarily Western industrial powers bring other nations into their sphere of influence.[17] Examples of this can refer to post–World War II Japan, where the industrial workplace became a kind of norm, or contemporary China, where industrialization is pulling millions from the agricultural economy and subjecting them to the rigors of confined living and work spaces, as well as to the discipline of working a shift in a factory. In its extreme, this imposition includes a kind of slave-like condition for the worker. This distinction has implications for our characters and for the season more generally, since those in prison constitute the underclass, nonparticipants in the core social and economic activities of the United States. Cutty and, to some degree, Wee-Bey experience time as an imposed norm, and their efforts to alter that norm are met with assertions of power. Wee-Bey's plastic fish, which he keeps in an ersatz aquarium in his cell, are destroyed by a guard because they give the prisoner a kind of meditative pleasure—they may make time seem to pass more quickly.

This distinction between the time and space of prison and that of capitalist production and distribution complicates one of the key concepts of the neoliberal orthodoxy. In that vision and explanation of the world, market logic reigns and the laws of the market are inexorable. Yet here we have people who are ostensibly removed from that arena of trade. Prisoners have been excised from the system of capital production and consumption because they have been judged as needing "correction." Unlike those involved in trade, prisoners experience time as undifferentiated duration, something that is constant and seems perpetual. The discipline of prison is to note the passage of time through the monotony of the life experienced.

Avon's refrain about serving two days has a kind of salience, and his removal from the larger world is far less complete than Cutty's. Avon can talk of having control over his perception of relative time, because he has access to the wonders of the outside world—nonprison food, some insulation from the harassment of the guards, greater freedom of movement than other prisoners, and a kind of status among the other convicts for his ability to game the system. Unlike other prisoners, then, Avon has devised a lifestyle that allows for a kind of time-space compression that emulates that which capitalists seek and exact on the outside. And Avon is, indeed, the freebooting capitalist seeking to expand his empire of trade—by any means necessary. The others have no such advantages, so they must do time in a way that is apparently without amenities. Prisoners like Cutty and Wee-Bey, who are simply part of the general population, are impressed into a system that is intensely hierarchical and controlled by others. That Avon is a relatively privileged participant in the system that physically represses him limits this analogy and highlights how access to devices that will ease the impact of such restrictions makes the limits more tolerable. The vision of the prison as a relatively egalitarian place defined by its rules and the dictates of the justice system proves to be untrue. Even within the penal system, we see a kind of uneven social status based on access to food, cigarettes, and cash to bribe guards and to engage lawyers scheming on the outside.[18]

In the exchange between Cutty and Avon, we can see that Cutty feels robbed of his time, as though the years that have passed while he was penned up in Jessup have weighed on him and changed him. Avon, however, has little of that feeling of loss. When he returns to the streets, he will return to his wealth, power, and position. Such distinctions make Avon other than a cog in a system that he has not made, so his vision of restricting time through his perspective is a matter of position—all timeservers are not equal. Neither time nor space is a natural concept; rather, each is relative and contingent on a variety of factors connected to position. When each man emerges from prison, he faces a distinct situation and responds to it differently. These areas of contrast further illuminate the role of capital, even if they are less clear on matters of class.

Barksdale returns to the world of his drug empire. When he is picked up at the gate, he mockingly complains about being transported in a Ford SUV. He immediately fills the frame and becomes the central figure in his crew. He is fitted with new and stylish clothes, and we hear him whoop with delight as he throws his prison garb out of the window.

Barksdale returns to a new penthouse with his name on the lease in one of Bell's buildings, as well as to drugs, alcohol, and women. Cutty, on the other hand, returns to the world he knew—except that he no longer knows it. As he muses while in prison, there have been "a lot of changes," and indeed, he is thrown into an environment that is far more

Season 3, episode 5, Avon returns.

entrepreneurial—as is the more general economic system—than the one from fourteen years before, and Cutty is not fully up to it. In effect, the passage of time has altered the meaning of the space to which he returns. The terrain has become far more violent and unforgiving—and the world that Cutty traversed in his years before incarceration was no one's idea of a garden. In this world, there is little honor among thieves. Avon, as a coming-home present, provides him with heroin to sell, but he is quickly scammed out of it. His choice is either to kill the scammer or to walk away. Though he accepts, however grudgingly, the bad faith of the drug seller, he is not certain of his future. His work prospects outside the Game are quite limited, and he becomes a casual laborer in a Hispanic lawn-cutting crew. As in prison, his time is not his own: he labors in the sun until the truck that brought him from West Baltimore returns him there.

The visual language of the episode, and indeed of the season, emphasizes the significance of Cutty's choice. When he works as a casual laborer, mowing lawns as part of a landscaping crew, he is physically out of place among the smaller brown men with whom he works. As he rides to the suburbs in the back of a pickup truck, he encounters some mid-level cogs in the Barksdale organization driving another car. They make eye contact as the drug workers scoff and drive away. In this encoun-

Season 3, episode 4, Cutty joins a lawn crew.

ter, we can see the life choices for this middle-aged, uneducated African American ex-convict. He can return to the street as an enforcer, or he can become one of the masses who seek any vaguely remunerative type of labor.

Being on the lawn crew places Cutty in an alien and unsatisfying environment—though in the next season we see him grow comfortable in it. It is no wonder, then, that he returns to the familiar, physically compact, and substantially African American city streets. Cutty's position in the visual presentation of his plight is often seen from an indirect angle: his body is often not quite at the center of the frame. When he mows lawns, the view is distanced, so we see him diminished as a kind of everyman among the others who have no status in the system. Cutty, like the immigrant workers, has no right to vote, no capital, and no status.

This depiction of Cutty's choices elaborates the economic predicament of many we encounter in this season, and for that matter, in all of the seasons. That he is among immigrant laborers is revealing. Since he has no education or conventional work resume, but does have a prison record, he is among those defined as surplus labor. Thus, we see Cutty working off the books, as needed, for a low wage. The lack of promise in his lawn-cutting career sends him back to street life, a choice that, given the options, we can define as rational. But being an enforcer is not suitable for a man in his midthirties. Like a professional athlete, Cutty is now too old for the life he previously led. We see this when we locate him among those who are much younger: his fellow gangsters refer to his age, and he frequently invokes the phrase "back in the day." He inhabits the same space, but not exactly the same time, as these younger men. The end of Cutty's gangster life is noted when he is unable to pull the trigger on a young man that Avon has sent him to kill. He explains, "It just wasn't in me no more." Avon asks, "What will you do?" Cutty replies, "I don't know, but I can't do this." Cutty has opted for a choice that is other than market-based. He forgoes easy money for drudgery, and this choice is treated with deference within the narrative. This choice is a matter of how the world and Cutty have changed over the past fourteen years.

After finding that he no longer has the heart of a gangster, Dennis (formerly Cutty) decides to address the problems of young people and the attractions of gangster culture by providing boxing instruction—in effect, replacing one game with another, more socially acceptable one. He attempts to navigate the city bureaucracy without assistance. In a montage that shows him literally run from city office to city office, through a whirl of uncooperative workers and aversive regulation, we see him frustrated by the process. It is only with the help of the politically connected deacon and the financially flush Avon that he is able to open his gym. Such assistance reveals how will alone is not sufficient to navigate urban bureaucracy and financial exigency. No wonder Dennis prefers the regimented spaces of the ring. In such an environment, the rules obtain in a more uniform and less mysterious way. The boxing ring becomes another circumscribed space defined by its own rules—though, as in Hamsterdam, the violence it teaches easily spills out into the world. Within the ropes of the ring, violence is circumscribed and generally nonlethal.

Dennis's commitment to the gym as an alternative to street life is intriguing, since the boxing ring possesses many of the features of life on the streets. It is compact, violent, and rewards both boldness of action and nimbleness of body. There are distinctions, of course. Boxing is done in a certain way—no guns or knives, no hitting below the belt—and each round is governed by the clock. While perceptions of time may be relative, everyone who is in the ring and does not get knocked out stays for two minutes (amateur boxing) or three minutes (professional). There are no suspended sentences, nor are their special rules for special people. Success in the ring requires devoting time and energy to de-

Season 3, episode 11, Cutty's gym.

veloping both skill and fitness, and that devotion removes one from the streets. The regimentation of the ring in both time and space makes it a place apart, and in that way an anachronism, since advantage can be gained in that domain only through maximum skill and effort.

HAMSTERDAM AND THE DISCRETE SPACES OF BALTIMORE

Within the spaces of Hamsterdam, time is a mostly undifferentiated concept. People buy, sell, and use drugs at all hours. As Bubbles tells his young charge, Johnny, "Ain't no rules for dope fiends." They stand in an alley in a configuration resembling that of Barksdale, Cutty, and Wee-Bey at the prison baseball field fence. But what is the fate of addicts when there are no rules? Does this absence of limits suggest the beneficence of the market? This comment proves prescient, since the absence of rules in Hamsterdam allows Johnny to indulge himself in heroin until it kills him. This adage extends also to those more broadly concerned with the selling of drugs. But even in the zone without rules, the contours of the zone itself are enforced, and we subsequently see efforts to devise and enforce rules that will make dope sales and use more rule-bound and therefore less destructive socially.

Colvin's audacious plan does not come into being until the season is nearly one-third completed. The impact of his policy potentially has all kinds of unforeseen ramifications: aiding the process of gentrification, endangering state and federal grants, killing drug users, and fostering violent crime. From a shot of Colvin speaking, a hard cut shows a view of a map of his sector, and then the stationary camera records him reentering the frame and walking to the camera, enhancing his size and presence: "Beginning today you can sell drugs in West Baltimore, but only where we say you can. Push them." From our first meeting of Colvin, he has been obsessively concerned with specific geography, asking new officers in his division to provide their exact locations. It as though he has internalized a map of the city and, in doing so, has defined its areas of social function and relative danger.

Explaining the concept of the drug zone and getting the dealers to use it is a difficult task. Sergeant Carver, a recurring character, tells the corner drug dealers: "Vincent Street is your Amsterdam in Baltimore." This is indeed ironic, since Amsterdam is a cosmopolitan center and a place where relative tolerance, for the most part, reigns. To some degree, its position as a cultural crossroads, a place that is porous both geographically and culturally, creates the proliferation of drugs as well as the judgment that the costs of attempting to prohibit drug use is not acceptable from a cost-benefit analysis.

Colvin's plan to use an abandoned area as the zone is not as easily executed as first thought. Is a discrete market generated by supply or demand? For the plan to succeed, he has to answer the question whether the area should be initially populated by users who attract the dealers, or, by dealers who will attract the users. In the end, both the dealers and the users are forcibly taken to the zone. After failing to move the users and low-level runners to Hamsterdam, Colvin tells them: "Middle management means you have just enough responsibility that you gotta listen when people talk." He realizes that not all economic actors are incentivized in the same manner.

This *rule* of spatial distinction attempts to confine the effects of the drug trade to its willing participants. This, of course, is impossible. Colvin's efforts to confine the drug trade to a discrete geography reveal a furthering of this conception. Colvin accepts this pathology as part of urban life and seeks not to eradicate it (by all evidence, it cannot be eradicated) but to define a space where the game is played—much as the fence defines the area of the softball game. We see that the de facto legalization of drugs in a particular area results in a thicket of unintended consequences. The drug zone becomes home to prostitution, violence, and disease, all of which require oversight and some degree of regulation. In effect, the experiment in libertarian drug policy fails—and not only for political reasons: it also fails as policy.

In our first sustained shot of Hamsterdam, we see the world from Johnny's point of view. He registers amazement as he looks at the police car sitting nearby to enforce the zone. The mobile camera follows the drug buyer and user, and we see Colvin's endeavor as a viable option. As the season progresses, the coercion of the police to enforce the zone becomes more pronounced. The zone can work only if all are required to patronize it; otherwise, drugs will continue to disrupt the city. In Hamsterdam itself, police are concerned only with enforcing its borders. As the action in the zone heats up, we see the results of the absence of police intervention. Drugs are stolen; holdups occur; murder becomes an option. The camera, frequently a handheld, becomes increasingly busy as it depicts the zone, producing a degree of shakiness and lurching shots. We experience the chaos and lack of orientation caused by the elaboration of this district. In the prelude to episode 8, titled "Moral Midgetry," we see a white, presumably suburban adolescent girl being served by an African American boy who could not be more than ten years old. We also see a drug customer being directed to a buyer, who promptly duct tapes his mouth, ties him up, steals his money, and leaves him bound in the abandoned building. The camera tracks to the police officers at the border of the zone, who are reading newspapers on the hoods of their cars. The culminating shot of the disaster that Hamsterdam has become occurs when Bubbles walks through in the evening hours, trying to sell his T-shirts. The scene is defined by the smoke of fires lit for warmth, but that have the effect of casting the district as a simmering hell. The point of view shifts between Bubbles and a camera that finds him amid the smoke and chaos. We see children engaged in all types of violence and illicit activities. The camera eventually cuts to a long shot of Bubbles pushing his cart through the smoky haze and chaotic movements of the district.

In a plot variation that extends the question of how free the free market is, we see that the existence of Hamsterdam causes dislocation for many who had formerly been employed in the drug trade. Since there is no longer a need for lookouts—the police are the lookouts—or servers or touts, the number of employees needed by the dealers drops dramatically. This downsizing leaves any number of youngsters with no work and no cash. They just mill around the zone. Such a condition

Season 3, episode 8, Bubbles in Hamsterdam.

mirrors the efficiencies of market forces and technology that produce structural unemployment in the age of neoliberalism. The idle children are akin to the many idle workers displaced by shifts in production methods, locales, and distribution. In response, Carver and Herc set up recreation—basketball—and extract an unemployment fund from the dealers; the policemen effectively extend their duties to include addressing structural unemployment.

It is because of Colvin's authority in his sector that Hamsterdam came into being. That authority derives from management strategies adapted from industry. He is exactly the middle manager he has spoken about, and he therefore possesses a limited autonomy. In creating Hamsterdam, he exceeded his charge, and his plan can succeed, even relatively, only because this portion of the city has, in effect, ceased to exist for most citizens and large sectors of government. It has only one resident and no city services. Since, as we have seen, Colvin is unduly concerned with specific geographic points of orientation, he tends to think of such spaces as more self-contained than they are. He has little regard for how those spaces necessarily spill out of their containers. While it is true that as a result of his experiment, crime in his sector is down, this is only because he has allowed all kinds of unreported crime to occur in Hamsterdam. His "decrease" in crime is a statistical trick, a matter of defining the drug zone as a discrete space where crime does not count and is not counted. The crime statistics reported in his sector are not a measure of actual "crime" in the sense that his superiors define it. The limits of Colvin's territorial imperative become apparent when Bodie and his crew are busted by Greggs and McNulty on the way to the zone. The drug dealers protest, saying they were on the way to Hamsterdam. Colvin eventually intervenes. Specific as Colvin attempts to be regarding matters of geography, space is always relative and contingent, and Hamsterdam defies his efforts to detach it from other spaces.

The publicizing of the existence of Hamsterdam occurs incrementally. Colvin takes the deacon on a tour, and the clergyman remarks, upon seeing what the major has done, "It's a great village of pain, and you're the mayor." This close friend of Colvin's provides a perspective that is other than one of expediency. It defines the zone in ways that attend to the moral dimension of the legalization of heroin—but not simplistically. He asks about any number of amenities that would reduce the danger of the zone—needle exchanges, condoms, water. In doing so, he is referring to physical danger, and he introduces the idea that such a social formation should include ancillary services. But the point of true disintegration occurs when Carver and Herc find a body within the contours of Hamsterdam and then move it outside the zone. When the homicide detectives arrive, they see almost immediately that the body has been dragged. The death is the last straw for Herc, who informs the press.

Hamsterdam, though, constitutes a start toward addressing the prohibition model of drug enforcement. But even this constrained notion of a free market results in many calamitous results. The neoliberal conception of space as fluid and contingent holds true. What is clear from the example of Hamsterdam is that no defined place or time is ultimately separate from other times and spaces. The zone fails because despite enforcement procedures, it cannot remain apart from other areas of the city.

And just as Hamsterdam cannot be divorced from other spaces and their social and historical definitions, Stringer Bell's movement into real estate also is based on fallacies of time and space. The new Bell cannot exist completely independent of the old one, and his gentrified property bears at least some relation to its past as substandard housing for poor people. The neoliberal city emerges from its prior incarnation as a city created in the service of productive enterprise. Thus, the residue of that era remains in any number of incarnations, including its residual population of un- and underemployed citizens who have been displaced by the decline of industrial production. Its half-life disrupts any neoliberal scheme to reconceive the city absolutely in those ideological terms. The apparent free market in real estate coexists with a numbing bureaucracy. The drug zone coexists with a policy of prohibition and harsh enforcement.

It is the leakage of the thin and restricted concepts of time and space that undoes efforts to recast the city in the moment. Bell relies on the business-friendly climate and the results of increasing inequality, since in neoliberal governance, as Harvey tells us, the rich get richer and the poor get poorer. This does not make the spaces of the increasingly economically polarized classes any more insulated from one another. In a macro sense, the problem of the drug trade can be seen as not necessarily resulting from growth in the number of users but rather from its increased visibility. That greater sense of its nuisance level and threat may well derive from the fact of gentrification. The winners of the post-industrial economy live close to the losers. While Colvin intends to make the world safe for working-class African American residents of his sector, the larger impulse to depress crime statistics comes from above and is deeply involved with the process of gentrification. If we look at the contingencies of three real estate practices—the corners, Hamsterdam, and the expanding gentrification zone near Baltimore's Inner Harbor—we can see how each elaborates a series of relationships that involve not only the politics of the city but also the macroeconomic forces of the world economy. Season 3 considers the ways in which organizational scales are mutually constituted.

In Jason Hackworth's apt discussion of how cities were motivated by the economic crisis of the 1970s to devise a "spatial fix" to their financial plights, he writes of the emergence of a remedy that was quite different from the one that marked the spatial fix of the 1930s. In that decade, significant capital was put into development that was, as Hackworth notes, centrifugal in its creation of roads and housing that radiated out from central business districts. This effort organized capital growth around the car and building industries, including the building of roads, as a means of responding to the economic conditions of the Great Depression. Much of this shift was, in a Keynesian way, initiated by governmental expenditure in the form of direct investment in infrastructure—roads, water and waste systems, and so forth—and tax credits for home buyers in the form of mortgage deductions.

For Bell and Colvin, then, insulating their redefined space from its temporal-spatial other is both imperative and impossible. Bell remains in many ways the gangster who amassed his capital by selling drugs. As Barksdale tells him, he is out of his element and does not recognize his situation. As a result, he is repeatedly fleeced by those in the know. Bell is new to the game, possessing only a broad conception and a desire to play. And if this entrepreneur with millions of dollars to dispose of cannot find his way to the center of the system of development, what does that say about such a system and the broader prospects for social mobility?

Two recurring reminders of Bell's gangster life are Omar and Brother Mouzone, the former a dope-robbing bandit and the latter a hit man. Omar afflicts Bell and Mouzone, who has been previously hired by Bell to kill Omar. And both exist as forces outside the free zone of Hamsterdam. In season 3, as Omar continues to rob Barksdale stash houses, the impact of the increasingly disrupted world of drug sales results in the attempt on Omar's life on a Sunday, a traditional truce day. Young and incompetent gunmen for the Barksdale gang shoot at Omar as he accompanies his grandmother to church. Intriguingly, it is Bell, the businessman, and not Avon, the gangster, who sets up this breach of the rules. That business is a matter of infinite contingencies makes commerce a dangerous game indeed. That Bell's ambition fails to respect the time constraints of a Sabbath day makes him an incarnation of the contemporary businessman.

Bell's murder occurs in one of the buildings he is renovating, just as he threatens a codeveloper (and recurring character) named Andy Krawczyk for not helping him overcome the obstacles that impede him in making his second, legitimate fortune. It is as though his gangster life and real estate life converge and explode. As Bell threatens Krawczyk, the residue of his drug life in the form of Brother Mouzone and Omar track him into his new place of business. The structure becomes a kind of trap; he is chased up the stairs and finally cornered and shot, accepting his fate before he dies. In theory at least, not too long ago, drug use in that building was not unknown. Bell attempted to go legitimate by moving away from a life of violent coercion; but by denying the role of violence in defining him and helping him succeed, he deluded himself into thinking that his business acumen would be enough to make him a major financial player. His efforts to wall off his past prove futile, recalling the scene just before D'Angelo's death in prison, when he expounds on the futility of Gatsby's flight from his past and more generally from the history in which his narrative is embedded.

Season 3, episode 11, The death of Stringer.

Season 3, episode 13, "It was a good thing, huh?"

The season ends with a montage that includes Councilman Carcetti responding to the spurious explanation of Hamsterdam, pontificating about crime with a full use of military metaphor. The camera seizes upon him and gradually moves straight in for a tight close-up. While his face is earnest, his words are clueless as he talks about how crime denies "economic freedom." In light of the nuanced treatment given this idea in season 3, these words have no clear meaning; but it is certain that economic freedom is not impeded just by criminal activity. All manner of entrenched social relationships and economic practices restrict its full expression, and it is not clear that its coming into being would be a social good. As we see lower-level figures of the Barksdale family being trundled off to jail after the busting of Hamsterdam, and Avon sitting in the court about to go back to prison, we see Marlo Stanfield in the courtroom, waiting to usher in a yet more brutal episode in the Baltimore drug trade.

In the final shot, Bubbles and his new ward—after Johnny died—push a shopping cart through the debris of the razed Hamsterdam. As Bubs and his friend move before the pile, they encounter Colvin staring off wistfully. As Bubs comments on what went on where there is now nothing, Colvin responds with a half question: "It was a good thing, huh?" But Bubbles cannot affirm that it was, and neither can the audience. Perhaps it was—as a limited gesture in the range of ineffectual efforts to fight the drug wars. But there was much that was at least problematic. As Bubbles wheels off, the shot shifts to a high angle, and we can see the pensive Colvin pacing before the rubble. As with the demise of the housing projects, the physical demise of Hamsterdam calls its historical existence into question. And we are back to a world of drug prohibition in which, as Bubbles has said, "Cops be banging on ya, hoppers be messing with ya." Bubbles's refrain sounds as though we have reverted to a world in which it is "more of the same." We are back to the blunt and crude instruments of drug enforcement. But some differences are plausible: Hamsterdam, now that it has been razed, can perhaps be redeveloped by people like Andy Krawczyk and rechristened: Hamsterdam Village: A Luxury Community.

{ FOUR }

Season 4

A NEOLIBERAL EDUCATION— SPACE, KNOWLEDGE, AND SCHOOLING

Season 4 focuses on the fact of the underclass's social isolation, by devoting itself to the greatest force for economic mobility in US social history: the public school. In this narrative, the series emphasizes factors that impinge on the education of inner-city adolescents. This season relies to a great degree on Ed Burns's seven years as a teacher in Baltimore public schools. Simon explains how he and Burns defined the focus of the season: "What do you want to say about the education system? The first step is sitting down and figuring that out. We kicked that around a lot in the writers' room. This year Ed was predominant in the writers' room because he had actual teaching experience."[1] Simon and Burns show how students are afflicted by the cupidity of politicians, the pervasiveness of an amoral culture dominated by ruthless drug dealers, and an education bureaucracy that seems clueless about their plight. In an intriguing treatment of the ways in which schooling connects with specific matters of practical knowledge, the season juxtaposes the terms and rigors of the classroom with that of the street as they apply to four eighth-grade boys: Namond, Randy, Duquan, and Michael.

All four attend the Tilghman Middle School, which is where the recurring characters of Colvin, now retired from the police force, and Pryzbylewski (Prez) both work. (Pryzbylewski's move from the police department to the public schools mirrors that of Burns.) Prez teaches math, and Colvin works on a research team attempting to identify and understand the school's most extreme behavioral problems. One of the season's parallel actions is the mayoral election pitting the white "law and order" candidate Tommy Carcetti against the incumbent African American mayor, Clarence Royce. Also featured is the tale of the further ascension of the young drug boss Marlo Stanfield.

These overlapping narratives trace the connections between the institutional theaters of schooling, politics, and the drug trade. Each structure corresponds to a specific space; yet each element shows some point of connection with the other, suggesting how one discrete systemic problem cannot be rectified without making adjustments in the larger structure of the city. Crime cannot be addressed because schools fail their job; schools cannot be fixed because children live in a world of crime; and in a world of limited resources, those used to fight crime cannot be used to address the problems of the school. Of course, within a restricted space, much of the significant knowledge needed to navigate those areas and to survive and prosper must be contextual, and it is this context that the early scenes describe. Knowledge that is particular and useful can lead a person to assume a higher place on the regional food chain, but such space-specific learning may be limited in its broad application.

Season 4 follows the fates of four adolescent boys who are deeply "at risk." Randy and Duquan have essentially no parent to assist them, and Namond and Michael are being raised by their largely dysfunctional mothers. Tilghman Middle School exists in a world of entrenched poverty and severely circumscribed opportunity. It is visually portrayed as a kind of fortress that is difficult to enter and even more difficult to leave. In a recurring scene, when students are allowed in at the morning bell, they overwhelm its front halls, creating the chaos of a stampede. As is so often the case in *The Wire*, the elaboration of context before defining the season's primary focus is the key to understanding that focus. In season 4, we are introduced to our eighth graders before the beginning of the school year, and we find Namond engaged in the drug trade as a low-level tout working with Bodie. We see how these eighth graders are different from the average: they are already deeply enmeshed in the social and economic systems of the spatially circumscribed underclass, with few apparent ways to stem their movement into an even deeper involvement.

Though the topic of urban education is at the center of the season, it takes a few episodes to establish the larger context of the region's social environment before we see children attending school. (This structuring parallels that of season 3, in which Colvin's drug zone plan—the event driving much of the action—is hatched after several early episodes.) Ultimately, the elaboration of the world in which Tilghman Middle is situated is vital to our understanding the school. That context well defines

Season 4, episode 3, Students begin the school day.

both the central metaphor of the season and its particular addition to the series' thematic. In the scene that precedes the credits in episode 1, we get a particular vision of education and knowledge when we see Marlo's enforcer Snoop in a hardware store with a middle-aged white man, trying to buy a nail gun. Snoop needs this gun so that when she and Chris, Marlo's other contract murderer, kill someone, they can nail the corpse inside one of the many vacant houses of West Baltimore. We can see that this young woman knows her business. The scene is well lighted and shot from the front. As the dialogue between her and the salesman develops, they move closer together. They are shot in a deep-focus two-shot, emphasizing both the degree to which they are ensconced in the store and their clear sympathy for each other.

This connection develops as they talk about which nail guns maintain a charge and possess significant force. When the salesman tells her that the gun has a force equivalent to that of a .27 caliber pistol, she understands, and when he tells her about its lack of kick, she also comprehends that. She goes on to stun the man as she talks about the force of a small-caliber shot and its relative ability to kill a person. At this point we see his stunned face in a reaction shot as she says, "Big joints, man, just break a bone, say fuck it." As she counts out her $800, he is further taken aback by the cash and her desire to leave him a substantial tip for his

Season 4, episode 1, Snoop buys a nail gun.

time. She tells him, "You earned that like a motherfucker." Snoop knows ballistics and the tools that she needs to do the work for which she is contracted. When she returns to the SUV with her nail gun, she tells Chris of her buying experience. She recounts that the salesman has called her purchase the Cadillac of nail guns, but reinterprets the comparison for her partner in crime: "He say Cadillac, but he mean Lexus . . . We can kill a couple of motherfucks with this right here." In the DVD commentary to this scene, David Simon asserts that this pre-credit scene establishes the theme for the season, that the salesman is "schooling" Snoop. But I see this exchange as more than unidirectional. Snoop is schooling the salesman even as she is being schooled; and both are involved in the mutual production of knowledge.

As the opening scene ends, Chris and Snoop take their nail gun and drive back to their neighborhood. While the contours of that place do not allow for the existence of such a retail establishment as the hardware store, it provides them with many opportunities for using the gun. Its purpose within that region is quite distinct from its likely use elsewhere. The problem is that those in one region have only a vague notion of what actually occurs in another. Though disquieted by Snoop, the salesman is unable to discern her true menace. In effect, all refined knowledge is necessarily space-specific, and the specificity of a particular knowledge is at least partially definitional for the spaces in which it obtains. Snoop's skill and knowledge is so impressive that the murder of those designated by Marlo, and the ultimate disappearance of their remains in vacant row houses, is one of the central narrative threads of the season.

Prominent within this season, and an explicit matter of the narrative significance of the Tommy Carcetti character, is an inquiry into the role of the political class in maintaining this system of spatial and social entrapment. In a return to the coda of season 3, we are posed to ask the question whether Carcetti is trying to change the city or, as Bodie said, "just doing the same." As the season proceeds, the figure of Carcetti becomes more and more prominent: he is elected mayor and then becomes indirectly involved in policy decisions affecting the schools and the police. These two city institutions find themselves at odds when Carcetti's promise to raise police salaries runs aground because of the lack of funding available for the city's school budget. This problem sends Carcetti to the state, where he is humiliated by a Republican governor, whose conditions for bailing out the schools is to put them into state receivership. For political purposes, Carcetti refuses the assistance, reasoning that if he can remain politically viable on the state level, he can assist the schools more effectively in the future. The school-versus-police debate emphasizes the interconnectedness of a range of urban spheres and the way in which those contingencies result in a kind of paralysis. Even the well-intentioned Carcetti lacks sufficient funds for running both the schools and the police department—assuming that he has a plan and a desire to make them perform their supposed functions.

In episode 2, we see Prez preparing his classroom in an ironically shot scene: the camera is a little too close to the former cop as he scrubs desks and chips away dried chewing gum from their bottoms. As Johnny Cash sings "Ring of Fire" in the background, we know only too well that what is about to take place in that room may be called education, but it is not; rather, it is a kind of social control. The school stands out in this season as a kind of controlled chaos: milling crowds, arbitrary and unenforceable rules, and willful resistance to learning. The neighborhood constitutes a form of social isolation, but the school is shot in a way that is so confining that the viewer may sigh with relief upon leaving its premises. In an abiding image, when Prez arrives to be assigned his class, he is unable to get through the locked front door. That this character has moved from one oppressive sector—policing—to another further affirms that education performs a vital social function in controlling young people and elaborating a predefined social and economic system. Prez's regard for his students ultimately is beside the point. As assistant principal Donnelly tells him, "These are not your children." And they are indeed not his children: they are of a different race and of a different class, and *both* facts are well recognized within the institution.

Soon after we see Prez's preparations, Namond and his mother go to visit his father, Wee-Bey, in prison. The analogies between the prison space and the school space are difficult to ignore. Indeed, this scene extends the visual emphases of season 3, but the restricted space related to prison is now the hallways of the public school. Both the school and the prison are self-contained, are apparently governed by fixed rules of comportment, and serve as places for the re-elaboration of social hierarchy. Clearly, despite the limits of life in the Baltimore underclass, prison is a far more confining and, particularly in Wee-Bey's case—he is serving a life sentence—hopeless. But prison is also an institution that is ever present in the lives of our middle-school students. All are connected to someone who has been or is in the penal system, and the possibility of experiencing this severe form of restriction is part of their everyday lives. It also looms as an outcome of the failures of public education.

These four children are failed in every way by the political and educational bureaucracies. The most effective types of support for them seem to come from ad hoc connections, interactions that are by definition unsystematic. Cutty mentors young men in his boxing gym; Bubbles befriends a young man, Sherrod, and encourages him to return to school; Namond develops a relationship with Colvin and eventually goes to live with him and his wife; Pryzbylewski makes sure that Duquan has clean clothes and lunch. Even McNulty's walking a beat and developing relationships in his assigned neighborhood is part of this informal network. This is not to say that almost all these efforts do not end tragically.

It is clear, though, that the city-sponsored bureaucracies have their own systems of protocol, and that those systems obstruct the people who labor in them and attempt to aid young men. The education project that separates the hard cases from those deemed educable at Tilghman Middle School exists as a matter of largesse by the school administration, but then is shut down. The foster care system is unbending when Randy's guardian is hospitalized—as a result of an act of vengeance directed at Randy for "snitching"—throwing him into a group home even though Carver offers to care for him. When Michael's sexually abusive stepfather returns to his home from prison, the system fails again, and Michael asks Snoop and Chris to remove—kill—him. Even as Pryzbylewski finds a way to teach math to many of his students by showing the application of his lessons to their everyday lives, the school administrators disrupt and reroute him, insisting that he adhere to a curriculum based on the standardized tests that define success or failure for the kids, teachers, and administrators.

Pryzbylewski confirms the ways in which education is connected with neoliberal dogma. As a teacher who was involved in the reification of crime and its victims when serving as an officer, he recognizes the same system at work in the test-driven public schools. Both systems operate on the basis of statistical reductions of a very complex social reality. When he realizes that he is not in the education profession but the numbers game, he knowingly questions his fellow teacher: "You mean we're juking the stats?" By this, he means that through the display of reified figures that show "progress," the schools create the illusion of improvement, just as the police force manufactures numbers to create the illusion of greater public safety. Such measures and their wide dissemination suggest how the narrow instrumentalism of the neoliberal moment has made more complex and potentially productive discussions of social issues all but impossible. As David Simon explained in an interview with Bill Moyers, "One of the themes of *The Wire* really was that statistics will always lie. Statistics can be made to say anything. You show me anything that depicts institutional progress in America: school test scores, crime stats, arrest reports, anything that a politician can run on, anything that somebody can get a promotion on, and as soon as you invent that statistical category, fifty people in that institution will be at work trying to figure out a way to make it look as if progress is actually occurring when actually no progress is."[2] This view explicitly links season 3 with season 4: just as crime statistics have little to do with actual safety, school statistics have little to do with actual learning.

And just as the schools fail to educate, so the police fail to protect. The season ends with the discovery of twenty-two bodies in the vacant row house—bodies that many in the community knew were there but that law enforcement officials could not find, because of their remoteness from the world they try to police. Following the logic of this nondetection of corpses, it is the department's desire, defined by Rawls, not to investigate the vacant houses, since that would add to the official murder rate. In the aftermath of this breakdown in detection and enforcement, the police department's inept efforts lead to the demise of both Randy and Bodie. In each case, the young man comes forward to cooperate with the police in a murder investigation—though not without coercion—and as a result of his efforts, one young man is executed and the other is ostracized. Both Randy and Bodie, wise denizens of West Baltimore, have knowledge to share that will unlock the murder mystery, but this insight seems beyond the comprehension of the officers. In each case, the officers involved—Herc and McNulty—are oddly clueless regarding the potential consequences of their interactions with these young men, since within the regional code, cooperating with the police can be a death sentence. The ineffectiveness of these systems is emblematic of the decline of the public sphere, a tale that is told repeatedly in the season as the fiscal chaos that defines the city creates comprehensive dysfunction.

The accrued effects of this confluence of policies and historical factors manifest themselves in any number of ways. Certainly, the legacy of racism defines the spatial and social isolation of this neighborhood. One of the key characters for explaining and showing these structural changes in the world is Bunny Colvin, who serves as a bridge between a range of worlds and provides a window into the complex relationships between institutions in those discrete social spaces. Colvin, the man who legalized drugs and was dismissed from the police force in season 3, reemerges as a central character in season 4. We find out that he lost his lucrative security job with Johns Hopkins University because of the publicity and controversy regarding Hamsterdam. Initially, he is a security guard at a downtown hotel, but loses that job when he refuses to let a visiting businessman, who has physically abused a prostitute, go free. He finds that his sense of right and wrong and his sense of authority are not suited to the conventions of the business world.

Eventually he finds himself, through his connection with the deacon, working as an assistant to a social scientist named David Parenti from the University of Maryland, who is studying inner-city adolescents. Colvin's role is to translate the professor's words into a form that can be understood by less-educated adults and the subjects of the study. We can see from the beginning that Colvin has an affinity for communicating with people from all aspects of life: he may be the one character in the series capable of doing so. In working with adolescents who are defined as "corner boys," children who have already cast their lot in the world of the drugs and the streets, Colvin is the device that seems not to be spatially restricted and to operate within a frame of knowledge that he can translate for both worlds.

But what defines this one character as other than bound within his circumstances? Colvin is one of the figures in the series who thinks beyond his circumstances and who therefore allows his circumstances to change. We see him move from being a regional commander to one who considers the possibility of decriminalizing drugs, a significant leap of the imagination. We see him behave empathetically with any number of people, including the battered prostitute, the children in the social experiment, and the jailed murderer Wee-Bey. As he talks to the prisoner about allowing him and his wife to become guardians of Wee-Bey's son Namond, he invokes a common experience of the streets of Baltimore and growing up in the 1960s and 1970s. Such depth of biographical detail allows the viewer to gain a greater sense of this figure's motivation for attempting to redress social calamities. That he becomes an ex-cop and something of an educator—but not within the system—situates him perfectly to produce alternative knowledge.

Colvin is exceptional. We saw in season 3 that his view of law and policing stood outside the norms of the bureaucracy. Further, we learn in his exchange with Wee-Bey at the prison that he is a product of the streets. He also stands as a middle-class African American who has moved to a middle-class neighborhood abutting the ghetto but standing as a distinctive and uncompromised place. This perch next to, but not in the thick of, West Baltimore is a matter of changes in housing patterns caused by white flight in the 1960s. His well-kept yard, porch, and house show us the prospect of a kind of safety zone. That this space functions as such for Namond exhibits a kind of logic, since Namond's disadvantages are primarily a matter of parenting and less a matter of economic situation.

In season 4, the implications of inner-city geography are clearly demarcated. Because students are bound to a particular range of schools as a result of their place of residence, the prospect of receiving adequate social capital through education becomes remote. Featured in this season are methods that attempt to mitigate this condition, all bureaucratic and all largely ineffectual: tracking students so that they are grouped by "ability"; teaching to the test, so that real learning is subordinated to narrowly applied lessons focused on the state proficiency exam; and employing strict discipline.

But more than dwelling on the formal means by which education is supposed to occur, season 4 asks questions about how capitalism in the early twenty-first century reproduces itself. How does it create the conditions by which it remains unchallenged as the dominant model for exchange in the urban United States—even as it absolutely fails more and more of the residents of those locales? Arguably, the "success" of this system in West Baltimore tells us much about its power to replicate itself as an unimpeachable ideology. Indeed, an important dimension of this replication is a matter of its defining and policing of marginal spaces, a social act with implications that extend far beyond West Baltimore. Season 3 considered the means and consequences of decriminalizing hard drugs, but in a specific locale that was policed at its borders and lodged within a place where urban desolation had largely run its course. This emphasis was part of a broader discussion of the varieties of real estate and their relationships to one another. In season 4, space is far more amorphous in its physical boundaries, but very clear in its social definitions. The ghetttoized space of West Baltimore is a domain of ideological replication, a place where we can view the role of the production and reproduction of knowledge in articulating the spaces of the underclass. This idea of ideological reproduction is a recurring one within the series. Indeed, season 1 introduces the concept of spatial isolation within the ideological constructs of Americanism in its very first pre-credit scene. A young man explains to McNulty, upon being asked about why the dead Snot Boogie was allowed to play dice even though he repeatedly tried to run away with the pot of money: "Got to. This [is] America, man."

In season 4, the school-age characters and the older drug dealers have naturalized the borders of West Baltimore: the area seems to be where many people live their entire lives. Arguably, this spatial isolation both intensifies the drug problem and creates the conditions in which the school fails. In a telling comment, Bubbles, just as he begins to nod after shooting heroin in episode 4, muses to Sherrod, an adolescent he attempts to mentor: "I remember when I was a kid, if you had a map of the world, the playground over at Baker and Moreland would be at the center of it. And as I got older, the playground just kept on getting bigger, went beyond the neighborhood. Everything changes, you know? One minute the ice cream truck be the only thing you want to hear. Next thing, them touts calling out the heroin be the only thing you can hear." This is an intriguing sentiment, since as one grows older, the centrality and size of the space of one's school playground should diminish. Theoretically, one's sense of the world should expand with the attendant experiences of life. But Bubbles's life is so spatially constrained that he cannot shrink the space that lies beyond his immediate locale; and in his musing, he defines his focused desire—the want of that one thing, whether it is ice cream or heroin—as that which keeps him lost.

In this season, the West Baltimore ghetto is both limited in its population and in its cultural capital, and teeming with both at the same time. If we look at the opening scene, we can see Snoop's lack of the conventional niceties of middle-class life, as well as her deep knowledge of ballistics and nail guns. As we see in the streetscapes, much of the district's population has moved on to other spaces, leaving it a patchwork of inhabited and empty row houses—the very structures that enable Snoop's work. It is also an area inhabited by many who lack marketable skills. Such attributes could create the basis for those persons' economic success in the more conventional world economy of the early twenty-first century. But they largely lack access to means of acquiring those particular attributes. As we move among the neighborhood, we see who is there, how they live, and how their sense of place and space creates an environment defined by a certain knowledge and expectation. These conceptual limits enhance the isolation of the region and make this area a system of social life parallel to that of middle- and upper-class Baltimore. This system includes its own, alternative means of commerce. This is not to say that West Baltimore's world is equal in wealth and comity to other parts of the city, the state, the nation, or the world. Rather, we see an alternative ecology occur when conventional means of mobility—both social and spatial—are removed from the area. Since the scale of the world we see is grossly reduced in wealth, diversity, and opportunity, the social dynamics within this relatively closed system change dramatically. The problem of the ghetto is its *social* distance from other parts of the city; as a result, its knowledge is too specialized and untranslatable to be applied in "mainstream" sectors. This was a significant problem in seasons 2 and 3 when Stringer Bell tried to move from the drug trade to real estate. Season 4 takes the geographic focus on discrete spaces that has been at the forefront of the previous three seasons and further refines it and provides it with a particular thematic: ideological replication within a "failed" region.

As always in *The Wire*, the drug trade looms and beckons. Drugs are the device through which a funhouse-mirror version of neoliberal capitalism is reinscribed. In season 4 we see the continuing rise of Marlo Stanfield as a drug kingpin as he further consolidates his control of the west side, and as a consequence of this, we see Bodie harassed, intimidated, and then co-opted by the Marlo gang. Within the spaces of the ghetto, Marlo's power far eclipses that of any other drug-dealing king; the Barksdale gang is barely a shadow of its former self. Marlo's outsize dominance is a matter of his rapaciousness, his brutal and calculating use of violence, and the isolation of this area from the domain of more fluid networks of trade. Marlo's methods and virtual monopoly of the regional drug trade re-elaborate a version of the capitalist model of the late nineteenth century, a world defined by notions of laissez-faire economics, the ideological obfuscations of social Darwinism, and the violence enforced physically by state militias and private enforcers such as Pinkerton.[3]

While Marlo dominates West Baltimore, Proposition Joe seeks to rationalize drug trading throughout the city by organizing a drug co-op. In providing us this "reasonable" businessman, Simon provides an alternative to Marlo's economic model. But this vision of a kind of corporate socialism in the end is no less dynamic, no less closed, and likely no less brutal. The difference seems to be that more businesspeople share the spoils. As always, Simon employs the drug trade as a metaphoric expression of broader domains of economic activity in a neoliberal world. As he explains it: "In some ways it's the most destructive form of welfare that we've established, the illegal drug trade in these neighborhoods. It's basically like opening up a Bethlehem Steel in the middle of the South Bronx or in West Baltimore and saying, 'You guys are all steelworkers.' Just say no? That's our answer to that? And by the way, if it was chewing up white folk, it wouldn't have gone on for as long as it did."[4]

While Marlo is initially a figure of laissez-faire, dominating markets and employees by any means necessary, he ultimately joins the co-op, though he is far from fully committed to it. Even though this modest gesture toward cooperation suggests his desire for regularity of product and protection from unforeseen events, he remains a devotee of pirate capitalism, and his association with the drug dealers' guild does not stop him from undermining its efforts and ultimately killing its organizer. In opposing these two visions of commerce and then showing their reconciliation, Simon once again reveals a world where there is no "outside" to reigning economic modes, only adjustments to be made in their top-down implementation.

True to the series' emphasis on crime and enforcement, however various the scenarios to which those emphases take us, season 4 counterpoises the story of miseducation in an urban locale with the outsize violence of Stanfield and his gang. Snoop and Chris account for any number of murders, taking their victims to vacant row houses and using murder as the first and usual tool for punishing perceived transgressors of Marlo's rule. The row houses are a kind of recurring visual image of the city, and many blocks are defined by their relative absence of residents. In season 3 this lack of population allowed for the existence of Hamsterdam. Here the houses become a kind of unmarked tomb for those who have crossed Marlo. The victims include adolescents with subordinate roles in the drug trade—Lex and Little Kevin—and those who have displeased Marlo in any way, such as the security guard at a local convenience store, whom Marlo goads by openly stealing two lollipops.

This use of violence and the reappropriating of existing structures calls to mind late-nineteenth-century methods of urban social control, a kind of gangster capitalism in which the ad hoc creation of urban streetscapes was defined by those with local power. Eventually, the problems of rampant overcrowding, the spread of communicable disease, and the persistence of criminality in these teeming, unregulated spaces of larger US cities led to the reforms of urban progressivism, which redefined the commons in a way that placed them outside a model of laissez-faire and utilitarian notions of maximum economic exploitation. Such intervention provides a point of emphasis in the neoliberal narrative of the nefarious rise of the regulatory state.

Simon's West Baltimore is not beset by teeming numbers of live bodies; rather, it is defined by a disproportion of dead ones. The deacon told Colvin about Hamsterdam in season 3, "It's a city of pain and you're its mayor," and Marlo is the emperor of the dead in season 4. He is able to reappropriate the commons, redefined as streets and abandoned structures, for his own mercenary purposes.[5] West Baltimore has become, in effect, his enterprise zone, much as Times Square in New York became the domain of private interests. He ensures a kind of commerce and a kind of order that make him both the only sheriff and the only factory owner in town. The prevalence of drug money infesting the political domain of Baltimore further recalls how the development of late-twentieth-century public-private projects such as Inner Harbor in Baltimore and the South Street Seaport of New York was greased by political contributions and kickbacks.

This strategy of making the bodies, in effect, disappear, is so successful that it appears to the police that the murder rate in the city has dropped significantly, since no bodies associated with Marlo ever turn up. But this is due to the lack of an effective police presence in the region more than to Marlo's wiliness. Intriguingly, within the structure of the season, the schoolchildren well know that there are corpses in the vacant houses. We see this in episode 5 when Dukie (Duquan), Randy,

Season 4, episode 5, "Not special dead, just dead."

and Michael enter a vacant row house to find a corpse and thereby prove that Snoop and Chris's victims are not "special dead" (zombies), but only dead. This knowledge becomes relatively common as the season moves on, though Bunk and Freamon solve this puzzle only in episode 11. That these adolescents invoke the supernatural to explain the powers of the killers further defines how the Marlo organization has an almost transcendent status in West Baltimore. For these youngsters, the extraordinary violence that surrounds their lives can be accounted for only irrationally, since it otherwise defies explanation.

The world that Simon portrays calls out for some historical context, since his ghetto locale has hardened and calcified, exhibiting its own ecology and seeming to offer few ways of escaping from it. By dramatizing this spatial system of constrained lives and economic opportunity, Simon rebuts the concept that the twenty-first century marks the onset of the postracial era. Indeed, the history and fact of economic and spatial segregation—and now, in the neoliberal era of hypersegregation—shows that the legacy of race has a life that extends far beyond its apparent legal dismantling. Since urban education remains a vexed and infinitely discussed issue of this era, *The Wire*'s complex dramatization of it provides a trenchant further commentary.[6]

THE ECOLOGY OF THE GHETTO

How you expect to run with the wolves come night when you spend all day sporting wit' the puppies?

OMAR

The production and reproduction of knowledge tends to be place-specific, however far-flung that space. A central discourse of globalized commerce is that of cosmopolitanism, a vision of knowledge that distends its spatial application. Cosmopolitanism's other is a kind of narrow tribalism, a vision of knowing that is far more geographically circumscribed. Such notions of circumscribed space bring to mind earlier versions of capitalism, a system of commerce that was narrowly bound by the technological limits of travel and communication, although even nineteenth-century commerce had a vision of international circulation. That earlier model was primarily focused on the national and subnational production and circulation of commodities and the accumulation of wealth. Arguably, it was at the point when commerce began to look more resolutely beyond the local or regional, in the late nineteenth century, that ideologies of extreme nationalism and localism developed their particular hold on a general public. Visions of nation and affiliation were necessarily derived from a need to reaffirm the local and affirm affiliation within a distinct geography just as that sense of the inviolability of borders was beginning to be contested. Simon shows this process as recursive within *The Wire*. We see in this season the need to affirm the smallness and self-contained nature of specific places: the west side of Baltimore over the east, or Baltimore over New York, for example.

As an effect of this sense of space and affiliation, as well as through the limits of wealth, class, and opportunity, *The Wire* delineates the terms of ghetto life in Baltimore, showing us in dramatic detail a self-contained sector of that city. In doing so, it develops a detailed sociological view of a region working in relative isolation. In season 2 we saw the waterfront defined as an island that projects into the world beyond, but remains a discrete space with its own specific social definitions. In season 3 we saw Colvin defining a region within the region. In season 4 we see the pervasive effects of the world as a closed system. In such a self-contained space, which is to some degree constrained from without and to some degree—and ideologically—constrained from within, over-

Season 4, episode 4, The ring.

all wealth tends to be finite, since one of the area's definitional qualities is its economic remoteness. In this context, if someone is getting more, then someone else is likely getting less. It is this sense of limited resources within a zero-sum game that fosters the intense competition that marks West Baltimore, a sense of contest that creates the intense violence of the season. This competitive environment, which is shown again and again, is affirmed by the circulation of a diamond ring, clearly one of the spoils of the drug trade. It passes from Andre, a drug conduit who owns a convenience store, to Marlo to Omar to the rogue officer Walker to Michael over the course of the season, and in each case we see how theft is a matter of domination. The ring comes to stand for the concept of ostentatious wealth within a constrained space and defines a predatory circle that is notably circumscribed. In each case, the ring is captured in close-up, a fetishistic object with local meaning beyond its monetary value.

This focus on the circulation of resources and goods within a circumscribed space seems to lead to the logic of the hierarchy of the food chain. As a further articulation of the impact of spatial constraints, Simon provides us with a system of assertions that show a kind of natural order, with its terms self-defined, which has come to define social relations in West Baltimore. And this assertion of such an order seems an intentional means of invoking the rhetoric of late-nineteenth-century explanations of inequality, including laissez-faire economics and social Darwinism. The inscription of this system defines its ideological impact and the resulting vision of the inevitability of cutthroat capitalism, an apparent inevitability that Simon critiques with this parallel.

Within the world defined by the season, this apparent reversion to the laws of nature is a by-product of the centrality of drugs in the local economy, and a result of how life in this region forestalls other opportunities. The violence and immorality of the drug trade leave its victims with little recourse; after all, what are you going to do: call a cop? This market, limited to a single commodity and a small geographic space, sets up a fierce and violent competition for status and wealth. As even Stringer Bell learns, it is not just about product but also about corners, since even a superior product cannot find its market if it cannot be accessed by those who would buy it. The fight for this limited turf results in intimidation, violence, and murder. In such a vision of a specific and constrained environment, it is no surprise that eventually the emphasis of the show moves toward a neo–social Darwinist worldview, which it critiques, as it explores the contours of human ecology within the spaces of West Baltimore. As we move through this season, we can see that Simon has developed an ongoing though recessed narrative of neoliberalism as a means of revisiting regressive late-nineteenth-century social thought. In doing so, he has also reiterated key aspects of one of its major expressive modes, literary naturalism. In season 4 in particular, we are provided a narrative that devises a vision of social life that makes its vicissitudes all but inevitable and all but intractable.

This focus takes many forms. In the picturesque quotation above, Omar explains how he feels about "finding" a bag of heroin when he is out looking for Honey Nut Cheerios, which he fails to find at the nearby convenience store. (It is easier to find heroin than Honey Nut Cheerios!) He expresses disappointment at the ease of his acquisition, elaborating further, "It's not what you take, but who you take it from." As one who has dedicated his life to feeding off those who feed off others, Omar's assertion shows his attention to the food chain: he seeks to feed at its highest point. For Omar, larceny is not necessarily about what he has gained; rather, it is also about the place of those he has stolen from on the local scale of fitness. He acquires status through his targeted acts of theft. Such attention to social or biological hierarchies turns our attention to explanations of such systems of wealth distribution.

Simon and Burns invoke definitions of natural systems that lead us to consider how neoliberalism undoes means of addressing social inequality enacted in the United States during the twentieth century. The season can be understood as a dramatic exposition of how late-nineteenth-century ideas of human social fitness remain at the core of free-market ideologies, even as they are losing influence in their home disciplines. The term "ecology," which refers to natural systems, has a deep structure that leads back to late-nineteenth-century race theory. The notion of natural systems then included social life, a view that was part of the origin of the social sciences. These social theories largely derived from the pioneering social scientist Herbert Spencer, who sought a field theory of human fitness that would naturalize social hierarchies.[7] William Catton explains:

> As was pointed out by [the pioneering sociologist William Graham] Sumner, the ratio between a population and the available quantity of an essential resource is an important determinant of the intensity of competition among members of that population. Insofar as the members of the population make identical demands on their environment, they relate to each other competitively. As their number increases, competition intensifies among them, unless they become further differentiated (Durkheim). These insights of Sumner and Durkheim are accepted as principles of sociology, but they are no less truly principles of ecology. Competition may apply not only to resource acquisition but also to disposal of life's products.[8]

This is not to say that Sumner and Durkheim are unrefuted by contemporary sociologists, only that their ideas live on in surprising and often embedded forms. This idea of animals competing for resources informs not only contemporary ecology but also theories of the market.

As previously noted, Herbert Spencer, a key figure in forming the concept of social Darwinism and quasi-racist notions of geographic determinism, was central in the development of the idea that humans were part of an overall ecology and that the biological systems defined by Darwin could provide an explanation for social life. In this regard, human ecology is connected with social Darwinism. Similarly, human ecology drank from the poison well of race theory when scientistic notions of race connected with late-nineteenth-century nationalism were used to define certain lands as being commensurate with certain peoples and their reified traits. This idea was central in the delineation of "nations" and the belief that such social entities had a right to a specific geography.

This association between people and place was important to those devising the post–World War I Treaty of Versailles.[9] Subsequently, for example, the Nazis saw the introduction of "foreign" species, such as Jews and Gypsies, as causing systemic decline; as a matter of "hygiene," National Socialists attempted to vanquish those peoples so that they would not "reinfect" Germanic culture.[10]

These notions of biological fitness being the ordering device for economic and social success are the gist of late-nineteenth- and early-twentieth-century social theory, and they also find their expression in eugenics. These notions persisted not only into the age of fascism but are also alive and well in today's neoliberal social theories, particularly in the works of Charles Murray, a key figure in both neoliberal and neoconservative thought. As noted earlier, his books, *Losing Ground* (1984), *The Bell Curve* (with Richard J. Herrnstein; 1994), and *Coming Apart* (2012), provide a contemporary application of Spencer's views.[11] If we apply Murray's views to season 4, we can say that three of the young men—Namond is the exception—are unfit, and that no social amelioration can undo that "fact." It is Simon and Burns's providing of context that shows us how they are products of a distinct social and historical situation. Duquan, Michael, and Randy possess many abilities, but their means of developing and applying those talents is constrained by their lack of access to a larger world.

This is not to place the pioneering urban sociologist Robert Park, who coined the term "human ecology," or David Simon in the company of Joseph Goebbels. Rather, I am simply defining the concept of human ecology at its extreme for the sake of clarity. The textual elements that lead us to consider this concept are so prominently placed that it is difficult not to see that Simon advanced his definition of the ghetto and its social isolation over the first four seasons of the show. For the idea of human ecology to have salience, the space to which it refers must be relatively distinct and closed. As Simon explains:

> The people most affected by this [the drug war] are black and brown and poor. It's the abandoned inner cores of our urban areas. As we said before, economically, we don't need those people; the American economy doesn't need them. So as long as they stay in their ghettos and they only kill each other, we're willing to pay for a police presence to keep them out of our America. And to let them fight over scraps, which is what the drug war, effectively, is. Since we basically have become a market-based culture, that's what we know, and it's what's led us to this

> sad dénouement. I think we're going to follow market-based logic right to the bitter end.[12]

So the ways in which this idea obtains in season 4 is a culmination of the ongoing explication of the idea of the ghetto that was focal in seasons 1 and 3. It is arguable that the introduction of urban education—as practiced—further refines the conceptual parameters that define this enclosed urban space. And the more isolated the space, the more intense the competition for resources.

Unlike Hamsterdam, the ghetto we see in season 4 *seems* organic, though it is indeed human created. It is a result of historically based de jure and de facto separation by race, which became urban practice in the twentieth century. This system became even more entrenched by the intraracial divisions of class that were a product of the economic and social policies of the era that immediately followed 1964—deindustrialization, neoliberalism, and a related return to the dominant conservative legal principles of the pre-civil-rights era. According to a common colloquial description of the effects of the civil rights movement, it provided access to the freeway just when the on-ramps were closing. And in this vision of Baltimore, the on-ramps are nowhere to be found.

In West Baltimore, people define their place in the food chain primarily through their connection with the wealth that derives from the drug trade. As a commodity, drugs fill the place where all other types of commerce used to proliferate. When Namond and his mother are removed from the Barksdale payroll, she pushes him to the corner as a full-time drug dealer. When Michael apprentices in a career, he goes to work in the drug trade. When Sherrod disappears, Bubbles finds him on a stoop, working for a drug seller. When drug dealers from New York attempt to develop a Baltimore presence, Snoop and Chris enforce Marlo's preeminence, as they do throughout the season, thus maintaining their boss's control over the local market. Drugs are the only commodity that creates significant profit in the community at large, though commerce in drugs seems to redistribute wealth rather than to create it: as Bodie loses, Marlo gains. As a confirmation of Marlo's place at the top of the food chain, he offers gifts, money for kids in his orbit to buy items for returning to school, so that the streets will make his "name ring out." He seems more concerned with status in this specific domain than with absolute wealth. Many of his murders are prompted by indignation, not theft.

The season defines West Baltimore as a place of enhanced com-

Season 4, episode 2, Marlo provides, Michael resists.

petition and violence. Marlo's amoral approach to business and money makes contextual sense, since his aspirations are not a matter of expanding his market but of maximizing market share. He is the businessman as literalist. The entire world he knows or needs to know is the one right in front of him. When he confronts Andre in the rim shop, after Andre's stash has been stolen by Omar, he is not interested in hearing about the analogies between West Baltimore and the post-9/11 world. He tells Andre, in a close two-shot, that he is responsible for replacing the stolen goods. Marlo's goal is to control drug commerce in the world as he knows it. He understands violence as the ultimate guarantor of his success, so his executioners, Chris and Snoop, kill not out of sadism, but for the ends of commerce. Marlo is a big fish that is ever eager to devour smaller fish. His sense of the world, then, is that of a fairly small pond, a view he seems to share with many others in West Baltimore.

This structuring metaphor of the food chain finds its way into the season's narrative through the repeated use of "natural" imagery. The season takes pains to show vacant lots suffused by weeds and wild bushes as a sign that the natural world is overwhelming what was once a place of far more concentrated human activity. Streets are shown reverting to dirt paths as the pavement erupts and crumbles. In an early scene of episode 1, we see boys who will be in Pryzbylewski's class at Tilghman

Season 4, episode 1, The wilds of West Baltimore.

playing in a deserted alley, with encroaching and reemergent "nature" all around. This scene is indicative of the back-to-cruel-nature narrative of *Lord of the Flies*; we observe the relative place in the natural pecking order of each boy, with Michael at the top and Duquan on the bottom. When Duquan blows up a bottle that contains a bug, the pigeon that Michael, Namond, and Randy are pursuing flies away. They rush toward Duquan, angry that they might have lost a "homing" pigeon that they (erroneously) believe that they could sell. But again, this emphasis on birds in the emergent wild, and even on the way in which "hunting" defines relative fitness within this peer group, shows us the narrative of neo–social Darwinism at work.

That Simon's vision of the 2000s should connect with that of a late-nineteenth-century social Darwinist is revealing. It takes little imagination to see that the contemporary rhetoric of the deserving rich and its complementary discourse of the undeserving poor is deeply embedded in US society—specific rhetoric that Simon addresses throughout the five seasons. Season 4's sprawling narrative allows us to see that failing schools reconfirm spatial segregation and the ghetto, and that the proliferation of drugs in the same spaces makes a kind of social sense. Heroin is like other commodities, as Stringer Bell found out in his economics class; but it is also unlike shoes and telephones and cars in that its effects on a community can be profound. The alternatives to the drug trade become Bubbles's shopping cart "depo," a level of enterprise that also harks back to the nineteenth century, when immigrant entrepreneurs pushed their carts through chaotic urban streets in hopes of one day opening a store with doors and walls. Bubbles finds only a bigger fish that robs and beats him, and an ineffectual police presence unable to secure his place at the low-end of capitalist enterprise.

SPACE, "EDUCATION," AND LOCAL KNOWLEDGE

Urban education in this dramatization is an important aspect of Simon's deep ecology of the ghetto. Education might lead to upward mobility, and historically it often has for immigrant populations and their heirs. But as practiced in the early-twenty-first-century inner city, it becomes another means of reinforcing isolation. True to the ecological concept of a permeable but constrained system defined spatially, the Baltimore city schools exemplify an institution that has become extrinsic to the space of the ghetto but that, in order to become effective, must become more intrinsic. In becoming more intrinsic, the schools might become part of the problem of spatial segregation in yet a different way. Schools replicate the contours of capitalist ideology in their reinscribing of class distinctions, of ever-elaborating relative hierarchies, and of the need to "get ahead." The problem with Tilghman Middle School is that virtually none of its students will move forward in a conventional sense, which allows us to see that the rhetoric of mobility, despite its implicit and explicit assertions of the fluidity of class, merely serves to entrap the disadvantaged further in a system of class rigidity.

This emphasis on applicable and local knowledge tracks with a certain means-end worldview connected with neoliberalism. That is, this type of education strongly emphasizes hands-on experience and minimizes the impact of abstraction. Simon and Burns employ this emphasis as a reading of contemporary culture rather than as an attempt to valorize this type of reductive paradigm. If we look at the frames of knowing elaborated and their specific areas of applicability, we can see their limits. For example, one important element of this season, and indeed of all seasons, is how crimes are solved. Simon notes the show's genesis as a police procedural, and in many ways, a strain of the show remains true to that formula. In season 4 this aspect is reemphasized through Kima's move to the homicide division and by the apparent unsolvability of the murders that are a by-product of Marlo's rise to power. It is only by exercising "soft eyes"—that is, viewing a scene as though for the first time and without socially learned blinders—that Lester Freamon can see the vacant houses as the places where the bodies are hidden.

This issue of spatial segregation and social mobility has vexed sociologists all through the twentieth and twenty-first centuries. It is compounded by the legacy of racism. As Elijah Anderson and Douglas S. Massey tell us, race and space have a long and deep connection in social science theory, and the failures of a system defined by spatially articulated hierarchies should not be surprising:

> According to Robert Park's widely cited dictum, social relations *were* spatial relations. Thus in building theories and conducting research, American sociologists concerned themselves fundamentally with understanding how ecological factors shaped and constrained interpersonal behavior and social structure. No analysis of racial stratification was complete without describing the ecological configurations of class, race, and ethnicity or outlining how their intersection influenced the life chances and social worlds experienced by individuals.
>
> One of the most important structural settings considered by sociologists was the neighborhood. From the early writings of Park and Burgess through the later work of Frazier, Janowitz, Blau, Duncan, and Lieberson, neighborhoods were seen as fundamental to the broader system of American stratification.[13]

The stratification of neighborhoods in Baltimore, depicted repeatedly during this season, is vital for elaborating how the school meets the local culture. When Prez is most successful in reaching his students, he teaches them probabilities, employing craps as his teaching tool. But, for example, Randy learns not the broader lesson of probabilities, but the narrower one of how to win at dice, leaving us to wonder whether this applied instructional mode loses the forest completely as it focuses on very specific trees. The teachers are *in* the neighborhood—but not *of* the neighborhood—and still must reach students whose lives have been distinctively isolated.

In a telling scene, we see one student slash the face of another with a razor blade. This is a response to persistent and low-level torment, but speaks of the level of violence that pervades the school as a matter of its situation in the world. It also shows the classroom to be a dangerous space, one where proximity can lead to violence. And as the camera

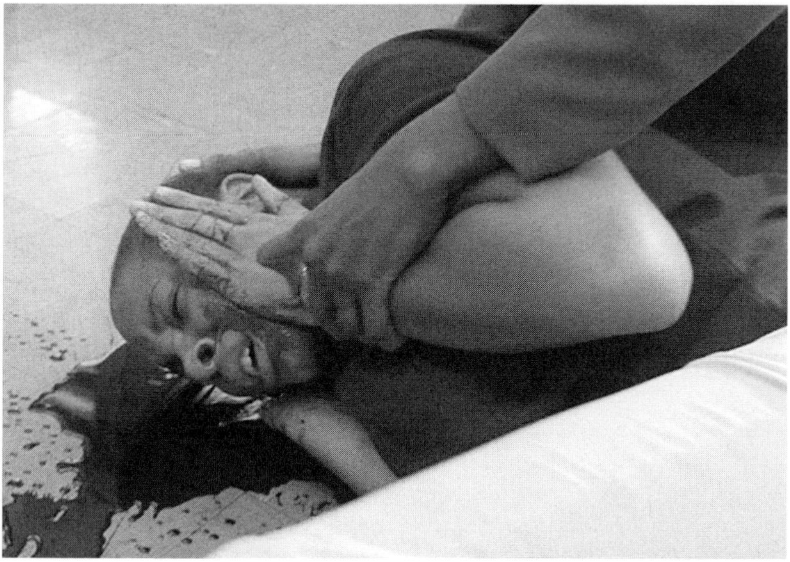

Season 4, episode 3, Violence in the classroom.

work of the scene shows us, the teacher is so far from the students that he can do little to prevent it. This act confirms for Prez that all schoolrooms are not alike, that it depends on the location of the building that houses the room. Prez spends the weekend puzzling over what lesson to derive from the incident, what he can tell his students. It turns out that his students accept the violence as routine, distracting Prez from his speech. His inability to find the means of having a conversation about the slashing confirms his great distance from his students, even though he remains spatially proximate within a closed space. The children are creatures of the street, and the refusal of the institution and its surrogates—the teachers and administrators—to recognize this clearly results in a major disconnection.

The role of the police in the spaces of West Baltimore is also questioned. In a defining scene, Doughnut, a car thief, is apprehended by the rogue officer Walker. As Walker brutally breaks the youngster's fingers, the scene is the site of the abandoned loading dock that serves as a hangout for our adolescent characters. As Doughnut tries to run away, he is caught in a shot in which he is centered and framed by a blank brick wall that faces the loading dock and is behind a chain-link fence. The lack of activity in this enclosure speaks both to the opportunity it allows Walker for violence and to the prospects for the future that face Dough-

Season 4, episode 10, Walker catches Doughnut.

nut and his contemporaries. In a physical composition that looks much like Bubbles being beaten by his tormentor, Walker literally surrounds Doughnut, leaving him nowhere to go, and then asserts his dominance.

Walker's portrayal as a rogue cop reiterates a sense of West Baltimore as a place where conventional assumptions of order are not operative. Officer Bunk Moreland notes this in episode 12 when Lester and Jimmy drunkenly enter a vacant house to settle a bet about Lester's theory that if you find newer nails on the outside of the vacant houses, inside will be corpses. When Lester's theory is affirmed, Bunk says: "Up is down, black is white, right is wrong." And indeed, the basic problem of the season—that authority exists in sectors that have no ethical vision or effective power—pulls together a range of plot threads. We are seeing nothing less than a breakdown in human function. In such a world, Marlo is king, and no counterpoised power questions his stature. And he is king because he has conquered the space created by poverty, deindustrialization, racism, and disinvestment. Indeed, globalization may reign in the macro economy, but Marlo controls the space left behind.

The recognition of the dictates of particular spaces constitutes the precondition for a useful local knowledge. For example, Namond's father, Wee-Bey, has made his peace with institutional life because it is a world he has come to know and understand. Similarly, we see Dennis (Cutty) making his peace with his life as a mentor to young men, through his boxing program, and as a lawn man. In each case, we see in Dennis a kind of solidity that comes with situated knowledge. In the gym, we find him as a dispenser of the knowledge of the ring; on the lawn crew, his fellow workers have taught him enough Spanish to engage in repartee, though he tells his crew chief that it is just "a few curse words" and little more. In opposition to the Cutty in season 3, he has mastered a trade of sorts and seems fully out of the life of crime. That he knows that life and its implications allows him to live within the neighborhood even as he eschews criminality. It is only when he misjudges the role and possibilities of violence in his specific moment that he falls victim to it: his attempts to intervene in the life of one of his boxers results in his being shot. Perhaps he is not sufficiently schooled in the new ways of West Baltimore; knowledge of the managed violence of the ring has little salience when he is confronted with a gun on a street corner. The boxing ring, with its attendant rules, emerges as a kind of safety zone that he cannot maintain or enforce in the world beyond it.

Such a view of the discrete space of a particularized knowledge has implications for the portrayal of Tilghman, since the school seems to be a specific site of particularized learning, a view that resituates public education in the extant narrative of social mobility in the United States. In their synthetic rewriting of Michel Foucault and Pierre Bourdieu, the education scholars Edward Buendía and Nancy Ares discuss inner-city education as not being primarily focused on the dissemination of knowledge; they argue that the discursive production of knowledge occurs concurrently with the production of the spaces—which are defined by the locale where that knowledge occurs. They paraphrase Foucault to argue that knowledge includes a "spatial dimension . . . that is mobilized by a wide array of spatially dispersed and buttressing discursive and material relations."[14] They go on to elaborate how the production of knowledge is commensurate with the production of space, since there may be no delimiting of a discrete area without its signifying a particular meaning or set of meanings.

Such a vision applies Henri Lefebvre's general vision of space and of abstract space in particular. In his *Production of Space,* Lefebvre defines representations of space as those of planners and bureaucrats, and within that category there exists the notion of abstract space, which is imposed from above. Abstract space, according to Lefebvre is instrumentalized and made a part of a reigning capitalist system.[15] The school is of that system, even within a world largely forgotten by all other institutions but

Season 4, episode 11, "They are tombs."

law enforcement. And while Buendía and Ares make the connection between space and specific knowledge, Lefebvre allows us to see the conflicts over the definition of space that are central to the season, and the ways in which those conflicts are emblematic of the issues that define the ghetto. The local knowledge of characters like Snoop, Marlo, and Omar, for example, is clearly outside this bureaucratic realm. As Zyong Zhang explains, "The term of lived space is balanced carefully between the two poles of conceived space (purely idealism) and perceived space (pure materialism). It embodies both elements without being reducible to either. It is the space of connaissance."[16]

This linking of knowledge and lived space is a vital means of differentiating the school from its environs, even as it remains linked with them. The school is an institution that is remote from the lives of its students and from the facts of the street. Such a model shows us Michael's rationale as he leaves the classroom, where he is clearly talented, for a life as Marlo's henchman. It also shows us why the police cannot deduce that the bodies are in the vacant houses: their routine ways of seeing and knowing preclude their employing "soft eyes," vision that defamiliarizes and resituates information. Since those structures have been reappropriated by Snoop and Chris, they no longer are defined by their original purpose. When Bunk tells us they are now "tombs," we see how the lived experience of those in the neighborhood allows for that knowledge, whereas it takes investigators a willed effort to look at the scene with soft eyes in order to see what has been before them for months.

The school is also a place where students bring their corporeal and cognitive beings, and those beings redound with the lives they live outside this institution. Public education becomes a device that shows them a world different from their customary one, and that, while not irrelevant, elaborates social conditions very unlikely to become theirs. It is a place where their local forms of knowledge come into direct conflict with the curriculum. Students are powerless to change this, and if they could, the result would not alter their social world. Thus, when certain incorrigibles are tracked, what is being noted is that some students will allow instruction to take place and some will preempt it with their own behaviors. But neither group seems to be learning anything that will alter their spatial isolation. The space of *connaissance* becomes that of a kind of stalemate, a place where time is served before, or as, lives are lived.

Intensely local knowledge emerges as the other of globalization and neoliberalism in ways that parallel the broader assertions of the narratives of seasons 2 and 3. For those left behind, knowledge of the spaces of their geographically circumscribed lives intensifies as those spaces acquire depth and nuance. Knowing which colors define which gang, how one serves drugs, who works for Marlo and who for Proposition Joe, may define a kind of success and safety in West Baltimore, but the applicability of such knowledge in predicting the arc of Asian financial markets in the next month will be necessarily limited. As worldwide systems of trade and communication sprawl across far-flung networks, the spaces outside those systems become increasingly parochial and particular. Indeed, this is the very dialectic of regional sectarianism within the age of world trade. It is no less than a comprehensive distending of one system from the other, a means of reorganizing space so that physical proximity may not matter. Definitional for this reconceiving of effective contiguity is the movement and penetration of capital. Since the ghetto is explicitly outside the major currents of neoliberal capital flow, it exists as a place of underdevelopment. Nearby are all sorts of places that seem to have little impact on or exchange with our slice of West Baltimore—particularly that of the downtown business world.

In a revealing scene, Colvin takes three of his "corner" children to Ruth's Chris Steak House in the Inner Harbor as a reward for working together and building a model of the Eiffel Tower in their class. This

Season 4, episode 9, Dining at Ruth's Chris.

scene brings to mind a very similar one involving D'Angelo and Donette at a similar restaurant in episode 5 of season 1. As in that earlier scene, but perhaps even more pronounced here, we see our fish out of water. And though the level of discomfort among the adolescents is palpable, that they can be brought into a distinctly different environment portends a world of possibility—even if few will partake of it. The world of this very expensive restaurant is socially remote, though geographically proximate. As the four walk to their table, we get reaction shots from the three children, who visibly show discomfort with their glancing looks at the other patrons and their stiff, uncomfortable body positions. Immediately upon sitting down, a succession of mid-close-ups shows each student expressing some lack of knowledge of the conventions of the restaurant, whether it is not knowing the difference between the hostess and waitress, not knowing that the specials are not cheaper than the regular menu items, or not knowing that napkins are not tucked under your chin. By the time they emerge from the restaurant, they are emotionally exhausted and surly. Safe to say, the two adolescents who are not Namond will not be going back anytime soon, and Namond might only because of his change in circumstances, having become a ward of the Colvins. Clearly the knowledge produced through experience is quite different from that produced by proximity.

MONEY AND CAPITAL

Season 4 powerfully considers how spatially specific knowing leads to the gaining of capital; but to have capital is not necessarily to have control over one's domain. The aspiration of fitting into the structure of a preexisting economic system is one that serves as a default desire throughout the season. There is no alternative imagined, no organizational energy to devise a means of modifying the institutional structures that elaborate capitalism. Politics is corrupt, schooling seeks to articulate a further form of social control, and community icons can imagine nothing but getting theirs. Thus, within this narrow geographic region, we see the worst aspects of vulture capitalism being replicated.

Capital, of course, comes in all forms—social, intellectual, economic. But in West Baltimore, these varieties of transactionable wealth largely collapse into the realm of the economic, and into a spatially circumscribed vision of that sector at that. Michael, through his physical bearing and his intellectual capacity, possesses both social and intellectual capital, which he leverages in his relationship with Marlo, a connection that brings relative wealth and a burgeoning career as a drug capitalist controlling a corner. Still, the prospect that this arrangement will result in Michael ascending fully into the capitalist class is dim. Omar has the soul and spirit of a thief, as well as the habits of patience and thoroughness that translate into wealth—and we see him achieve his payoff. But he is *only* a thief who uses his wiles to steal money; he is not a capitalist who will reinvest his wealth to make more. Snoop's knowledge of killing and places to stow the bodies is also transactionable, since both she and Chris are well compensated for their actions. But neither will supplant Marlo. It is in this collapsing of the category of knowledge into the realm of the economic that we can see the brutal logic of a world in which value had largely been reduced to cash value and in which cash rarely reaches the scale of capital, and thus cannot provide a basis for economic mobility. This distinction is one of economic scale and, to some degree, a matter of neoliberalism's effect of redistributing capital upward to the point that those in the middle class—and below—struggle and become increasingly remote from the top tier of the economic system. (What we currently refer to as the 1 percent is actually only a fraction of that percentage.) Still, despite the intransigence of class barriers, all play the game as conventionally defined.

Marx argues that money is the objectified form of the abstract quality of social value as well as a device both for exchange and for defining relative value. In West Baltimore, we can see the first definition eclipse the other two, since there are few goods to buy and therefore few goods through which to define value. Within this domain of limited and highly disproportionate wealth, the local equivalent of the capitalist class reigns supreme, and the means and morality of acquisition barely enter the equation. Figures like Marlo and Omar become local legends even as they engage in acts that defy conventional morality. Because of the spatial limitations of this system, capital accumulation is necessarily limited; still, the system valorizes the ethos of individual accumulation at a scale that defines a market. Within that market, having the cash for lower-level consumption and enterprise is vitally distinct from having capital to invest. Simon sets up a complex dynamic in which money is both defined as necessary and seen as a device that is not necessarily equally powerful in all contexts. While most residents could not articulate these distinctions in scales of wealth, or the ways in which investment can lead to the accumulation of cash for the sake of generating a geometrically enhanced scale of wealth, on some level the paucity of money and wealth in this district generates outsize desire.

In West Baltimore, that object quality of cash creates a mind-set that equates money with such abstract ideas as stability, security, and power. But we see that such effects cannot occur at a lower scale of enterprise and accumulation, thus affirming the need to join the capitalist class. It is the distinction between money and capital that defines the former's efficacy and its relative power even within this spatially circumscribed world. But all are constrained, either by formal devices that limit physical space or by conceptual ones that perform similar functions. Unlike Marlo, Randy and Bubbles find themselves selling goods that are easily procured elsewhere. In the ways that they are shot, they are diminished by their limited scale of commerce: Bubbles's cart is typically shot slightly distantly, emphasizing the smallness of his person, market, and stock. Randy typically sits at a lunchroom table, a small boy among smaller boys, shot from a slightly skewed angle, selling candy and other treats to his captive—literally—audience. They are able to develop their clientele only because of their buyers' spatial limits and the limits of their entrepreneurial "schooling." And indeed, that schooling is very much a matter of class position, a limit with clear spatial implications. So what they offer is merely convenience for those who are similarly spatially restricted. Bubbles's cart would have no place outside the self-defined region of this neighborhood. He cannot push his cart downtown, nor will there be much demand for his wares there. Randy's market is the school, and even it is limited by the rules of the institution, which has its own spatial definition and limits. His relative access depends on purloined hall passes and passing for a younger student as he enters the lunchroom.

As a contrast to Marlo's vast accumulation of wealth, we see the modest entrepreneurial efforts of Bubbles and Randy. These characters introduce the problem of scale in this self-contained area. Both small entrepreneurs are engaged in enterprises that siphon off very circumscribed aspects of local capital. This is clearer in the case of Randy, who lives as a foster child with Miss Anna. Understanding the insecurities of his life and the ways in which cash payments to foster parents create the system in which he lives, he believes that if he has enough cash, he will attain security. But he will never attain that amount of capital. Similarly, Bubbles develops his modern version of the pushcart as a means of providing a modest income so that he can maintain his drug habit but not be fully enveloped by the world of drug use and commerce. Bubbles and Randy are stuck in a world of relative self-sufficiency but low yield. Both seek only a modest level of security and some insulation from the risks of their precarious positions. Their mistake is to equate capital with security, since capital, by definition, is not risk averse and therefore is never fully secure. Marlo kills because of this inherent insecurity regarding his place in the market. He could go elsewhere, but is limited by the violence of the drug business and his dominance within his appointed zone of sales. In any case, these restraints define the scope of each market, and the ability of each to grow is limited. Such an illustration points to the problems of market orthodoxy and the almost inevitable existence of anomalies and constraints.

Such a market places them clearly outside the flow of international exchange. As Saskia Sassen explains, these are small operations that work off a discrete supply of labor and consumers: "establishments that are small, rely on family labor, and often fall below minimum safety and health standards."[17] By seeing Bubbles and Randy, who is a much younger version of the former, as part of the casual labor force, we are further reminded how those who theorize the global network declare such enterprises to be below the concern of larger capital. They have nothing to fear from Walmart, because Walmart has ceded the West Baltimore T-shirt and toilet paper market to Bubbles and his ilk. Clearly, drugs are a far more lucrative commodity than candy or household sundries. This low level of commerce defines the mundane contours of this particular economic space. Such a vision of a decentralized and disorganized system well fits the broader model defining the neoliberal moment, since that mode of production resituates labor as dispersed rather than as concentrated, as it was in the Fordist model. While Bubbles and Randy are constrained by space, they seem to temporally reach into an earlier capitalist moment—the world of small entrepreneurs in the late nineteenth and early twentieth centuries, before the consolidation of commerce in the form of hypermarkets and big box stores.

In ways reminiscent of the dredging up of late-nineteenth-century ideologies in Simon's evocation of social Darwinism and human ecology, so Bubbles's "depo" reminds us of how immigrants from southern and eastern Europe made their cash in the late nineteenth century. They devised small businesses with little capital, and they were subject to little regulation. Indeed, they constituted the lowest rung on the economic ladder, and though some became rich through their enterprise, most failed. To see Bubbles and Randy as analogous to those peddlers is to see the degree to which those left behind by the globalized economy are stuck in the same unproductive and precarious spaces of those of the era of laissez-faire. Perhaps their businesses are even more precarious even than those of the late nineteenth century, since these contemporary ventures exist within a broader landscape of mature capitalism, a system with few spaces outside its organizational structure.

This recalling of late-nineteenth-century modes of commerce brings us full circle to the issues of space, race, and education within circumscribed zones. Bubbles talks of how his lack of education led to his limited opportunities, and as the season ends we find him deeply disrupted by having provided a cyanide-laced dose of heroin that kills Sherrod. This dose is the direct result of Bubbles's inability to avoid being beaten and having his wares and money stolen. He is vulnerable as a result of his business and his place outside any protected zone of commerce and safety. Sherrod chose life with Bubbles despite the older man's desire to send him to school; however, that was an extremely short-lived exercise.

Marlo's case becomes the key to comprehending the dysfunction of the community and the broader vicissitudes of malapportioned wealth. David Harvey defines the economic situation of the moment (late twentieth and early twenty-first centuries) as "surplus capital and surplus labour existing side by side with seemingly no way to put them back together."[18] This results in idleness and poverty for those left behind. Marlo has sucked up an enormous disproportion of the spatially circumscribed capital of the ghetto, leaving little available for other uses. While he does employ a significant workforce, his lack of desire to invest more strategically in the space from which his capital derives and in broader diversification that could create relative wealth in West Baltimore leaves his environs underserved by his wealth. Marlo seems analogous to a contemporary rapacious businessman who shields his wealth from taxes and stows it in tax-free havens offshore. Simon even employs Marlo's condition as an opportunity to gloss the role of charity. Though we see a smiling drug dealer giving out cash to schoolchildren, such apparent largesse does nothing to alter the conditions that create poverty.

The idleness that defines West Baltimore seems to call for a kind of beneficent feudalism, one in which the lord—in this case, Marlo—assumes responsibility for his retainers. But since, in this case, economic status is an end in itself, there is no social necessity for such a system; nor is there an economic one, since Marlo is already in control of a disproportion of the area's resources. Indeed, the drug lord's job is only to maintain his own place at the top of the hierarchy of drug dealers. Thus, he ruthlessly controls his turf while more generally creating an atmosphere of exploitation and violence. Clearly, the trickle-down effects of such a system are limited. With such a large and static pot of money, Marlo becomes a target. Not of local competitors, who, as we see in the case of the co-op, are unable to compete with his considerable network and simply seek to make peace with it and proffer their drugs in relatively small amounts at the edges of his empire. He is targeted, ineffectively, by New York–based dealers who have little local knowledge. On the other hand, a figure like Omar, who is not seeking to compete with Marlo but only to steal his wealth—whether in cash or drugs—poses a threat to the dealer but not to his broader enterprise. This act of theft is confirming of the system rather and merely disruptive, affirming it as the only enterprise worth robbing but not substantially altering its ongoing power.

As the season goes on, we can see Marlo's difficulty with capital enhancement, and thus he falls prey to the problems of overaccumulation. He neither moves beyond the spaces of his enterprise nor, unlike Stringer Bell, does he invest in Baltimore real estate. As a result, he fails the capitalist test of using his money to make more. As Benjamin Kunkel writes in his review of David Harvey's *The Enigma of Capital: And the Crises of Capitalism* and *A Companion to Marx's "Capital"*:

> Overaccumulated capital can be defined as capital unable to realise the expected rate of profit. Whether in the form of money, physical plant, commodities for sale or labour power (the latter being, in Marx's terms, mere "variable capital"), it can only be invested, utilised, sold or

> hired, as the case may be, with reduced profitability or at a loss. Overaccumulation will then be variously reflected in money hoarded or gambled rather than invested; in underused factories or vacant storefronts; in half-finished goods or unsold inventories; and in idle workers, even as the need for all these things goes unmet.[19]

As Harvey writes, "If the crisis cannot be resolved, then the result is massive devaluation of both capital and labor (bankruptcies, idle factories and machines, unsold commodities, and unemployed laborers)."[20] Indeed, Marlo's excessive interest in poker speaks to this problem, as does the general scenario of dispossessed people and empty buildings—including commercial structures. In an ideal world of commerce, those buildings would house tenants and not corpses. That they house dead bodies rather than live ones speaks to the cycle of overaccumulation. Since labor is devalued in this world, and consumption operates at its virtual maximum, the elimination of some number of individuals has no macroeconomic effect. Indeed, lower-level workers like Little Kevin are worth more dead than alive.

In season 4 we can see the fact that all capital is not created equally and that though the accruing of wealth is advantageous to Marlo, it fails to create a larger social good. In season 5 we see Marlo move his cash offshore, to the Cayman Islands. This constitutes the spatial fix for Marlo and his enterprise while illustrating how even the most geographically circumscribed capital can fail to benefit those in its immediate vicinity. Marlo's wealth becomes intertwined with a far-flung system of finance. West Baltimore remains impoverished, and even its drug money has become systematized in a global network of commerce.

The failure of schools to define and exact economic opportunity is made clear in the season's last episode. Simon affirms that those outside a viable economic system tend to remain so, despite well-intentioned efforts to bring them in. As the season ends, we see Duquan in his new school but clearly headed toward dropping out; Randy is being harassed in the group home; and the pilot project for incorrigible students has been dismantled because of school funding cuts—a result of the defunding of the public sector, which is a key component of this economic regime. As the Paul Weller version of the song "Walk on Gilded Splinters," composed by Mac Rebennack (aka Doctor John), plays, we see the failure of capital circulation as the lodging of an underclass in an unredemptive space. As Freamon and Daniels survey the many bodies taken from the vacant row houses and put into a makeshift morgue, Daniels

Season 4, episode 13, The school as a morgue.

notes that the morgue was once the grammar school he attended. In a close-up he offers, "I got a decent education." But those days are clearly gone, and what is left is a life made precarious by lack of opportunity. The houses became tombs, and the school became a morgue, suggesting the outcome that can occur when a community falls off the known world and becomes its own zone of unregulated commerce. Such a scene develops the intense pessimism of Simon's vision; and although there is a space outside globalized networks of commerce that operate on neoliberal principles, that space is exceedingly narrow and uninviting.

Namond Brice finally finds a means of extrication from this world: in a telling recapitulation of the Horatio Alger, rags-to-respectability story (another aspect of late-nineteenth-century conservative cultural assertion), he is adopted by the middle-class Colvins and freed from his fate as a corner boy. And if Namond's deliverance offers the only, very slim margin of hope, then the cultural logic of "running with the wolves" is all but confirmed. And indeed, if this is the environment that prevails and the terms that articulate the social system, then the mode of economic organization associated with rapacious capitalism seems to reign without comment or contest. Indeed, the other three boys are clearly worse off through the direct intervention of guardians of the public weal.

{ FIVE }

Season 5

THE DEMISE OF THE PUBLIC SPHERE—NEWS, LIES, AND POLICING

Though this season is quite interesting in its means of addressing significant problems affecting contemporary urban life—the role of the news media, the impact of neoliberal polices of governance, the relationship between scales of government—it is also the weakest dramatically, and it is more problematic historically than the other four seasons. Whereas the other seasons were dramatically complex and nuanced, this one is far more circumscribed and didactic. The possible reasons for this are multiple, though two readily come to mind: creative fatigue after four seasons and Simon's emotional proximity to the events he dramatizes at the newspaper. Nevertheless, despite its limitations, season 5 remains provocative and, conceptually, a fitting end to the series.

Season 5 begins with a brilliant set piece in which Bunk, Landsman, and two other homicide detectives convince a young suspect both of his friend's duplicity *and* of the efficacy of the "lie detector" machine. That machine is the office copier, which has been loaded with pieces of paper that say "true" and "false." But the suspect, who knows no better, is convinced by the sincerity with which the officers assert that which is patently untrue. Detective Ed Norris says, "Americans are stupid people by and large. We pretty much believe whatever we're told." Such a statement after season 4's focus on knowledge and public education links the two seasons. The ruse results in a confession; when the suspect's assertion that he was not the murderer triggers a "false" piece of paper from the copier, he promptly admits his guilt, thus proving Norris's insight.

Like earlier first-of-the-season scenes, this incident serves as a broad introduction to the theme that binds the season. While maintaining a focus on the ravages of Baltimore in the neoliberal age, season 5 places

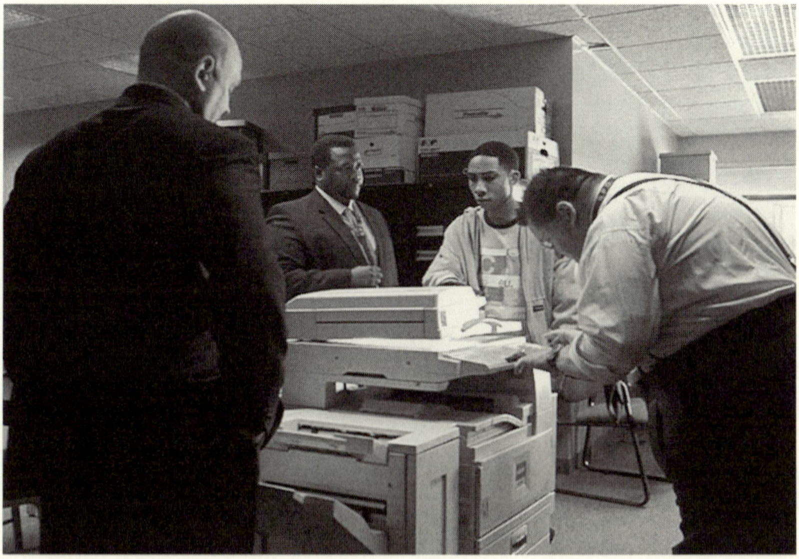

Season 5, episode 1, "Americans are stupid people by and large."

at its center the corruption and decline of the urban daily press, employing as its very effective example the case of the *Baltimore Sun*, a fictional journal. But as commentators have pointed out, the fictional *Sun* and the actual *Baltimore Sun* have quite a bit in common. Both are fully owned properties of the Tribune Company, and both are under duress—not because they lose money, but because they do not make enough. Simon focuses on the paper as part of the cultural and political landscape of Baltimore. He is particularly concerned with its status because it is where he began his career as a crime reporter and where he worked for twelve years. This experience led Simon to develop the police drama *Homicide: Life on the Street* (from his book *Homicide: A Year on the Killing Streets*) and the subsequent productions that led to *The Wire*. In season 5, we witness two rounds of buyouts in which newspaper employees receive some extra compensation and agree to take early retirement. The season tells a tale of a newspaper staff too small to cover civic life in a way that sufficiently informs citizens and keeps city leaders, especially politicians, feeling accountable. Simon, it is worth noting, accepted a buyout in 1995, and had been an officer in the union. At the actual *Sun*, unionized employees lost significant benefits in a 1987 negotiation. The ever-evolving corporate model of management at the *Sun* embittered Simon, and his antipathy, which remains to this day, is widely evident in this season. As he explained in a 2008 interview: "That's my critique of what happened to *The Sun* and to many other second-tier regional papers. When the money was there, when the paper was fat, the out-of-town ownership took profits. When the Internet arrived, they had not improved the product in any manner that actually made the newspaper more essential to readers."[1]

It is undeniable that the era of cable news and the Internet has not been kind to the daily newspaper. The newer portions of the mediascape have made the daily newspaper look lumbering and irrelevant. The daily press has been challenged to find ways to define its particular place and to make certain that place results in economic viability. The fictional *Baltimore Sun* of *The Wire* devotes a disproportionate amount of its diminished resources to chasing prizes, particularly the Pulitzer, as well as to finding feature stories that appeal to an affluent demographic more interested in human interest stories than in hard news. Simon locates this focus and employs it as a further means of critiquing the state of journalism. We are repeatedly apprised of significant events that do not become stories because there is no one to write them, while precious resources are employed for things like covering the Orioles' opening day. The derailing of the historical mission of the paper results in an increasingly top-down model of management, which is also critiqued harshly. We see the heavy hand of the managing editor and the executive editor as they repurpose the newsroom toward producing gauzy and flashy urban tales. Stories about drug violence and black-on-black crime take on a decidedly subordinate role to those that intrigue a more upscale and economically invested audience. To paraphrase a barroom conversation between Detectives Lester Freamon, Bunk Moreland, and Jimmy McNulty: "What if it was three hundred white middle-class citizens who were killed every year? Then you'd see some outrage."

The ultimate versions of these urban tales are two fabrications, each involving an ambitious young reporter, Scott Templeton. In the first case, we find him unable or unwilling to develop a piece about opening day at the Orioles' Camden Yards ballpark, so he fabricates a tale about a crippled boy who was shot in West Baltimore, a sentimental tale of lurid urban violence with a racial dimension. He refers to the young man only by his initials and cannot identify him further—because he has fabricated both the boy and the quotations. Gus Haynes, the city desk editor, already suspicious of the reporter, looks into the archives of the paper to find similar tales of such shootings, but is unable to do so. The story does not meet the sourcing standards of the paper, yet the executive ed-

Season 5, episode 2, McNulty creates a serial killer.

itor chooses to print it anyway. The second instance, and one of the major threads of the season, is the tale of a homeless serial killer marauding through the city. But there is no homeless killer. McNulty has taken the corpses of homeless men and staged their death scenes to make it appear as if their deaths were homicides. In episode 2, McNulty begins laying the groundwork for his creation of a serial killer: he investigates the corpse of a homeless man with Bunk and then chooses to create a scene suggestive of a violent crime. He bruises the dead man's neck, repositions the body, and makes the scene look like a place where a physical altercation has taken place.

Upon returning to the homicide office, McNulty combs through unsolved murder cases involving the homeless and devises a way to make those deaths appear to be related to one another. McNulty's nemesis throughout is his former partner Bunk Moreland, who advises him that he will go to jail for his efforts. Nevertheless, McNulty goes fully rogue, and in episode 5 we see him feeding the story to Templeton. He involves the ambitious reporter by impersonating the murderer and making repeated calls to him. There is much about the story that would not pass even limited scrutiny, but neither the reporter nor his superiors ask effective questions. The case of Templeton highlights the extent to which news ceases to be not only sufficiently informing but even true as the civic role of the daily newspaper morphs fully into a source of amusement rather than information.

One of the ironic aspects of McNulty's tale is that it refocuses the department's attention from the twenty-two bodies found in the vacant row houses. Since attention to those murders has run its course, the funding for their investigation is one of the things cut, but then is increased as the "homeless killer" is sought. This meshing of these two narratives of civic decline resulting from institutional impoverishment and corruption fully occupies the center of this season, and Simon takes pains to show their complementary relationship. McNulty becomes more and more empowered as a result of the media coverage of his false tale. Funds flow to him almost without limit, since Carcetti does not wish to add the onus of presiding over the reign of a mass murderer to his failed promises on crime reduction. Jimmy becomes, in effect, the captain of a small brigade as he directs his resources to officers who are in the act of solving real crimes. These cops must only fill out false time sheets, documentation that attests to their work on McNulty's case. We see one lie leading to another, and the truth becoming more and more remote and abstract. Of course, involving Templeton not only accelerates the investigation, but also produces a new maze of prevarications. The press plays a major role in the cycle of lies, and its emphasis on the sensational at the expense of the actual makes it a central aspect of civic decline. And although McNulty and his eventual accomplice, Lester Freamon, assert that the ends justify the means, they never fully accomplish any of their goals; they neither incarcerate Marlo nor reduce other crimes significantly.

Simon creates a parallel situation to that of the downsizing of the *Sun* in his depiction of both the gutting of the police department and the consequences of that move. The police department, unlike the newspaper, is reduced not as a direct result of corporate cupidity but rather because of the declining tax base of the city, which is a given throughout the five seasons, and Mayor Carcetti's oversight of a fiscal debacle. The core of that chaos results from the revelation that the schools are running at a significant deficit and that the deficit must be covered by the city's general funds—unless other funding can be found. This all but eliminates other possible programs and results in the downsizing of the police force. These budget cuts take the form of eliminating overtime, paying the officers in scrip—as opposed to real money—ceasing to maintain the department's vehicles, and limiting payment for laboratory services, as well as other economies. And since the department is unable to pay overtime, special investigations, such as the one to find those re-

Season 5, episode 1, "Sit!!"

sponsible for the bodies found in the empty row houses at the end of season 4, are reduced or terminated. In episode 1, we see Carver, now the shift-leading sergeant in the Western District, addressing his rank and file. They are understandably peeved and contrary.

This breakdown of the public sector is pointedly shown in this second scene of the season. As Carver addresses his fellow officers, the camera is behind the podium and watches him walk up the room's center aisle. As he speaks, the camera frames him in a tight close-up, and then reaction shots from cops are shown in quick cuts as a sequence of individuals and smaller groups. Since Carver stands alone at the front, the quick cuts emphasize the officers' mass and general disquiet. The issue immediately ceases to be actual policing and becomes instead the problem of city finances and the degradation of the department because of a lack of funds. One cop, Brown, who we will see multiple times, is shown in mid-close-up as he produces a thick pad of paper, which he identifies as the scrip he has received in lieu of an actual check for his overtime. He slams the paper to the desk and begins to walk out of the room, only to be reprimanded by Carver, who finally screams, "Sit you ass down"; we see his face and neck straining with the effort of his assertion. Carver then goes on to berate his charges, telling them that they are professionals and should behave accordingly.

The scene ends with a cut to the special investigations unit tailing Marlo. Again, this unit is a result of Carcetti becoming mayor and a follow-up to the murders that ended season 4. But the unit at this point is undermanned and has no active wiretaps. When we return to the Western District, we find Carver in his lieutenant's office, telling of his experience. The lieutenant says, "You gave them the professionalism bit, right?" Carver responds, "Yes, but in the real world, they pay professionals. That's why we call them pros." They are informed of an altercation in the parking lot, where two officers have come to blows over the condition of a squad car. The lieutenant comments, "These guys haven't had an honest paycheck in weeks. We have no morale." Again, the leaders stand outside the din and are portrayed in a two-shot that elaborates their relationship with each other but also their distinctness from the mass.

The police officers' resentments are made more profound by the fact that they were promised significant increases in their operating budgets and paychecks by Carcetti. But he has, as his aide Norm tells him, left "sixty million dollars on the table" for political reasons, since he rejects the governor's offer to bail out the Baltimore schools; he does not want to empower the state's chief executive, a Republican who could use his political leverage to thwart Carcetti's statehouse ambitions. This naked political decision is clearly not in the best interest of the city, and its execution reveals a world where self-interest extends into the world of public servants who fail to serve the public.

Similarly, as the police department fails, Carcetti requests that the FBI devote resources to solving the murders in the row houses that occurred during season 4. But the federal agency's "price" is the prosecution of local politician Clay Davis, who will become a trophy for the Republican national administration and a resonant symbol of black urban corruption. But the newly elected state's attorney, Rupert Bond, who has his own political ambitions, seeks to convict Davis, to symbolize his willingness to prosecute criminals and corruption even if the criminal is of his own party and his own race.

As a result of these political impasses, Carcetti's law-and-order campaign has led to an administration that can barely marshal the resources to keep crime rates at their current levels and has little hope of keeping his campaign promise to reduce them—except by, as Pryzbylewski said, "juking the stats."

Around these central actions, and thematically connected plot threads, spirals a maze of causally and thematically related actions. The unsuccessful prosecution of the corrupt politician Clay Davis, for example, is connected with the propensity toward lying dramatized throughout the season. We can surmise that Davis is not less believable than McNulty or Templeton, and that what is more broadly at issue is the lack of a pervasive standard of truth. McNulty finally admits his lies to Kima in the eighth episode of the season when he sees her wasting her time paging through files that *might* be, but in fact could not be, connected with the illusory homeless killer. He is moved by the waste of time he has created and the way in which it diverts from actual police work. Soon, Kima tells Carver of McNulty's ruse, and then Daniels. It is no accident that McNulty is not prosecuted—though he is dismissed from the force. His public trial would certainly redound to the humiliation of his superiors. Instead, the web of lies is completed by the "confession" of a mentally ill homeless man to all the murders, which, in effect, closes the case. As a bitter conclusion, Templeton and the paper receive their desired Pulitzer Prize.

CRIME, NEWS, AND THE NEOLIBERAL CITY

The civic polity of Baltimore depicted in this season suffers from a lack of revenue. We see this in a complex web of connected circumstances, including the negative synergy of a declining tax base—visually articulated by the mass of abandoned property that is off the city tax rolls, which is both an effect and a cause of middle-class homeowners moving to the county, that is, across the political boundaries of the city to abutting suburban municipalities. But the county offers only a limited haven for those migrants. We find out at the end of the season that the county is beginning to experience some of the difficulties associated with the inner city, a common phenomenon of the 2000s, suggesting how "urban" space easily supersedes "suburban" and how political boundaries can be reduced in significance.

Mayor Carcetti's strategy for dealing with his multiple fiscal woes is patterned after the policies of Mayor William Donald Schaefer. Schaefer is mentioned several times in the season. He was a four-time mayor of Baltimore and later a governor of Maryland, best known for revitalizing the city by inviting in developers and embarking on major landscape-altering plans, such as the city's Inner Harbor project. Unsurprisingly, this took place substantially in the 1980s as forlorn postindustrial cities began remaking themselves in the image of emerging neoliberalism by devising plans for city development that effectively embraced trickle-down theories of economic distribution. One astute commentator notes, "Schaefer, who continued to focus on real estate, retail, and tourism sectors rather than manufacturing, sought to create what one academic, Marc Levine, called a 'developer's city,' offering below-market loans, land write-downs, sale lease-back agreements and property tax abatements."[2] Tax abatements have been one of the primary means of inducing development, but the result over time has been to limit the impact of those who might contribute to the city's broader revitalization. To epitomize the plight of Baltimore and to provide context for the season, the city became somewhat notorious for contracting with a private security firm to police its police headquarters. Such a lack of confidence in its civic law enforcement agency, as well as its resources, found its way into the fictional series in any number of ways, including the portrayal of a highly evolved commerce in drugs, in which large and wealthy dealers have little to fear from law enforcement. In *The Wire*, the city spins toward a kind of anarchy as a result of its lack of funds.

In season 5, the relative autonomy of the crime world is well expressed by the further consolidation of Marlo Stanfield's empire. His ruthlessness takes him to new heights as he comes to see the police department's somewhat skeletal investigative unit as a laughable adversary. He feels sufficiently empowered to abrogate the co-op and develop his own connection with the Greek. The reintroduction of the Greek again brings attention to the phenomenon of international trade, revealing how a selective aspect of the global system of trade reaches into secondary cities to squeeze out further revenue. In this regard, Marlo may be the king of Baltimore, but now we see that he is only a pawn of international drug traffickers. Simon further develops this play on geographic and economic scale as he explores the local ramifications of Marlo's extraordinary profits. Marlo finds he has nothing to do with the enormous quantity of cash that has come to him directly from a very specific, self-contained local community. Through the advice of Proposition Joe, whom Marlo later has killed, he learns of the world of offshore accounts, telling Marlo that at some point there are not enough mattresses in which to stuff that much cash. Placing his wealth in a form and a place where it is no longer tangible requires a major intellectual leap for the drug dealer, a transition that Joe notes. Even with his cash safely stashed in the Caribbean, Marlo feels he must go to the place where it is ostensibly kept so that he can make his electronic investment concrete in his own mind. When he arrives, with no knowledge of the local language and as one depositor among many—and likely not nearly the largest—he

Season 5, episode 3, Marlo checks on his money.

sees his relative unimportance on the international stage, but does satisfy his need to know that there is a there there to which he sends his cash.

As Marlo actually and metaphorically moves into the international class of finance, he remains parochial in many ways: the need to see his bank and touch his money is only one, and the most overt, example. As the season proceeds, he becomes obsessed with his street credibility, with his "name." It is this concern, which may or may not have economic implications, that leads him to track Omar and to try to kill Michael. Indeed, although Marlo is a cold and calculating businessman who doggedly pursues his own monopolistic goals, he is also exceedingly thin-skinned and wedded to violence as an adjunct to his enterprise. He brings to his work the calculation of Stringer Bell and the love of violence that we associate with Avon Barksdale. Marlo ends up leaving the drug-dealing business as part of a plea deal that his lawyer makes to keep him out of jail. But he is far from happy in his new life as a very well-funded Baltimore businessman, feeling deeply his insignificance in this larger world with its different, though related, values.

One of the notable moments of this season is the death of Omar. As he enters a convenience store to buy cigarettes, a boy not older than

Season 5, episode 8, The death of Omar.

eleven, whom we previously encountered as a very young and very violent member of Namond's crew in season 4, shoots him in the back. He is shown cornered, utterly at the mercy of this youngster. His death becomes known in the community, but it takes on a kind of legendary gloss as time passes. In the homicide division, an accurate sense of his cause of death and of the life he lived prevails; Bunk notes that he has reached the end of his trail, but that his demise was quite unheroic. In an added note, we see how his death registers in the world of the *Sun*. As Haynes decides on what stories will make the daily paper, he judges that the death of a black man in a predominantly black region is too much a "dog bites man" sort of story, and so he scrubs it. Thus, Omar resists being mainstreamed, even as this ensures the line of demarcation between certain types of fame. The remoteness of the world of the *Sun*—and particularly the *Sun* in its reduced form and capacity—from the world we have spent these past seasons viewing is notable. It is as though the world of drugs, gangs, and spatial insularity exists on a different plane. While names such as Avon Barksdale, Marlo Stanfield, and Omar Little are famous and infamous in the predominantly African American regions of East and West Baltimore, these figures have no visibility whatsoever in the world of downtown offices. The *Sun* is, in the end, more concerned with the world of the middle and upper classes than that of the underclass. But this critique of contemporary news-gathering organizations has as its apparent alternative a past where such coverage occurred, and that was clearly not the case.

While this season presents a critique of the mainstream media, the broader view of the *Sun* is one filled with nostalgia. The name of the larger-than-life *Sun* editor and Baltimorean H. L. Mencken is invoked more than once; and we hear multiple conversations between editors and reporters noting the glory days of the urban press. As he sits in a comfortable and sedately lighted bar, shot from a side angle and then in a respectful close-up, Gus Haynes tells of the reverence with which his father treated the daily broadsheet when it arrived on his doorstep, explaining that such reverence was the stuff that drew him toward the paper. In the same scene, Twigg, a downsized employee, remembers watching a bus rider folding the paper with the care befitting its place in the public trust. But this central role in the public sphere has been relinquished, leaving the public less informed, the financial sector more powerful, and the political class less accountable. Simon's critique and lament focuses on the erosion of the mediating role of the media, one that placed responsible individuals between the public and events, allowing an engaged reporter to employ a rational perspective and voice. In this telling, the absence of such stewardship results in corruption and mendacity.

But Simon's vision of the mainstream media providing disinterested information to an attentive populace is neither an accurate vision of the past nor a plausible vision of the present; rather, it is one suffused with nostalgia. It largely flies in the face of many, but not all, of the critical insights informing the previous four seasons in that it valorizes a "then and now" narrative—although we do see elements of a similar nostalgia informing season 2. In that season, the chronicling of the institutional racism of the earlier time cuts through otherwise fond memories of that apparently better past. Such mitigating insights could also find their way into this season, but do not.

The *Sun* is but one example of a declining institution grasping at straws for a secure place in the contemporary media landscape. But by the early 2000s, the urban daily had been declining for over fifty years. In that time, the number of dailies has shrunk precipitously, and even more so in the last decades as the rise of cable news and the mass implementation of online sources have seriously impinged upon the turf of the newspaper. A report from the Project for Excellence in Journalism summarizes the figures: "Over the last 20 years, the number of daily American newspapers has decreased slowly but steadily. From 1,611 in 1990, the number fell to 1,387 in 2009, the most recent year for which figures are available. That is a decline of 14%. Since yearly declines for the last five years measured were consistently between 14 and 21 papers, it is a reasonable estimate that 1,350 dailies are still being published."[3] According to the same report: "Estimates for newspaper newsroom cutbacks in 2012 put the industry down 30% since 2000 and below 40,000 full-time professional employees for the first time since 1978. In local TV, . . . sports, weather and traffic now account on average for 40% of the content produced on the newscasts studied while story lengths shrink."[4]

The disjunction here is between overall decline and a problematic historical model. Newspapers have historically been owned by the wealthy and the politically conservative, and their content has to some degree reflected the interests of their owners. Although the cases of some of the most successful papers of recent generations, such as the *New York Times* and the *Washington Post*, somewhat rebut this trend, these journals tend to be exceptions. Figures such as Robert McCormick (*Chicago Tribune*), Harry Chandler (*Los Angeles Times*), Roy W. Howard (Scripps Howard syndicate), and Frank Gannett (upstate New York newspapers), not to mention the virulently anticommunist Hearst papers, dominated a large part of the US market during the heyday of the daily.[5] Newsrooms were virtually all-white and all-male, and barely covered events on the other side of the historically well-articulated color line.

Simon's presentation of a dichotomous relationship between a problematic and nostalgic vision of the past and a critical vision of the present seems to leave little room for reconceiving the problem of the decline of the urban daily. To realize a more comprehensive democratic polity through the auspices of informed activism, the polity must have some means of engaging the devices of power that are definitional socially, economically, and politically. Season 5 locates the hub of that cycle of decline in the state of the *Sun*. Yet the problem seems miscast within the context of the season, since that system of cause and effect, while embedded in the narrative, is broadly assumptive. If we step away from the embedded tale focused on daily journalism, the issue need not be the decline of the daily press but the *impact* of that decline on civic life. And to what degree is the decline of the press an effect and not a cause?

THE PRESS AND THE NEOLIBERAL PUBLIC SPHERE

In paying necessary narrative attention to the tying up of loose ends, the sprawling structure of season 5 results in a culminating critique of neoliberalism as an entire way of life. This vision moves from the public spheres, defined in a number of salient ways, to the private. The result is an atomized society (one in which collectivity by any definition almost fails to exist), a state that leaves the landscape to the most avaricious and cynical. Indeed, the remaining Baltimore we see is one where cynicism and self-involvement justify their own rewards. Season 5 tends to frame its characters in single shots: two-shots and shots of larger groups are relatively rare. This isolation of subjects seems a means of affirming the breakdown of interpersonal relations on any level. People are detached from a larger social body and at the mercy of social forces; in effect, one's fortunes are overdetermined by social structures and motivations that are beyond any one person's control. This strategy defines a visual emphasis that recalls the character-centered naturalistic novels of the late nineteenth and early twentieth centuries. Like *The Wire*, these social fictions had important historical emphases, and were often written by those who, like David Simon, had a background in journalism. In these naturalistic fictions, authors such as Stephen Crane, Theodore Dreiser, Frank Norris, and Upton Sinclair show how individuals are subject to and at the mercy of social forces, with no means of redress or insulation. Characters like Maggie (in Crane), and Hurstwood (in Dreiser), McTeague (in Norris) succumb to those forces, much as Bodie and Proposition Joe (among others) do in *The Wire*. Even the death of Omar has an aura of inevitability around it, since the number of places he is able to go without being accosted becomes more and more circumscribed. This visual strategy, then, is a vital aspect of the season's broader assertions and a way of affirming the common social ground that links the early twentieth and the early twenty-first centuries, a connection discussed at greater length in the last chapter.

In season 5 the decline of the daily newspaper is both causal and emblematic of the vicissitudes of contemporary life. Its failure defines the relative impotence of the polity and provides a means of maintaining and enhancing that ineffectuality. The fictional *Baltimore Sun* finds itself in an untenable market position. It has been bought successively by two large media companies with primary footholds in larger cities: first by the *Los Angeles Times* and then by the company that controls the *Chicago Tribune*. The initial shots of the newsroom emphasize the relative

Season 5, episode 1, The democracy of the newsroom staff.

camaraderie among those who practice the craft of journalism. Opening shots of the *Sun* complex show a group of middle-aged men smoking on the loading dock, and then a group of three newsroom workers looking at the smoke from a fire outside the newsroom window.

But this vision of mutuality soon breaks down. The next scene in the newsroom features an editorial meeting of the metro staff at which ten or so people sit around a conference table with the paper's managing editor; tellingly, no two people are ever in the same frame. It is in this scene that we find that the paper is now understaffed because of cutbacks. The managing editor, Tom Klebanow, states the obvious: "We simply have to do more with less." Such a sentiment aligns the paper with many aspects of the shrunken neoliberal public sector, including the schools, fire departments, and police departments. Such a statement is the mantra of neoliberalism, but nowhere is it more frequently invoked than in the public sector, a part of the economy that does not yield private profit—unless it is "freed" to become privatized.

Revealingly, this phrase turns up almost immediately in a Google search on the accounting and consulting firm Deloitte's site. A report from the firm on "disruptive innovation" includes the statement that in the wake of "the deep austerity facing most governments around the Western world," there is "a steady refrain from politicians and pundits to '*do more with less*'" (emphasis added). Deloitte is an important management consulting firm, one that specializes in reducing overhead, particularly in the area of labor costs—salary and benefits. The report early on offers a rationale for downsizing and outsourcing that is almost laughably obfuscating: "Creating the conditions for disruption will require policymakers to view government through a different lens. Instead of seeing only endless programs and bureaucracies, the myriad responsibilities and customers of government can be seen as a series of *markets* that can be shaped in ways to find and cultivate very different, less expensive—and ultimately more effective—ways of supplying public services" (emphasis in the original).[6] This language echoes that of the *Sun*'s editor and publisher; the concept of the public and of service has fallen away from the paper's self-description and been replaced by notions of clients and economies of scale.

Such a model reduces journalism to a business, a view that introduces a process that is increasingly top-down and that fails to recognize the significant impact that the loss of staff has on the newspaper's public mission. Immediately after this scene, we see a general conference chaired by the executive editor. Sector editors offer "what they have" for the next edition. The education editor reports that the University of Maryland is failing to meet its desegregation goals, but she is corrected by the executive editor, James Whiting, who tells her that he knows differently. He scrubs the story based on his source, an old friend who works at the university, telling her heavy-handedly that the story will have to wait until it can be delivered with more nuance and "better" sources—those who agree with his former colleague, who is now the dean of the school of journalism. Haynes takes exception to his superior flexing his bureaucratic muscles, but wins nothing except the jaundiced glare of his superiors as the class bias of the bosses wins out. Gus reminds them, "A healthy newsroom is a place where people argue about everything, all the time." Such a sentiment echoes Jürgen Habermas's idealized vision of the eighteenth-century public sphere, an era when, in his telling, wide discussion ultimately created rational discourse.[7]

In the next newsroom scene, we see the role of the section editors in ensuring precision of language and clarity of mission. The first involves knowing the difference between evacuating a person and evacuating a building. In the second, attention is paid to the transfer of property from the city to a drug dealer who contributes to political campaigns. In his attention to linguistic precision, Simon seems to invoke George Orwell's argument regarding the necessity of words having distinct meanings and being employed with clarity as a precondition for a healthy civil society. If actions and ideas with political consequence are rendered imprecise, then the polity will be undermined by its citizens' lack of knowledge. In the second instance, the surreptitious transfer of property can be seen as a payoff to city council president Nerese Campbell, and it will benefit a notorious drug dealer by over one million dollars. If there is no local coverage of such a transfer, then politicians may corruptly employ public conveyances for their own gain.

Although the nefarious act by the head of the city council is uncovered, it seems to have little impact. This result leads us to ask questions about what Scott Templeton calls a story's legs: that is, its visibility over a period of at least weeks and maybe months. When Scott's cynical comment about Baltimore being a "shit" news town is rejoined by his colleague Alma Gutierrez's example of the bodies in the vacant row houses, he notes that story's "lack of legs." (Alma is something of an antithesis to Scott: conscientious, diligent, service oriented.) But in a world where tales of politicians showing their bare flesh on Twitter dominates the news cycle for weeks, or where the disappearance of a tourist in the tropics becomes the stuff of weeks of television coverage and discussion, it is difficult to define a story as inherently newsworthy. Indeed, the problem seems to be more than a matter of sheer coverage; audiences seem to suffer from a notable difficulty in defining what is germane and what is of interest. That this is not an explicit part of *The Wire* is a glaring omission, as is the fact that cable and online news create very different environments for both news production and consumption. Indeed, we can broaden the concept of the "wire" to refer to the electronic means by which news has been disseminated, such as the telegraph and telephone wire, means now supplanted by wireless forms of transmission.

Simon asserts dramatically how the demise of the newsroom was caused by an imbalance between professionalism and market ethics. On the side of professionalism is the commitment to the public mission of informing a generalized community and making judgments that will help that populace make informed choices about their everyday lives. This vision of professionalism is distinctly opposed to the neoliberal conception of all activities being reducible to relatively profitable or unprofitable quantities on a ledger sheet. In the newsroom overseen by Gus Haynes, journalism as a public-spirited activity has its own value, making marketplace calculations no better than a secondary consideration.

Such a view makes him the custodian of residual social values, those traceable to the writings of the sociologist Talcott Parsons in the late

1930s, who advised that "the professional man is not thought of as engaged in the pursuit of his personal profit, but in performing services to his patient or client." Parsons goes on to emphasize that the realm of the professional is technical knowledge; thus, the social status of the individual recognized as able in a particular area need not spill over into a generalized social elevation. Parsons defines such knowledge as rational and "disinterested," making it a nonparticular, generalized domain of knowing. He also notes that the type of competence associated with such knowledge is generally adequately, even if not generously, compensated.[8] All this is illuminating for elaborating the disagreements that define the newsroom and the broader cultural disjunctions. We see Haynes as a guardian of an older liberalism, one that resists being engulfed in an enveloping system of cost-benefit analyses. Such a separation of conceptual markers places the newsroom ethos affirmed by Simon as a residual modernism, one that asserts the logic of both distinction and hierarchy.

In his excellent essay on neoliberalism in the contemporary media, Daniel Hallin astutely notes, "Neoliberals do not believe, as Parsons did, in differentiation and are contemptuous of the ideas that professionals have responsibilities that transcend market values."[9] Indeed, a cornerstone of neoliberal orientation is cost-benefit analysis, a mode of consideration that assumes all acts must have benefits that can be recorded on a ledger's bottom line. In the case of the *Sun*, the existence of a reporter to cover, say, urban transportation is a cost sink with no discernible financial benefit. Season 5 takes pains to emphasize how politics is not a sphere of entertainment or a group of activities taking place in a firmament above the city. It is that which influences the everyday life of citizens in a variety of ways. The *Sun* covers murders and scandals—but it also covers—or used to and still should cover—public transportation, fires, and schools. By including such coverage as part of the journal's rightful breadth of interest, *The Wire* enlists viewers in a critical project to make visible all that was and should be, but may no longer be, part of the journalistic enterprise: precision, astute judgment of newsworthiness, and a commitment to coverage at all scales—local, regional, national and international.

Simon's critique of the contemporary newspaper business touches on a range of practices and trends. In episode 3, we witness an announcement of further cutbacks at the paper. James Whiting delivers the news while standing in the middle of a mass of newspaper employees: "It's a bad time for newspapers. . . . Our circulation numbers are down as we compete with a variety of media." With this preamble, he announces the

Season 5, episode 3, Whiting announces cuts in staff.

closing of all international bureaus and "a fresh round of buyouts." This moment further shows the early 2000s to be a time of steep decline for the newspaper. We learn of the commodification of the paper as yet another "property" in an enveloping system of the financialization of everything. This is not to say that the product necessarily becomes a "thing," only that the enterprise becomes, in many ways, indistinguishable from other enterprises and so becomes just an engine of potential profit. This scene's visual language confirms that the newsroom has become an intensely hierarchical enterprise: it moves from a wide shot of the staff to one that diminishes the group by focusing on Whiting at the center, raised above the masses. In a reiteration of the language we have heard from the managing editor, Tom Klebanow, he entreats the remaining staff to "do more with less."

At the meeting, Klebanow follows Whiting, but rather than being shot from above the group, he is shown on the same vertical plane. It is his job to address the details of the retrenchment and to answer any questions. Seen as one of the crowd, he is subject to hostile questions and comments such as "kiss any raise goodbye" and, from Haynes, "How come there's cuts in the newsroom when the company's still profitable?" In response, one reporter notes, "Fact of the matter is, it's more profitable these days to run a worse paper for less money. Cut back people and pages, you increase revenue." These insights place the *Sun* in the position of most large-scale enterprises in the era of neoliberalism. Simon explains, "*The Wire* is about capital and labor, and when capital triumphs, labor is diminished." He goes on note that the process he shows occurring at the *Sun* "is the same as what happens to middle management at every other [depicted] institution."[10] Both Klebanow and Whiting are cast as outsiders in the relatively egalitarian newsroom. In Simon's vision of daily journalism, the camaraderie among equals is definitional. It is strategic that the only reporter who seems at all sympathetic to the doings of management is Scott Templeton, the serial prevaricator, one who places self-gain above any sense of the worth of the journalistic enterprise.

In *The Sociology of News*, Michael Schudson further explains the situation of the *Sun* in a way that enlarges its example. In looking at the issue of relative, rather than absolute, profitability, Schudson shows how a paper with fewer reporters and readers may derive a higher-percentage profit by targeting key, upper-end demographics and thus increasing its relative advertising rates. Schudson described this emergent shift in the late 1980s and 1990s at the *Philadelphia Inquirer*, the paper for which the fictional character Whiting once worked: "Readership in leafy suburbs was growing; readership in poor neighborhoods was falling away. New coverage, many observers in and out of journalism agree, tends to mirror these patterns: less coverage of delayed welfare checks and more coverage of where to get the next cappuccino." According to Schudson, between 1977 and 1997, general readership for daily papers declined from 67 percent of the population to 39 percent. In a 2007 survey, only 49 percent of those over thirty and 29 percent of those between eighteen and thirty were daily readers.[11] The analogue of this in heavy industry is the downscaling of production and labor by major car manufacturers while significantly increasing their profits per unit.

Intriguingly, the radical historian and gadfly Christopher Lasch in 1988 wrote of the demise of the public sphere in ways that anticipate Simon's dramatization and demonstrates that the chronology between the 1980s and the 2000s can be used to describe emergent and regnant neoliberalism. Lasch, in response to an essay elevating the continuing project of liberalism as a social and political movement, asserted: "Apathy and cynicism about politics, abstention from voting, the decline of party loyalties—these familiar symptoms of political alienation register the transformation of politics from a central component of popular culture into a spectator sport. . . . It is not some vague feeling of security that has been lost, but the opportunity to exercise the virtues associated with deliberation and participation in public debate. The atrophy of these virtues in the common people: judgment, prudence, eloquence, courage, self-reliance, resourcefulness, common sense—is a loss potentially fatal to the future of democracy."[12] Lasch's stance is that of a left populist, though it is arguable that at that moment he was tracking increasingly to the right.[13] But his argument asserts that traditional journalism—which Simon affirms as necessary for the definition and health of the public sphere—was in itself part of the problem of the day. He puts forth the idea that the bureaucratic mainstream press and its privileged cultural position—as a matter of its mass and corporate definitions—is not a force that promotes democracy, but rather a device that creates political inertia, a state that allows for the dominance of the moneyed classes.

Balancing the populist critique of the news establishment and the defense of the necessity of the profession of journalism is a vexed process. To some degree, I believe, critiques such as Lasch's are of their time. This is not to say that the newspaper industry was not retrenching even in the late 1980s, because it most certainly was. But Lasch's critique was articulated a full eight years before the advent of Rupert Murdoch and Roger Ailes's Fox News, a watershed event in the history of the contemporary US press, and just before the national syndication of Rush Limbaugh's radio show and, later, its many imitators. It is also worth noting that these radio shows were made possible by the FCC's elimination of the "fairness doctrine" in 1987, which would have required that any station licensed by the FCC that contained political programming would have to "balance" its presentation of points of view. Further, that change in the legal structure of the media landscape was contemporaneous with the evolution of the Internet as a news source.

Simon's critique is aimed mainly at the further corporatization of the US newsroom. When the repeated ethos of doing "more with less" becomes paramount, there is an inevitable winnowing of mission. As Klebanow puts it: "Just because Chicago does a little belt tightening, it's no excuse for us to fall down." "Chicago" refers to the paper's corporate owners, the Tribune company, publishers of the *Chicago Tribune* and other media properties; the reference draws the fictional *Sun* back to the actual *Sun*, which was bought by the Times Mirror Corporation in 1986, during David Simon's tenure there. Under the management of that Los Angeles–based company, the paper began downsizing, including a major buyout in the mid-1990s. Simon explains:

> Amid buyout after buyout, the *Baltimore Sun* conceded much of its institutional memory, its beat structure, its ability to penetrate municipal institutions and report qualitatively on substantive issues in a way that explains not just the symptomatic problems of the city, but the root causes of those problems.
>
> The *Sun* began doing so in the 1990s—before the internet, before the Tribune Company did its worst—when beat reporting and any serious, systemic examination of issues was eschewed in favor of "impact" journalism, special projects and Pulitzer sniffing. It continued doing so into the present decade as the Tribune Company followed the Times-Mirror buyouts with even more ruthless abandon. And now, with the economic vise that is the internet tight around her, The *Sun*—like so many once-worthy regional newspapers—is fighting for relevance and readers.[14]

Season 5, then, invokes the circumstances of the real *Baltimore Sun* and then contextualizes them within an involved fictional narrative in order to show both the broader causes and effects of the demise of the daily urban newspaper. In keeping with the narrative line of the season—neoliberalism and the corporatization of the press—it is worth noting that the Times Mirror Corporation was led after 1995 not by a newsman but by a former General Mills executive named Mark Willes, a fact that elaborates the perspective Simon employs in season 5, in which mission is ancillary to profit. This view was further confirmed by subsequent history when the Tribune Company bought the paper (and all of Times Mirror) in 2000, again making it a "property" and gutting it with efficiencies of scale that further reduced the ability of the paper to perform its residual mission. Indeed, after the purchase, the Tribune Company was capable of reaching over 75 percent of the US population. In an article from 2006, a writer for the *New York Observer* asserted, "A newspaper is only as strong as its purpose. For nearly 20 years, step by step, the *Sun* has been acting out the crisis of the newspaper industry: cutting staff, losing readers, shedding content, shrinking the comics. Like Amtrak trimming service because ridership is down, the less it does, the less it can do."[15]

But in a greater irony, *just* before season 5's airing in early 2008, the *Sun* was again sold, this time as part of the purchase of the Tribune Company by the real estate magnate Sam Zell, whose only interest in the media was its ability to turn a profit. Zell had made his fortune through massive purchases of undervalued assets, which he sold off strategically; some parts ended up having higher valuations than that of the entire original purchase. Zell was not in it for the long haul, and was not much interested in stewarding papers like the *Sun*. But the mismanagement of the massive media conglomerate and the global downturn of 2007 drove the Tribune Company into bankruptcy, from which it only recently emerged. Currently, it is owned by a group of Zell's creditors, who are looking for buyers for its properties, including the *Sun*.

Simon's iteration of the repeated buying and selling of the *Sun* as a property tells us that the paper is now most significant as a commodity, and consequently less important as a civic institution. And if the paper is functioning not as a relative cooperative, a workplace that shows throughout the need for mutual respect and conjoined effort to produce something vital for civic life, then its skewed value system allows for all kinds of reordering of its mission. It is here that the season sutures its historical critique to a central plot element of its fiction. Focal in this degeneration of mission and product is Scott Templeton, a relatively young reporter used as a pawn in the war between the corporate bosses and the newsroom staff. Scott is the new member of the staff who is most indicative of the erosion of mission that afflicts the *Sun*. Scott's ultimate crime is his fabrication of quotations, sources, and whole stories. Through this character we come to understand Simon's take on the further reasons for the failure of the urban daily newspaper, and on its broad range of deleterious effects, both on civic culture and on the institution of journalism itself.

In the first episode of the season, we see that Scott has an antipathetic relationship with the city editor, Gus Haynes. As the season progresses, we see the basis of that rancor: Scott is not a very good reporter, lacking the energy or initiative either to find stories or to cover those assigned to him. When we first meet Scott, the managing editor, Whiting, is proposing a series about the public schools in Baltimore, obviously looking for something pithy and affecting. In a reiteration of the dominant visual language of the season, the staff is pictured as a group of individuals: the direction emphasizes mid-close-ups and eschews aggregated groups. As those sitting at the table respond to Whiting's idea, we see the scene transition defined by an off-center shot of Whiting in the group; but the shot is from the left, and only half his face is to the camera. Such a view, a Janus face, almost immediately places the legitimacy of his authority in question. His begins by saying, "The word I'm thinking of is 'Dickensian.' We want to depict the Dickensian lives of city children." It is clear that the suggestion is almost uniformly unpopular as reporters and editors take issue with a perspective on Baltimore's schoolchildren that lacks context. The most passionate rebuttal comes from Gus, analogizing such a view to that of showing a house falling down without broadening the frame to reveal the hurricane that caused the damage. As Gus speaks, the camera provides a tight off-center reaction shot of Whiting, who clearly disagrees. In the context of the series, of course, this is a setup: the preceding season examined extensively the context in which the schools failed—poverty, drugs, isolation, and criminality—and showed their institutional problems of funding, bureaucracy, and uninspired leadership. Scott rejoins, "You don't need a lot of context to seriously examine what goes on in one classroom." Whiting chimes in: "I think we need to limit the scope. Not get bogged down in a lot of details." Gus gets to the heart of the matter: "For what: To address the problem or to win a prize? What are we doing here?" But Whiting affirms his desire to define a situation where "the problems and solutions can be measured clearly," citing his wife's volunteer work in the public schools as the basis for his "expertise." He concludes that the reader "doesn't want a litany of excuses," and besides, "if you leave in everything, then you have nothing." He decides that "Scott is the man to lead the charge."

Such a view of content reflects a tabloid ethos. Whiting and Templeton are interested in shocking their readership while playing to their prejudices. They logically surmise that their target readers do not send their children to those inner-city schools and would never consider doing so. Indeed, although newspaper circulation is dwindling, it dwindles less among those in higher education and income brackets.[16] By appealing to those groups, the paper is able to maintain a certain level of advertising revenue. The paper's strategy plays to the attitudes and beliefs of the desired demographic for the product, people who possess sufficient disposable income to appeal to advertisers or prospective advertisers.

"The Dickensian Aspect" is used ironically as the title of the sixth episode of the season, in which Scott develops false narratives about the city's homeless population. The term "Dickensian" is both broad and plastic, qualities that place it in opposition to the kinds of nuts-and-bolts writing and reporting valued by Simon and depicted as eroding during this season. The editorial meeting argument over context and, especially, its heavy-handed conclusion reveal how news has ceased to be about informing a public and instead about titillating them. That Whiting knows the outcome of his series before any reporting is done is problematic enough; that he invokes Charles Dickens as a model shows him reveling in the tragedy and melodrama associated with that Victorian novelist.

This association is a broader comment on the state of second- and third-tier US newspapers—like the *Sun*. With the devaluation of reporting, ornate types of writing in the service of soft-focus pieces of human interest become increasingly the norm. This style is in opposition to most of the prose found in the major papers of record: the *Washington Post* and the *New York Times*, and maybe the *Los Angeles Times* and the *Wall Street Journal*. As Scott's ambitions and lack of ethics conjoin to form a career of outright fabrication, he becomes the central area of conflict between Haynes and the corporate heads of the paper, Whiting and Klebanow. And the more ornate and deceitful Templeton's prose becomes, the more the Pulitzer-starved managers love him.

Scott's professional trajectory moves up and down concurrently. On one hand, he becomes an increasingly unreliable purveyor of news, moving from small lies to big lies. But as he tries to use his cachet with his superiors to move on to the *Washington Post*, he finds himself thwarted by the very means he employed to succeed at the down-market *Sun*. The editor and interviewer at the *Post* remarks, "Some of your feature work is a little wrought for what we do at the *Post* language-wise." Though Scott tries to explain away his purple prose, he leaves Washington and returns to the *Sun*, where his prose becomes even more purple and more filled with imaginary characters and situations. Later, Scott's coverage of the homeless, an event inspired by the fabrication of a public panic by McNulty, reveals his further flight from fact; he creates characters and tales and then adorns them with overheated language—all with the support and encouragement of Klebanow and Whiting. In episode 8, we see Scott being confronted by a homeless man whose story he steals and embellishes, showing us further his ethical lapses. In episode 9, we see him fabricating a tale of a man kidnapping homeless people. In episode 10 he wins the Pulitzer for his efforts.

Scott is symptomatic of what is wrong with the press in a neoliberal regime. Once the press abrogates its connection with an articulated public sphere, its residual function is to titillate the public and to garner recognition and awards for its reporters and editors. The desire for such recognition results in a willingness to do the journalistic equivalent of "juking the stats": writing stories that are less than vital to the health of the polity and composing them in a way that inflames rather than informs. Ultimately, Haynes's skepticism regarding the reporter—well founded though it may be—results in increasingly heated confrontations with his superiors. In the end, Gus is demoted to a position as a line editor because of his efforts to maintain the integrity of the paper and its mission. His stewardship is connected with his sense of the paper serving the public, and his fall constitutes a further erosion of the public sphere. In a sense, the season—and perhaps all five seasons—devote themselves to a world that has become invisible to the local press except primarily to distance it and pathologize it for the increasingly disproportionate middle-class readers. In the changed "game" of journalism, the fearless independence of reporters wanes. None but Gus are willing to stand up for their ethics, and the reporter Alma Gutierrez, who values her community role and the ethos of professionalism exemplified by Haynes, is exiled to a distant suburban bureau.

LIES, POLITICS, AND POLICING

Simon takes pains to draw parallels between the demise of the *Sun* and the decline of the Baltimore Police Department. Arguably the root cause of the latter, which is synergistically connected to the former, is the erosion of the political sphere as an area concerned with the common good. Again, there is some degree of nostalgia at work here, since politics, and urban politics in the United States in particular, has long been the domain of the scurrilous; the rogues' gallery includes Boss Tweed, James Curley, William Thompson, Marion Barry, and Kwame Kilpatrick. But Simon's particular vision of urban politics dwells primarily on the vicissitudes of the present. As we watch the public sphere break down, it is instructive to keep our eyes on the ways in which the debased world of daily journalism enables that breakdown through its inattention or through its complicity in the lies that pass as truth.

Lies permeate the social fabric, and newspapers are either not interested in bringing them to light or not able to do so. Similarly, politicians often operate on the basis of narrow self-interest, an orientation that results in acts that are contrary to those that were promised or that do not serve the public. Our paradigmatic politicians are Mayor Tommy Carcetti, a would-be do-gooder, and Clay Davis, a cynical and notorious liar who only ever seems interested in his own financial gain. Yet despite their obvious differences, these two men share too many characteristics to ignore. Carcetti's political calculation has him refuse the cash to shore up the public schools—because he otherwise could not maintain his political viability as a statewide candidate—which in turn causes the degradation of the police department. And the absence of probing political reportage allows Carcetti to go unpunished for his cynical choice. Political calculations are, finally, the major concern of his regime, and they become its only truth. All his promises regarding the good of the city therefore go unrealized. And while the world of politics becomes something of a narrative backdrop, it comes to the center of the season causally. The police department's corruption and ineffectiveness is a direct result of its political situation.

While self-serving politicians are not unique to the present age, the extreme cynicism that Simon highlights invites comment. There seems to be little that motivates politicians beyond self-interest. In a well-conceived and compelling essay, Wendy Brown offers a clear description of the fate of the public sphere, and of the political public sphere in particular, as neoliberal logic becomes broadly applied. Brown's conjoining of the broader economic world and the logic of the political illuminates the terrain in which Carcetti operates. She develops the concept of neoliberal political rationality as a corollary to neoliberal economic rationality, arguing that "neoliberal rationality, while foregrounding the market, is not only or even primarily focused on the economy; it involves extending and disseminating market values to all institutions and social action, even as the market itself remains a distinctive player."[17] In Brown's view, neoliberalism becomes a kind of instrumentalism that applies a means-end logic—analogous to cost-benefit analysis—to all matters of public life. Politics becomes a calculation based fully on self-interest and not at all a matter of a conception of the political body. She writes further of the ways in which precepts of economic rationality become a means of constructing the individual subject and thus permeate all aspects of behavior, paradoxically circumscribing the actions of individuals by asserting and reasserting their atomized role in a "free" society. She quotes the German sociologist Thomas Lemke in articulating the vexed role of the state in neoliberal theory and practice: "The state leads and controls its subjects while not being responsible for them."[18] In this formulation, no poor person constitutes a deserving subsection of the public, since individuals are ultimately responsible only for themselves. This system functions as a perfect tautology: as Ray Charles famously sang, "Them that has are them that gets."

But beyond this means of reducing the poor, the system eliminates the notion of mutuality, even if the individual in question has taken on the role of public servant. In the realm of social policy, this logic articulates the public servant as a rational actor in the domain of his or her own selfishness. Thomas Carcetti thus serves his own political interests while rhetorically remaining a "caring" leader. The implications of this self-interest are seen throughout the season as they fundamentally affect public services and life. It is this vision of the political public sphere that results in a world where social bonds have become fully distended.

The most cynical of all politicians is state assemblyman Clay Davis. Davis has long been a target of the special investigative unit, one of the objects of Freamon's focus on the money trail that leads from drug dealers to politicians. This was a recurring aspect of the prior seasons. But when shown the evidence that Davis has falsified a mortgage application, Freamon refers to it as the "head shot." The newly elected prosecutor, Rupert Bond, takes the case as a career maker, resisting attempts by the federal prosecutor to move it to his own jurisdiction. As the trial proceeds, Davis seems to have little going for him beyond a stirring style of making speeches and a belief that he is invulnerable. He goes on a radio talk show and proclaims his innocence and righteousness, taking up the mantle of martyrs who have defended the downtrodden, from Jesus to Martin Luther King. His former allies, including Carcetti, Police Chief Burrell, and council president Nerese Campbell, all advise him to resign and take a plea deal. In his closing statements, Davis admits to the all–African American jury his "bad bookkeeping" in the service of the needy of the inner city, and asks them whether he should be punished for his good intentions. Davis's resorting to a kind of race-based strategy to influence the jury shows the polarized terms of urban life, how spatial and social segregation lead to an ultimate mistrust of even legitimate legal institutions. Indeed, we are in an era when the truth becomes anything you can make people believe. And while it is abundantly clear that Davis is exactly the criminal that the prosecution defines, Davis's lies win the day, as he is acquitted.

The narrative of Davis is extreme; we see him as a willful and wanton liar who never receives his due. He is the apotheosis of a public figure that cares little about the public. A telling example of this occurs during his meeting with his lawyer, Billy Murphy (an actual Baltimore attorney who plays himself), just before Davis's testimony, at a point when it appears that the prosecution cannot lose, having documented all manner of corruption and malfeasance. Murphy, who occupies a lavish office overlooking the harbor, is as slick as Davis. Davis tries to get him to alter his policy of getting his full fee up front, arguing, ultimately, that the case is a boon for the lawyer, who will gain astronomically in reputation from Davis's inevitable acquittal. Davis goes on to tell Murphy that

Season 5, episode 7, Clay Davis and the real Billy Murphy.

the defendant is the one who should be getting paid. Definitional in this scene of two great hustlers squaring off is the absence of a shot that includes both. As the scene ends, Murray says in close-up, "Why don't you save some of the silver-tongue bullshit for the jury?" As the camera cuts to Davis, he is smiling, but alone. This scene is a kind of commentary on racial solidarity, a stance and rhetoric that has been co-opted by these two men. They play to the jury, people of color who possess far fewer of the trappings of economic success, by appealing to their naïve sense of commonality.

The corollary to Davis is Carcetti, whom we met in season 3 as a vaguely ambitious but unpolished city councilman. We now see him having grown into a fully cynical politician. A telling index of this is the fact that perpetually at his side are his two political advisors, and he never makes a move without their approval. In episode 7 we see him raising money over the phone, an act we first saw in season 4 when he was just at the start of his mayoral campaign. The large difference between the two scenes is the ease with which he now asks for money and the success he has in getting it. Doing this seems to delight him in ways that the actual job of mayor never can. As he enters his main office, he is positively jubilant, dancing as he proclaims that he raised $92,000 in a morning.

Despite his boyish looks and mawkish sincerity, his heart is nearly as cold as Davis's. As episode 6 begins, Carcetti invokes the legacy of W. Donald Schaefer as he introduces the development project, "with his name on it," which will propel him to the statehouse. Says the mayor, invoking a line of connection: "It all started with the Charles Center and Tommy D'Alessandro. And it continued with William Donald Schaefer and Harbor Place. And following that, there were Mayors Schmoke and O'Malley with Inner Harbor East. Well, today it is my administration's turn to lay claim to the middle branch of the Patapsco." Once again, the major developer is Andy Krawczyk, a wealthy Baltimore businessman who turns up in several seasons and is notable as the developer who bled Stringer Bell dry. We know that he has paid for his access with political contributions, both legal and illegal. Within the context of the show, Krawczyk is indicative of a city run for the benefit of the few. If the Andy Krawczyks of the world paid their fair share of taxes, there might be money for both schools and policing. But since people of his ilk would never send their children to public schools—for that matter, neither does Carcetti—and since they can afford their own security guards, these matters of public funding are not compelling. As the New Westport development is announced, we see Nick Sobotka from season 2 in the crowd, heckling both the mayor and the developer. What is notable is that he is alone; there is no populist outcry against this use of public lands and resources. In season 2, the longshoreman had tried to have this site improved as a place for deepwater shipping. The union had lobbied actively for the state government to devote resources to improve Baltimore's place as an international shipping center and thus to create working-class jobs. That this is now a place for tax-abated condos where the owners will live behind gates is a sad coda to that effort.

While such development creates the illusion of a city that is prospering widely, the facts are different. This is indeed a dysfunctional city, but it is broken because it lacks politicians who will run it for the good of its public, and newspapers that will call those politicians to account. This lack of funds results in moral chaos, some of which is a matter of the condition of the police department. With the erosion of the public sphere, the neoliberal city becomes the place for those with means to buy their own services.[19]

What remains of the public sector is that which cannot or has not yet been recast into the world of profit, that is, privatized. Such a definition points us to the necessity of the "commons," which I explore in the next chapter. The connection between policing and newspaper work triggers

Season 5, episode 6, Carcetti and Andy Krawczyk announce their new waterfront development.

a consideration of a presumptive aspect of the public sphere that has in the last two decades ceased to be so. I am thinking of all kinds of services: municipal, state, and federal activities. The list includes the privatization of many of the functions of the military, the privatization of prisons, the increasing privatization of the "public" schools through charter schools and voucher programs, and the demise of state-supported systems of higher education, as well as functions of municipal governments including parking enforcement, trash collection, and street repairs. And some police functions have been privatized, particularly street-level security in urban development zones, Times Square in New York being the most visible one. Those privatized functions increasingly sprawl beyond citizen oversight and provide opportunities for capitalists to create new domains of geometric profit while further degrading the value of work. The profit margin for private contractors in many of these areas—schools, municipal work, street security—is a direct result of replacing skilled permanent employees with part-time, temporary, and minimally trained labor, creating a kind of precariousness that is definitional for the biopolitical city. The "biopolitical," a term employed in important ways by Michel Foucault, defines the ways in which human life is managed by regimes of power. In such a situation, time is both relatively free—as a result of the diminishing of traditional employer-employee relationships, and with them the normative workday—and less free, since all time, in a world of casual labor, is subject to being work time—as it is for those in the drug trade.[20]

As we have seen in recent examples of cities and states selling their toll roads and parking franchises, the private buyers often pay relatively few cents on the dollar to their cash-strapped public owners, and then are able to reap significant profits over time, since public oversight is weak and distended. In this season, the police department's extreme dysfunction is a matter of its involvement in the dysfunction of local politics. The lack of funding results in a failure to solve crimes. In response, McNulty and Freamon ingeniously decide to develop their own parallel police force, which is not quite privatized but which is decidedly an ad hoc operation. The funding source is the emergency cash appropriated by the mayor to solve the case of the serial killer who is preying on the homeless. Of course, there is no such killer. He is fully a creation of McNulty.

In episode 6, the mayor convenes a press conference to announce his full efforts to apprehend the (nonexistent) serial killer. As the mayor speaks, he is shot with relative reverence, located in the depth of the image as seen from the back of the room, and then in a gradual zoom that enhances his size, earnest facial gestures, and ultimately his authority. This visual language replicates that used during his performance at the end of season 3 when he announced his war on drugs and his intolerance for any form of drug legalization, a moment just before announcing his run for mayor in season 4. As was true in the earlier scene, his words are empty, filled with the gestures of sincerity but utterly ineffectual. In two telling moments that define the press conference, a reporter asks Rawls whether there is a connection between these murders and the ones in the vacant houses last year. "No connection," replies Rawls. Of course, we know that the *only* reason this ruse exists is that McNulty has employed it to funnel money precisely into that investigation. But at this point only the audience, McNulty, and Freamon know the degree of relationship between the two crime sprees—the actual one and the fabricated one. In the second telling moment, after Daniels has been called upon to convince the reporters of the efforts that will be taken to find this murderer, Rawls tells Daniels, out of sight of the cameras, that there will be few resources: "The cupboard is bare." When Daniels protests, he asserts," You're running with the big dogs now." This can only mean that the more authority one has, the more one is expected to lie.

Season 5, episode 6, Carcetti resolves to catch the "serial killer."

Ultimately the mayor comes across with significant resources, primarily because doing so allows him to position himself as a "caring" politician, unlike the Republican governor he will soon oppose. As a result of this largesse, McNulty is able to funnel resources into "real police work" by making it seem as though those working on all types of other cases are now ceaselessly pursuing the murderer of those whom Carcetti sanctimoniously refers to as our "most vulnerable." But to reroute his funds, McNulty must engage in his own malfeasance as well as continue to lie about the existence of the fictitious killer. In a tricornered plot flourish, Simon shows us Scott Templeton, McNulty, and Carcetti equally engaged in the fiction of a serial killer. In the pre-credit scene of episode 10 there is a colloquy in the mayor's office in which the befuddled Carcetti apparently holds the central position of authority. The scene begins with a very tight shot of the mayor, his body slightly canted, sunk in his red leather chair. His face shows confusion, and the lack of context—we have yet to see who else is on the room—makes him seem somewhat absurd. This scene almost replicates the one in season 3 when Mayor Clarence Royce found out about Hamsterdam. Clearly, executive power is not the same as executive control.

We see the mayor sigh and shift in the chair for a few seconds, and the shot shifts to a low-angle panorama of the room, which diminishes

Carcetti and shows us that the room is arranged with great symmetry. Immediately before him and side by side are Bond and Rawls; directly behind them are Pearlman and Daniels; and off to the sides, but on the same plane as Carcetti, are his political advisors, Norman and Michael (his chief of staff). As Carcetti stumbles for words, now standing, the shot reverses so that the configuration of people, which he was formerly addressing, now surrounds him in a semicircle. He is trapped. Carcetti's concern about the political fallout of his gullibility becomes the predominant reaction.

It is only his political advisor, the former newspaperman Norman Wilson, who revels in the irony of the situation, noting that both the police and the politician had gained from the ruse. "Everyone's getting what he needs behind some make-believe," he says as he turns away from the camera to be shot in midrange profile as he snickers. The scene ends with Norman, first in a close-up and then in a three-shot with Rawls and Bond, leaning his body toward them and facing them from the side: "I wish I still worked at the newspaper so I could write on this mess. It's too fucking good." But the present-day *Sun* will never reveal its role in this public lie and resulting panic: the newspaper will eventually win a Pulitzer Prize for its coverage by a prevaricating reporter of a crisis that doesn't exist. Further, the editors of the *Sun* will manufacture a public effect of their coverage so that they further conform to the dictates of the prize criteria. To protect Carcetti, there is never any announcement of the scam, though Daniels and Freamon lose their jobs.

This emphasis on the homeless (and their murder and abuse) is a further means of commenting on the definition of public space in a city where preferred real estate—downtown and the harbor front—is morphing into a region for the few. Carcetti refers to them as "our most vulnerable," and McNulty defines them as those about whom "no one gives a shit." But this depiction of the "homeless," whose very aggregation is a matter of their objectification shows their extremely marginal place in contemporary Baltimore. Their world is that of spaces to which no one else lays claim—abandoned regions, places under overpasses, derelict factories, and vacant houses. Indeed, when we see McNulty or Templeton traversing their spaces, we are struck by the squalor and chaos. In a world where success is characterized by individuals having negotiated a basis of material comfort and stability, and where the responsibility of the comfortable for those who are without is all but nonexistent, the homeless are no more than an annoyance that reminds us of the precariousness of life.[21] It is telling that McNulty stages their abuse by bruising and repositioning the corpses, an act he would be loath to commit on the bodies of more important citizens. These bodies cease to be fully human, taking on an aura of things that had never been alive. Indeed, the only way they can be noticed is when they are constructed as part of a sensational narrative. In season 5, the homeless are those who are ignored until they cannot be. That is, they are treated as virtually invisible until they are at the center of a sensational tale. But otherwise, they are pushed to the physical margins of the city and ignored as fully as possible by the general populace.[22] To be homeless is to cease to have a place in the social life of the United States. They are virtual blank slates on which all manner of discourses can be written, including both murder victim and murderer.

The last, very long episode of the five seasons—ninety-three minutes—exudes pessimism and offers little in the way of resolution. True to the neoliberal world that Simon articulates, everything changes and most everything remains the same. And central to this whirling of the fortunes of individuals against a background of stasis in the broader world of social relations is the absence of a discernible public asserting its will to secure a world where the needs and desires of the few no longer take precedence.

REDEEMING NAMOND AND BUBBLES

As in other seasons, David Simon provides just enough hope to keep the narrative from being unduly oppressive. In the last season, this broader narrative returns to a range of characters—Avon Barksdale, Wee-Bey, the Greek, Sergei, Nick Sobotka, and others. All either perform their prior function with new clients, or reveal their circumstances as having further deteriorated. In some cases, these figures show how circumstances are not necessarily reliant on particular characters: they have a logic and sustainability of their own. The Greek now sells to Marlo and then to Slim Charles. Omar is dead, but Michael assumes his role. Wee-Bey remains in prison but now has Chris as a compadre; Haynes and Alma are demoted for their efforts to maintain journalistic integrity; Carcetti becomes governor as a reward for his cynicism. Meanwhile, the drug trade goes on. Daniels has left the force because he loses hope that it can be insulated from the mire of politics; Pearlman, a careerist, becomes a municipal judge. It is a wheel of fortunes, but the system produces an ever-downward spiral toward greater inequality and injustice.

Season 5, episode 2, Bubbles at NA.

There are two notable exceptions, both germane for considering the emphases of this season on the demise of the public sector: Namond Brice and Bubbles. Both are redeemed; their lives are improved; and in the final scenes of the season, each is shown heading away from the disastrous circumstances that seemed inevitable. We see Namond at a debate contest in which he discusses the need to provide resources to stop the spread of HIV in sub-Saharan Africa. Bubbles finds his way through the auspices of a church-based Narcotics Anonymous group led by a man named Walon (played by the musician and recovering addict Steve Earle), who takes a particular interest in him. While I will return to the exceptions in the conclusion, it is fair to say that neither suggests any system-wide means of addressing the dystopian aspects of the urban present.

In this season, Bubbles begins his journey away from the world of drug addiction, having decided to leave it after he inadvertently leaves a toxic dose of heroin and cyanide in his squat and Sherrod, the young man he is mentoring, shoots it and dies. Racked with guilt, Bubbles seeks out his sister, asking whether he can live in her basement. Since, she tells us, the last time he sought her help he ended up selling her household effects for drug money, she requires him to leave the house when she does, and she locks the door that provides access to the main part of the house.

Bubbles gradually comes to terms with his guilt, mostly through the assistance of Walon. In addition to NA, he avails himself of the help offered by religious organizations providing services to the homeless. Ever the entrepreneur, Bubbles also sells the daily *Sun*. As the season ends, he has been the subject of a feature story by one of the *Sun*'s "good" reporters, who scrupulously tells his tale. Bubble's redemption is incremental and plausible, but wholly a matter of nonpublic support systems, including friends and family. Indeed, the reason he finds himself in this situation is, to a degree, because the police have failed him. When he asks for protection from a man who beats and robs him on sight, Herc promises his help but fails to provide it. As a result, Bubbles is left to his own devices, which include the deadly dose of heroin that he had planned to provide for his tormenter.

Simon clearly likes this character and the actor who plays him, but his redemption seems like a long shot that happens to come through. It is not a mawkish resolution, but it does feel a little pat, as though Simon is looking for a way to mitigate the show's overarching critical view and negativity. Coming as it does in a series and season that chronicles the demise of the public sector, the story of this ex-addict seems to represent the limited probability of such occurrences, even as they remain possible. Contextually, this brings us back to season 3, when, after Hamsterdam is discovered, Royce and his aides, including some public health workers and academics, muse about the possibility of using that area as a basis for drug treatment and HIV prevention. Needless to say, Hamsterdam and its potential salutary effects are politically impossible in a neoliberal world defined by the demise of the public and the related subjugation of the weak.

In Namond's case, redemption is more a matter of luck than pluck—to paraphrase Horatio Alger. He benefits from the fact that circumstances have led Bunny Colvin to a job on a research team working in Baltimore public schools. After the Hamsterdam story becomes widely known, Colvin loses his postretirement job at Johns Hopkins and eventually ends up in Tilghman Middle School, where Namond attends eighth grade. When Namond is adopted by the Colvins, it is a discrete transaction—he is never in the foster care system, nor is he subject to any outcome other than landing with the Colvins. And the Colvins stand as a part of ever-diminishing inner-city African American middle class, a group dramatically reduced by the rise of neoliberalism and the decline of the public sector. In addition, as noted in the last chapter, Namond is economically not a member of the underclass: his family has some means. Rather, he

Season 5, episode 10, McNulty watches the new day dawn.

is a member of the underclass socially, but has been exposed to something of a larger world. His obvious intelligence and relative sophistication prepare him for his new status in life. There are no other children in the show who are so equipped.

These two characters are removed from the mass not as a means of asserting the value of hard work and the possibility of social mobility. We see three of Namond's fellow eighth graders fail utterly—Duquan, Randy, and, in a different way, Michael, who embarks on a life of crime. Similarly, for every Bubbles there are any number of untreated addicts in the city. In these two cases of personal success, the camera shows us their relative isolation from a larger social group, reminding us visually that this is a largely unforgiving social system. The emphasis of the season is affirmed by its ending. McNulty stares off into the sunrise over Baltimore as various scenarios occur out in the metaphoric distance, revealing the ways in which little changes: life goes on. (I return to this scene with an alternative reading in the next chapter.) Pleasures for the many remain small and localized, and systems beyond their control proceed with their own logic. Simon employs the failure of the daily newspaper as a means of developing a long and involved meditation on the decline of the public sector and leaves us with images of intermittent local and private contentment existing in a world of broader, and potentially catastrophic, public decline.

The question remains whether those few success stories constitute an anchor for an alternative vision of social life. Is it possible to employ these narrative elements as the beginning of a vision of a more hopeful future? As I have briefly suggested in this chapter, there does exist a means of devising an analytical strategy that sees Simon's well-founded vision as other than a nightmare without end. I explore that strategy further in the conclusion.

Conclusion

THE WIRE AND THE NEW DAWN (MAYBE)

You can't make this shit up.

DAVID SIMON

The Wire develops both depth of analysis and scope as it proceeds over its five seasons. The series takes us on a critical tour of Baltimore's police department and courts, its waterfront world of unionized labor, its system and precepts of drug enforcement, and its public school system. There is a kind of accruing logic to the emphases of each season. Arguably, if the city's schools worked well, then the issues of seasons 1 through 3 might diminish significantly. That is, the problems of drugs, crime, and the degrading of blue-collar work *could* be addressed by a public system of education that *truly* educated young people and began to address the social inequities of twenty-first-century life in the United States. Season 5 presents many dramatic problems, but also intriguingly poses fundamental social questions, since the focus on newspapers, journalists, and journalism calls into question the means by which we know the larger social world. If we could see how the media defines the parameters of our worldview, maybe we would demand a type of communication that reveals the means by which power and corruption become entrenched, and then we could effectively change that world. But in Simon's view, the role of the mass media is increasingly compromised by its place within the structure of corporate America, just as public schools are limited by the world in which they exist, along with the scourges of limited resources and increasing privatization.

As season 5 was wrapping up, Simon wrote a despairing piece about the situation of the commercial press in the early twenty-first century, asking, "Isn't the news itself still valuable to anyone? In any format, through any medium—isn't an understanding of the events of the day still a salable commodity? Or were we kidding ourselves? Was a newspaper a viable entity only so long as it had classifieds, comics and the latest sports scores? It's hard to say that, even harder to think it. By that premise, what all of us pretended to regard as a viable commodity—indeed, as the source of all that was purposeful and heroic—was in fact, an intellectual vanity."[1] Perhaps the fatal error of this question as posed is in its invoking the newspaper as a commodity rather than as a public trust. By accepting it as an object within commercial markets, Simon concedes the logic of capitalism and the mass media's problematic place within the current regime of capital. Such views need to be further theorized in order to see—and to rebuff—the systemic reign of neoliberalism and its coming to stand for all possible systems of social life.

In his recent book *Seventeen Contradictions and the End of Capitalism*, David Harvey articulates how the present has seen the domain of capitalist social reproduction expand and intensify to the point that market logic pervades a great expanse of social processes. He goes on to note that those processes stand as emblems of the rationality and inevitability of a kind of means-ends fiduciary view of the world. According to Harvey, this view threatens to become pervasive: "The sphere of social reproduction has in fact almost everywhere become the site of highly intrusive capitalist activities. The tentacles of the state's and capital's influence now proliferate within the spheres of social reproduction in myriad ways."[2] Harvey's focus in this chapter—titled "Social Reproduction"—is often the sphere of education, noting many of the features of that system that Simon touches on in season 4. But he also delineates how necessities like food and shelter predominantly assume commodity and market values, as opposed to use values, and how, in that conceptualization, they are subsumed by the predominant logic of the time, abrogating what could be conceptual spaces outside the logic of capitalism. Such a depiction of the pervasiveness of the prevailing economic system finds its way into all the seasons; the brutality of that regime drives not only the drug trade and its attendant violent and exploitive behavior, but also politics, business, and all types of social interactions.

In season 5, the lament for the glory days of the urban daily creates a kind of sepia-toned vision of the past, one that finds its way into many episodes of the show. Whether it is a longshoreman muttering in season 2, "It will never be what it was," or Daniels affirming at the end of season 4 that the former school where the corpses are being collected was a place where he received "a pretty good education," *The Wire* does, at times, look back with a wistful eye. Simon argues that the show is about the passing of an era of US primacy.[3] Such a vision of the ebbing US power does not necessarily suggest nostalgia, but it easily admits that feeling. The emotional tone and backward perspective is a matter of the *Wire*'s status as a work of fiction. Such a feeling is one enabled by the openness of the fictional form, however fact based it is in this instance, since that ability to build on and embellish the details of an idealized past derives from the writer's *imagining* another, better day.

By elaborating his show as one about the decline of the United States, Simon focuses our attention on what he feels are the components—both micro and macro—that define that retrenchment, and the spatial and historical aspects of it. On the macro level, there is an indictment of our failing public institutions, including politics, the legal system, the schools, and our ways of attaining information about the world. The malaise that *The Wire* dramatically presents most pressingly implicates the poorer classes, but in doing so suggests how the world that afflicts those without means creates social conditions that affect all. For example, in season 1, the emptying out of people and commerce from West Baltimore creates an environment of desperation in which the drug trade flourishes. And certainly the evils of drug addiction are not confined to the lower classes. Indeed, in season 2, we see beleaguered dockworkers increasingly caught up in the destruction of drug use. In season 4, the failure of the schools creates the situation in which a young man such as Michael can become a social scourge, afflicting and endangering untold victims from all walks of life. Simon has made his pessimism clear: "I would be happy to find out that *The Wire* was hyperbolic and ridiculous, and that the 'American Century' is still to come. I don't believe it, but I'd love to believe it, because I live in Baltimore and I'm an American. I want to sit in my house and see the game on Saturday along with everybody else. But I just don't see a lot of evidence of it."[4]

Simon's invoking of the show's location emphasizes the link between Baltimore and the rest of the nation. Though the show's repeated focus on one city provides a specific map and set of historical circumstances with which to test the show's relationship to a palpable reality, nothing that happens over the five seasons has not happened or could not happen in many other US urban centers. Baltimore, then, becomes a microcosm of more general decline. It allows us to see the relative isolation of areas beleaguered by poverty and historical racism, but it also shows us how that isolation is only relative. In season 4, we see that West Baltimore is only a short car ride away from the gentrified Inner Harbor. In season 2, condos are planned for areas abutting the piers where women were shipped in containers.

Simon's view is indicative of his definition of the dystopic present. That is, he catalogues in the five seasons of *The Wire* the many ways in which the present has become the site of a social life organized by the greedy and powerful, a situation that renders progressive impulses moot. But does that vision also contain a glimmer of a more hopeful future? This seems an apt question in light of the mass of evidence to the contrary. The further question one might ask of *The Wire*—as a production and as a sprawling narrative—is whether it produces a kind of documentary heft that is, in the end, both demoralizing and a source of inaction in response to the social ills it characterizes—broadly, those caused by racism and economic inequality.

Season 5 is a retrospective for the series as a whole in that it situates *The Wire* in the world that occurs after the relative demise of a city's newspaper. This world is, in addition, one defined by that which David Harvey has termed the regime of flexible accumulation and the cultural force of postmodernism. In keeping with these broad definitions of the 2000s, the season discusses a representational medium—the newspaper—that apparently shows us the domain of the actual and temporally proximate; conversely, it also discusses the crisis in conveying and disseminating information about that reality through that institution. One of the cruxes of the season is how that underresourced medium fails to cover the metropolis yet thoroughly covers things that are not there, namely, the homeless serial killer. And if the newspaper does not (and perhaps cannot) document life as it is, and if it also engages in documenting life as it is not, then what institution will assume the responsibility of informing the general public of significant civic affairs?

As noted in the previous chapter, the years since 1990 have not been kind to that type of enterprise, a trend that has become more pronounced lately as even the most prominent and successful newspapers have downsized both their staffs and the physical dimensions of their newspapers. Increasingly, journals have put paywalls around their online content in an effort to maintain economic viability.[5] The result of this, of course, has been reduced access for a general public. But not only is access a problem. As noted in the previous chapter, Simon views these financial difficulties as resulting in an erosion of mission. The urban daily survives in a shell-like state, but its impact, at least in the world that Simon imagines, ceases to be what it once was.

This emphasis on the impact of the macroeconomic changes of the last decades on the daily newspaper suggests both the destructiveness of neoliberalism for civic institutions and the centrality of the newspaper in civic life. As a screed against the specifically urban ravages of neoliberalism, *The Wire*, then, would seem to point toward a resolution that moves away from the pillars of that social theory. In the explicit realm of the newspaper, clearly an object of importance for Simon, he has spoken frequently and fairly extensively against the very thing that season 5 seems to endorse the commoning of the daily newspaper. He has persistently argued that in order to remain viable, Web-based sites connected to daily newspapers must have paywalls; that is, access to the news must be restricted, with none but subscribers able to view the content of an online journal. He has also argued that it was the complacency of an industry defined by single-paper monopolies in urban locales that led to the decline of the product, a decline fostered by the cupidity and greed of those owners, at first local and then absentee. As a result, when viable electronic competition emerged, the daily paper was no longer a commodity with significant value.[6]

This is a viable argument, but is, again, limited in its scope. Season 5's view of journalism in the early twenty-first century, especially when linked with the context of the four prior seasons, provides a much larger and more complex discussion. Simon's vision of the newspaper industry seems connected with these earlier seasons in that it shows neoliberalism and its attendant ethos subsuming all institutions in its path. But in its nostalgia, season 5 fails to note, as others have, that the commercial press has always suffered from inherent contradictions, and that the apparently dichotomous construction of the public and the private assumes a certain market situation of all things of value, the question being which master will be served.

The distinction between private and public was vexed for much of the twentieth century, and was far more so in the early twenty-first. As we well know, distinctions between that which is owned by the government and that which is owned by private and commercial entities can be extremely slippery in an age when the US Post Office is a quasi-private corporation, and when Medicare plans can be administered by private insurers. The concept of the newspaper—as a public trust owned by private entities—harks back to the first newspapers in the country and calls to mind the Franklinian notion of doing good to do well. But that exists as an idealized relationship between deed and outcome and is by no means a necessity of commerce. Even in the mid-twentieth century, a period valorized in this season, a newspaper had to turn a profit in order to survive, and evening dailies were vanishing in the 1950s and even more so in the 1960s as readership and advertising dollars gravitated toward morning editions. More broadly, Simon sees that erosion as emblematic of a broader disruption of the public sector. He explains that "it might have sprung from a journalistic impulse," but he "moved beyond simple reportage." Instead, it was more like a "big op-ed piece," and viewers should "consider it to be dissent." And according to Simon, the interconnectedness of the seasons reflects his view of the city's overall decline: "What I saw happen with the drug war, a series of political elections, and vague attempts at reform in Baltimore. . . . What I saw happen to the Port of Baltimore, and what I saw happen to the Baltimore *Sun*—I think it's all of a piece."[7]

Such statements seem to contradict the political content of his statements on the future of the newspaper, or at least to mitigate them. In the last comment, he defines the fate of the *Sun* as symptomatic of the social and cultural milieu of the 1990s and 2000s. More broadly, he asserts that which is dramatized at various points in *The Wire*: the political class is beholden to those with significant capital, so elections are bought, as are the elected. When we see the means by which moneyed interests funnel cash into the coffers of politicians and the policy results of such contributions, there can be little doubt about why condominiums get built on the site where a grain pier, if constructed, would have provided many working-class jobs. In season 5 the case of Clay Davis provides an extreme example, but his skullduggery is emblematic of the broader definition of "public service" that pervades the series.

Again, if we situate the newspaper as a key component of a revived public sphere, one that keeps the political class accountable, a couple of questions arise: Who shall gather the news? How shall it be disseminated in order to keep it both vital and unencumbered by the devices of the market, devices that restrict it both in definition and availability? Certainly, the answer would not be to revert to an earlier-century model of elite stewardship by moguls. Many news stories and beats were deemed not worthy of coverage in the first half of the twentieth century: racial discrimination by corporations and government, the collusion that led to blacklists in major industries in the 1950s (including in the entertainment industry), the elimination of women from professions, and others. In its current form in the service of capital, the journal abrogates its historical mission and ignores its complementary definition as a means of informing the public. In its reduction of mission, the newspaper in its current state suggests a related conundrum: as public space increasingly vanishes, both actually and conceptually, then what constitutes necessary common knowledge and experience? Is there a defined public for a body of information that will allow it to define itself as an informed polity?

Despite Simon's pragmatic acceptance of the commodified definition of the newspaper and its product, the news, there is a way of seeing public information as something other than a commodity belonging to the highest bidder. Within the broader contours of *The Wire*, the conceptual space formerly defined by the daily newspaper has been all but eradicated by the logic of neoliberalism and its attendant fetish for privatization: which is not to say that the newspaper has ever been anything but a privately held entity. But even as a privately owned entity, it defined a certain cognitive space that could be defined as public—though not owned by the state or even definable as a commodity—and to borrow a term from Michael Hardt and Antonio Negri, it articulated a "common" sphere of knowledge and information. In their intriguing study *Commonwealth*, Hardt and Negri, as noted in the last chapter, provide a term that disrupts the market assumptions involved in the private-public mode of conceptualization. They define the concept, called the "common," as a space of infinitely available—though not infinite in quantity—resources, a space "on a different plane from the public and private . . . fundamentally autonomous from both . . . the locus of freedom and innovation that stands against private control."[8] The "common," as Hardt and Negri conceive it, exists in the undefined fabric of culture and information, and in some formulations, it can constitute vital knowledge. They write of the need to keep separate "the common—such as common knowledge and common culture—and the public institutional arrangements that attempt to regulate access to it."[9] For these theorists, the domain of the common is essential, and it constitutes whatever is involved in producing knowledge (vital to production) but is outside the realm of private property, including intellectual property.

Such a concept allows for a counterreading of Simon's often-nightmarish historical emphases, enabling us to envision vital civic phenomena—particularly the press—as constitutive of a sphere that retains a utopian strain definable as capitalism's other, an entity that stands outside the binary of public and private ownership. If we extract the concept of news from that of private media entities, it becomes the provenance of the common. That is, there exists an entity that we can call germane information. Citizens may partake of it as a means of enhancing and producing an alternative civic life, one that we can tease out of the dystopian social carnage of the aggregated five seasons. Although Hardt and Negri's formulations tend to project toward the utopian, they potentially have the power of freeing us from the grip of nostalgia and hopelessness.[10] And while the notion of an *immaterial* common is most germane in regard to season 5, it is also possible to look at seasons 2 through 4 as at least gesturing toward that formulation.

Through this conceptual lens, the emphasis on the homeless and their placeless-ness that marks season 5 becomes a broader lament for the absence of a common that can allow for the existence and sustenance of those who have no role or investment in the productive economy. It suggests the ethics of a world that recognizes the necessity of the ready availability of the constituent qualities of life—shelter, water, food. That sentiment can also be seen as an explicit part of other seasons: in the decline of common knowledge and the public school in season 4; in the decline of common work, work with dignity and an ample recompense—unionized labor—in season 2; and in the decline of common space, including *public* housing as a result of gentrification in season 3.

The Wire has repeatedly been compared to a Victorian novel, and to one by Dickens at that.[11] But it is much more like the naturalistic novels that emerged in the early twentieth century. By noting affinities between *The Wire* and naturalistic works of fiction, we may see the force and limits of its cultural critique, as well as how we might redirect that critique and amplify it. Naturalistic novels, like Simon's television series, have their basis in the documentary impulse. As this emphasis developed, works such as Stephen Crane's *Maggie, A Girl of the Streets* (1893), Kate Chopin's *The Awakening* (1899), Theodore Dreiser's *Sister Carrie* (1900), Frank Norris's *The Octopus* (1901), Upton Sinclair's *The Jungle* (1906), and somewhat later novels such as Abraham Cahan's *The Rise of David Levinsky* (1917), and Dreiser's *American Tragedy* (1925)—among others—have at their center a documentary impulse, and all have a central cultural or economic condition around which they structure their narratives.[12] Each also has the death of a central character at its center, an affirmation of the overwhelming power of entrenched social forces to restrict an individual's arc of existence and, more profoundly, his or her ability to alter social life significantly. Arguably, these novels were a response to the consolidation of social possibilities that occurred in the wake of large-scale industrialization and urbanization, as well as the many social ills that emerged around those events, including economic inequality. The naturalistic form persisted in many guises through the twentieth century and regained a kind of significance during the era of the Depression, the 1930s, including the much-read and much-honored *Grapes of Wrath* (John Steinbeck, 1939) and *Native Son* (Richard Wright, 1940). *The Wire* reiterates elements of this form in many of its core features, which are made more salient and immediate through their visual presentation. Like naturalistic novels, it is about the ways in which large institutions cease to serve the interests of a general populace, and about the ruinous impact of this disservice on individuals and the broader social fabric.[13]

Analogies between the early twentieth century and the early twenty-first abound: a return to laissez-faire economics, the resulting massive social and economic inequality, and a broad sense that the system works only for those with amassed social capital and power. *The Wire* succeeds in repurposing the naturalistic form as a means of at least abutting and possibly superseding the anemic social insights of the corporatized primary organs of mass communication. Problematic, however, is its status as a commodity and a property of that corporatized media, in this case HBO. Despite the proprietary interest of this media corporation, there is still a quasi-public space (or common) that the show, in all of its poetic and economic complexity, may occupy. In that broader circulation of text and the resulting public discussion, it may become an aspect of the commons.

The Wire as an HBO production begins to function in ways that recall an older enterprise of news dissemination, but through clearly twenty-first-century devices, a means that relies on niche audiences, on quasi-public–quasi-private networks, and on the fictional form. The series was insulated from the brutality of the marketplace by its corporate sponsors. It was far from a hit and never won an Emmy; yet HBO allowed it to run for five full seasons. It is clearly a compelling and informing series that the network chose to support as a prestige production. It is very difficult to see this act of relative corporate largesse as a kind of "commoning," but Simon's show was not subject to the kind of fiduciary scrutiny that afflicts both the fictional and the actual *Baltimore Sun*. It therefore enters the public sphere and achieves a kind of trickle-down fame, notoriety, and effect. And indeed, through the conceptual lens afforded by Hardt and Negri, we can extract the insights of Simon's series from its particular corporate ownership.

Harvey further develops this idea of the *process* of delineating the common, in which the perspective of recognizing what may be viewed as lying outside the economic logic of the time may constitute a kind of social act that precedes an alternative politics. For our purposes, Harvey's idea of a "social process of commoning" is particularly useful: "This practice produces or establishes a social relation with a common whose uses are either exclusive to a social group or partially or fully open to all and sundry. At the heart of the practice of commoning lies the principle that the relation between the social group and that aspect of the environment being treated as common shall be both collective and non-commodified—off limits to the logic of market exchange and market valuations."[14] By commoning the news, for example—or the school in season 4, or the port in season 2—one need not entrust it to either a public or a private entity; it might exist strictly for a broad notion of the public weal and might be conceived of in that way.

Harvey defines the common as that which, functionally, belongs to no particular entity. He provides the example of a community garden, a plot of land within an urban zone that typically has reverted to the city as a result of its deeded owner ceasing to pay taxes over a period of time. For most owners, this is a market-based decision. The land is judged to be less valuable than the cost of maintaining title to it. Indeed, in all five seasons of *The Wire*, we see lot after lot of such property and in season 3, Hamsterdam was exactly this type of land. But, despite its juridical status as public land, the community garden exists as an entity that is available to anyone, even if not to everyone—because of its limits as a resource—and the fact that its produce may be sold does not reduce it to a market-based commodity. Similarly, the news may exist as a common trust without being owned by the state. In approaching the news as a public trust rather than a commodity, we begin to seize upon other ways of defining the public: ways that do not see it simply as a domain controlled by a political class and therefore subject to being subsumed by private, for-profit interests.[15] Such a funding system would not be a direct subsidy but a steady stream of unassailable public funding—in effect, a dedicated trust. Such a funding stream, if it could be exacted and placed outside politics, would resemble the financial setup of the BBC in the 1950s and 1960s, which was provided revenues through a television licensing fee. Then the idea of informing the public through the results of diligent inquiry could become a kind of professional model, though I am not putting forth the BBC of that era, with all of its biases of class and race, as an ideal.[16] But even more broadly, I am suggesting that we common the cultural critique embedded in the series in order to place it outside the show's commodity status and, in doing so, to define an active viewing audience resistant to the potential inertia caused by the weight of its considerable critique.

By looking at the series through a more active interpretive lens, we can mitigate an ethos that defines institutional ethics and law as necessarily correct. Rather, in a revised perspective we can see that such views are merely reflective of a corrupted bureaucracy; if we therefore reconsider some of the wrongdoers that Simon created, they may become heroic resisters, a view that Simon at least teases us to consider. This vision opens up a means of reconceiving the many acts of resistance that punctuate the five seasons, including the gestures of McNulty and Freamon in season 5. What appears as lawlessness and a waste of resources when these two detectives concoct a serial killer preying on the homeless easily becomes a heroic act of civil disobedience that has as its design, in effect, reappropriating power to the lower echelons of the bureaucracy and marshaling resources for legitimate investigations. The officers use the debased newspaper for their own purposes, but they are not the corruptors of that institution; rather, they simply employ it in its corrupted state. Such a recasting of *The Wire*'s central plot problem in many of the seasons allows us to reread the series' ethical arc and to see what otherwise might look like illegal or immoral actions as moral actions deemed illegal because of the many ways in which public stewards fail to imagine, and therefore fail to serve, the public. This shift in the locus of authority defines a kind of anarchic urge to reimagine a commons at the point where that reimagining takes the most conceptual effort. In some ways, *The Wire* can be seen as a gesture toward the consideration of civil disobedience in response to a thoroughly bureaucratized civic life put in the service of private interests.

In such a view, extreme as it might be, Frank Sobotka becomes a hero, attempting to repurpose the Baltimore waterfront for the working class and to keep it from development by private interests. Similarly, in season 3, Bunny Colvin reappropriates derelict space in order to create a drug commons, one insulated from the punishments of the state and one that, as suggested by others besides Colvin, with the cooperation of public health services could become a safe zone for drug use and, ultimately, the care and treatment of addicts. In season 4, we are able to see Pryzbylewski's moving his occupation from policing to schooling as a means of providing an earlier intervention into the lives of urban youths and an effort to repurpose the schools toward actual education. An act of reappropriation of the classroom occurs when he is instructed to help his students cram for the state exams, but instead subverts the directive by continuing his more relevant instruction.

Simon affirms that the show is about the passing of an era of US primacy.[17] Such a vision of ebbing US power need not be suffused with despair. It is possible to view the show not only as a lament for a social world gone awry, but also as a suggestion of a world that may yet come from the wreckage. The distinction between reportage and the broader possibilities of fiction is one that Simon affirms frequently. He makes this explicit in an interview: "In journalism, of course, you have to quote people accurately. When people have verbal idiosyncrasies, your job is not to clean those up. You're almost being clinical about how people talk, to be fair to the material. That was peculiarly good training for developing an ear. My ability to meet people on their own terms and gather not only facts but voices, mood, character and spirit. That comes out of reporting."[18] So without the imposed boundaries of journalism, one can go far more deeply into character and situation, since the writer is not constrained by the narrow limits of the actual. The narrative possibilities allow for more editorializing and potentially more resonance. In season 5, it is the confusing of these two types of writing that makes Scott Templeton morally questionable. For the reduced compass of journalism, he substitutes the more open expressions of fiction, without noting the important distinctions between them. In creating a fiction that he asserts as fact, he fools public servants into providing resources to solve a crime that was never committed. In the relative fluidity of the fictional form, the ideological emphases of the show emerge. But those assertions are nuanced and at times contradictory. Despite *The Wire*'s factual basis, its status as fiction is what creates its social resonance and textual density. Simon's fiction is distinct from Scott Templeton's in its hewing closer to the facts of social reality and in its willing assumption of a social mission. Simon believes in the political efficacy of his dramatic critique. According to Margaret Talbot: "Simon makes it clear that the show's ambitions were grand. *The Wire* is dissent, he says. It is perhaps the only storytelling on television that overtly suggests that our political and economic and social constructs are no longer viable, that our leadership has failed us relentlessly, and that no, we are not going to be all right."[19] Unlike Scott's free-floating tales, Simon's fiction seeks not to titillate, but to inform; and it is in his devotion to that mission and its dramatic portrayal that the series suggests a path to a different world.

As Simon tells us, *The Wire* invites us to see how it is not a found aspect of the world, but a narrative sutured together strategically that employs elements we may find in the world. For example, the character of Omar increasingly takes on the aura of a legend out of the idealized image of the Old West. (He repeatedly refers to his code; he survives all kinds of murder attempts; his name is whispered on the street.) Further, the editing that often emphasizes the spatial gaps between scenes, and the final shots of McNulty cosmically looking out over the whole of the city, both signal the prospect of a kind of reflexive reading. That is, they provide a means for a viewer to distance himself or herself and achieve an awareness of the machinations of the narrative, to break its hypnotic effect and develop an active, analytical angle of apprehension. Such a view moves toward questions of "what if" and "what else might be." Such a reading strategy, then, provides a means to undo its apparent determinism, empowering its viewers to develop the kind of critical consciousness it dialectically suggests.

Notes

INTRODUCTION

1. See Weisberg, "*The Wire* on Fire: Analyzing the Best Show on Television"; Welsh et al., "Is This the Best TV Series Ever Made?"; Wilde, "The Wire Named No. 1 TV Show Of All Time By Entertainment Weekly."

2. *The Wire: Truth Be Told*, compiled by Rafael Alvarez, a writer for the show and a former colleague of David Simon's at the *Baltimore Sun*, is largely a collection of the shooting scripts of the five seasons of the show; it also includes some brief essays and reflections by those involved in writing and production. For example, it includes an interview with the famous Baltimore drug dealer Little Melvin Williams, who, in part, provided the inspiration for Avon Barksdale, the major drug dealer, and a focal figure, of the first three seasons. Williams also has a small part as the deacon in seasons 3 and 4. Although a valuable collection, it is a very different type of companion from what I am proposing here. Indeed, it would complement my own, since it mainly refers to aspects of the show rather than interpreting them. Lacking the system and the intellectual scope of my project, it would be less valuable than mine for viewers with probing questions about emphases and historical references. For other able treatments, see Potter and Marshall, *The Wire: Urban Decay and American Television*; Busfield and Owen, *"The Wire" Re-Up: The "Guardian" Guide to the Greatest TV Show Ever Made*; Kennedy and Shapiro, *"The Wire": Race, Class, and Genre*; L. Williams, *On "The Wire."* There are also excellent essay treatments of the show in print and online. These include a special issue of *Criticism* (Summer and Fall 2010, nos. 3 and 4), which includes notable contributions by Fredric Jameson, Mark Anthony Neal, and Paul Farber; a thread in *Critical Inquiry* (Autumn 2011) includes an essay cowritten by William Julius Wilson and Anmol Chadha, as well as a number of astute responses to that essay; and a number of very good essays published online in *Dark Matter: In the Ruins of Imperial Culture*, May 2009. There have also been smart and engaging treatments in the *New Yorker*, the *Atlantic*, *Dissent*, and the *New York Review of Books*. Also notable are Toscano and

Kinkle, "Baltimore as World and Representation: Cognitive Mapping and Capitalism in 'The Wire'"; Kinder, "Re-Wiring Baltimore: The Emotive Power of Systemics, Seriality, and the City"; and Sheehan and Sweeney, "*The Wire* and the World: Narrative and Metanarrative." Single-author books about the show include Vint, *The Wire*, and L. Williams, *On "The Wire"* (mentioned above).

3. Schmoke, "*The Wire* and the Real Baltimore."

4. For a discussion of *The Wire* that, ultimately, emphasizes its status as a generic melodrama, see L. Williams, *On "The Wire."* Williams argues forcefully that the show's use of melodramatic tropes and ethnographic observations are what make extraordinary television: "The dramatic form forged out of the multisited ethnographic imaginary of this sixty-hour work can best be described as serial melodrama with occasional overtones of tragedy" (17). Williams's approach is quite different from my own, both in broad method and focus. I am less concerned with the show's generic emphasis than with its season-by-season sociohistorical commentary, a commentary that includes a significant spatio-geographic component.

5. See Navasky, *Naming Names*, 80–83; Langdon, *Caught in The Crossfire: Adrian Scott and the Politics of Americanism in 1940s Hollywood.*

6. For insightful discussions of this cycle of radical films, see Hirsch, "Film Gris Reconsidered"; Maland, "Crime, Critique and Cold War Culture, 1951."

7. See Jakobson "On Realism in Art."

8. *Telegraph*, "The Wire: Arguably the Greatest Television Programme Ever Made."

9. For very good treatments of the show's demographic, see Walters, "*The Wire* for Tourists"; Salam, "*The Wire* as High Art."

10. For discussions of teaching *The Wire*, see Bennett, "This Will Be on the Midterm. You Feel Me? Why So Many Colleges Are Teaching *The Wire*"; Mittell, "Teaching *The Wire.*"

11. See Alvarez, *The Wire*, 13–21.

12. Ibid., 19.

13. Quoted in Talbot, "Stealing Life: The Crusader behind *The Wire.*" More broadly, Brett Martin catalogues Simon's central but not monolithic role in the creation and execution of the show over its many years; see Martin, *Difficult Men: Behind the Scenes of a Creative Revolution; From "The Sopranos" and "The Wire" to "Mad Men" and "Breaking Bad,"* 133–153.

14. Currently, most Baltimoreans are African Americans, and most poor Baltimoreans are African American. That there is a racial component to poverty in the city makes it similar to all US cities. In 2000, Baltimore's population was 64.3 percent African American and 31.6 percent white (Baltimore Census Data). This demographic picture is important for recognizing the fact-based reasons for the preponderance of African American characters in the show.

15. In A *Brief History of Neoliberalism*, David Harvey offers a trenchant and lucid treatment of this regime, with a geographer's recognition of the contributing aspect of spatial definition in its execution.

16. Simon, "Down to the Wire."

17. For apt discussions of the processes of globalized trade and the costs that it imposes on urban centers, see Sassen, *The Global City: New York, London, Tokyo*; M. Smith, *City, State, and Market*; N. Smith, *The New Urban Frontier: Gentrification and the Revanchist City*; Harvey, *Justice, Nature, and the Geography of Difference*; Harvey, *Spaces of Hope*; Harvey, *A Brief History of Neoliberalism*.

18. Orr, *The Politics of School Reform in Baltimore, 1986–1998*, 69–70.

19. Simon, interview by Nick Hornby.

20. See Lemann, *The Promised Land: The Great Black Migration and How It Changed America* (New York: Vintage, 1992). For further discussion, see Jordan, "The Causes of Poverty: Cultural vs. Structural; Can There Be a Synthesis?"; Alterman, "Think Again: Charles Murray and the Power of Mainstream Media Amnesia"; Lemann, "Evening the Odds: Is There a Politics of Inequality?" Lemann interestingly notes Murray's ongoing war against the poor, which continued in his 2013 book, *Coming Apart: The State of White America, 1960–2010*. He lambastes Murray's determinist approach both as theory and as polemic: "'Coming Apart' is, in effect, an analysis of inequality that rules out a program of redistribution. In Murray's view, trying to shift resources away from the élite wouldn't do much good, because (as Murray and Richard Herrnstein argued, in far more detail, in 'The Bell Curve') the élite are genetically endowed with higher intelligence: as long as the United States is a meritocratic society, and as long as these people keep meeting at selective colleges, marrying, and improving their breeding stock, they'll keep doing better than everybody else. Anyway, what the non-élite need isn't money, Murray thinks; it's better values. Very little of 'Coming Apart' is devoted to government policy."

21. E. Friedman, "Vacant Properties in Baltimore: Strategies for Reuse."

22. R. Williams, *The Politics of Public Housing: Black Women's Struggles against Urban Inequality*, 29–37.

23. This historical information is widely available, but it is effectively distilled in "How We Got Here: The Historical Roots of Housing Segregation," on the website of the Leadership Conference on Civil and Human Rights: www.civilrights.org/publications/reports/fairhousing/historical.html.

24. R. Williams, 91–96.

25. See Rae, *City: Urbanism and Its End*, 274–282.

26. See Service Employees International Union, *Putting Baltimore's People First*, the chapter "A Brief Economic History of Modern Baltimore, available from the journal *Chicken Bones*, www.nathanielturner.com/robertmooreand1199union3.htm.

27. The best expressions of this view are Lemann, *Promised Land* and Murray, *Losing Ground: American Social Policy, 1950 to 1980*. Lemann is not nearly so scholastic or reductive as Murray, but both point strongly to "the culture of poverty" thesis. See also Jones, "Southern Diaspora: Origins of the Northern 'Underclass'"; Katz, "The Urban 'Underclass' as a Metaphor of Social Transformation."

28. Soja, *Seeking Spatial Justice*, 14–18.

29. Ibid., 17.

30. Agnew, "Space and Place."

31. See Lipsitz, *How Racism Takes Place*, 28.

32. This multidisciplinary approach has developed over the course of some forty years, but there is a clear line, influenced by Lefebvre, from *The Condition of Postmodernity* to *Justice, Nature, and the Geography of Difference*, in which he shows that what Fredric Jameson has called the "cultural dominant" of the postmodern has resulted in significant changes in the way we conceptualize space, and how those reconceptions have a vital economic dimension. This analytical method has developed and become more trenchantly political in a number of more recent works, including Harvey's *Spaces of Hope*, *Spaces of Capital: Towards a Critical Geography*, and *Spaces of Global Capitalism: A Theory of Uneven Geographical Development*.

33. See Harvey, *Brief History of Neoliberalism*; N. Smith, *Uneven Development: Nature, Capital, and the Production of Space*.

CHAPTER 1

1. Alvarez, "Season One: Overview," 48.

2. US Census, "Quick Facts, Baltimore, Maryland."

3. For statistics regarding the police force, see Ashkenas and Park, "The Race Gap in America's Police Departments"; for broader census information, see Baltimore Census Data.

4. See Haglund, "The Visual Style of *The Wire*."

5. This overview is largely gleaned from Simon and Burns, *The Corner*, 62–68.

6. Jameson, "Realism and Utopia in *The Wire*," 360.

7. Dos Passos, *The Big Money*, 460–464.

8. Jones, "Southern Diaspora," 32–33.

9. Simon, "Case Closed."

10. Orser, "Flight to the Suburbs." As the economic reorganization associated with neoliberalism increasingly moves wealth from the lower classes and concentrates it among the wealthy, it affects formerly stable middle-class individuals and their communities. According to Eric Siegel: "Part of Baltimore's demographic story of the 1990s, when it lost more people than any city in America, was that large numbers of middle-class blacks joined middle-class whites in leaving the city. That's why the number of non-Hispanic blacks living in the city, which had risen as the number of whites declined, dropped from 433,705 in 1990 to 417,009 in 2000 and continued to decline in the first two years of this decade. During the 1990s, the city's non-Hispanic white population declined from 284,187 to 201,566" ("White Flight Shows Signs of Declining"). And somewhat counterintuitively, to make up for this loss of taxpayers, the city increasingly granted tax abatements to developers and new property owners. The legacy of reducing the tax liabilities of developers and wealthy

homeowners has a deep structure that goes back to the days when cities despaired over declining populations and particularly "white flight."

11. See Simon and Burns, *The Corner*, 88–99.

12. Wilson, *When Work Disappears*, 58–59.

13. See Joseph, "Soldiers in Baltimore: *The Wire* and the New Global Wars."

CHAPTER 2

1. Simon, "Under the Wire."

2. US Department of Transportation, Research and Innovative Technology Administration, Bureau of Transportation Statistics, *America's Container Ports: Linking Markets at Home and Abroad*, 6.

3. Simon, "Case Closed."

4. Simon, interview by Nick Hornby.

5. Many excellent discussions of Kazan, Schulberg, and the Hollywood blacklist take into account the vexed circumstances of *On The Waterfront*; see Navasky, *Naming Names*; Braudy, *On the Waterfront*; and Rapf, *On the Waterfront*. Marsha Kinder notes this antecedent in "Re-Wiring Baltimore."

6. In April 2010, New Jersey Waterfront officials arrested four ILA officials on charges of extortion; see Waterfront Commission of New York Harbor, "Division of Criminal Justice and Waterfront Commission Arrest Top Union Official in Alleged Shake-Down of Dock Workers." Later headlines asserted that these union bosses were members of the Genovese crime family; see US Attorneys, District of New Jersey and Eastern District of New York, "Genovese Organized Crime Family Soldier and Associates Indicted on Racketeering Charges, Including Extortion of International Longshoremen's Association Members."

7. Simon, interview by Bob Andelman.

8. Sheehan and Sweeney, "*The Wire* and the World"; *Scandalum Magnatum*, "Balzac of Baltimore."

9. Appadurai, *Modernity at Large: Cultural Dimensions of Globalization*, 189; see also Appadurai, *Fear of Small Numbers: An Essay in the Geography of Anger*. Stephen Lucasi notes the connection of this season to Appadurai's writings about space and affiliation in a neoliberal world; see his "Networks of Affiliation: Familialism and Anticorporatism in Black and White."

10. Appadurai, *Modernity at Large*, 191.

11. Harvey, *Enigma of Capital*, 28

12. Harvey, *Spaces of Hope*, 109–113.

13. Ibid., 122.

14. Harvey, *The Enigma of Capital*, 158.

15. Ibid.

16. See Comaroff and Comaroff, "Millenial Capitalism: First Thoughts on a Second Coming"; Harvey, *Brief History of Neoliberalism*.

17. Wikrent, "Yes, Poverty Is Worse Than They Ever Admitted."
18. See Braziel, *Diaspora: An Introduction*, 85–104.
19. Harvey, *Spaces of Hope*, 117–121.
20. Ibid., 117.
21. Gibb and Sabin, "Who Loves Ya, David Simon?"

CHAPTER 3

1. Simon, "David Simon Says."

2. The impact of the demolition of Baltimore's public housing stock has been well documented by the Abell Foundation; its *Annual Report, 2007* reveals that the policy of eliminating publicly owned units has been catastrophic for the city's poor.

3. See L. Friedman, "Public Housing and the Poor: An Overview." Friedman writes with clarity of the shift in public-housing residents after World War II as economic requirements were created to force those in the middle class out of subsidized units in order to make them consumers of the new houses being built in the suburbs. They were replaced by African Americans migrating from the South (650–653).

4. For example, in season 2, we learned that the federal agents were no longer interested in drug dealers, because the post-9/11 landscape had moved them into terrorism and the hobbyhorse of corrupt unions. In season 1, we had some vision of politics when a bag man for the Barksdale syndicate is caught transporting a bag of money to state senator Clay Davis, a figure who plays a larger role in season 3 and an even larger one in season 5. Further, we come to see political pressure put on Commissioner Burrell, who in turn pressures Lieutenant Daniels, to close down the investigation of the Barksdales when they start following the money trail that leads to politicians, including the state's attorney's office. And who is to say that the logic of the free market, in which opportunity for financial gain is seen as an ideal condition, does not at least implicitly condone corruption?

5. See University of Maryland. "What Is Compstat?"

6. See, for example, Higgs, *Depression, War, and Cold War: Studies in Political Economy*; Rothbard, *A History of Money and Banking in the United States*. The focus of the season largely grew out of conversations between David Simon and Ed Burns about the social costs and ultimate failure of the war on drugs. This topic was a subtext in the first season, and even less prominent in the second. But it represents a thought experiment largely driven by Simon and critically agreed to, with many reservations, by Burns. Explains Simon to the reporter Bret McCabe, "We only started thinking about subsequent seasons in the middle of the [first] season as we were working on it." Problems with the entirety of the drug war readily came to mind: "Why does the police department continue to embrace a dysfunctional drug war and manage to solve less and less crime with every year? And what is the political element doing about these things? You can ask the questions spe-

cifically of those institutions, but in the end, the first question you have to ask is, what are we paying attention to?" (Simon, "Case Closed"). Season 3 was on Simon's mind. In a *Salon* interview, he expressed his concerns: "We bought in to a war metaphor that justifies anything. Once you're at war, you have an enemy. Once you have an enemy, you can do what you want. I don't think that the government will ever find a meaningful way to police desire and human frailty. I'm not supportive of the idea of drugs, but what drugs have not destroyed, the war on them has managed to pry apart" (Rothkerch, "What Drugs Have Not Destroyed"). This questioning of default urban drug enforcement policy is at the heart of the season and is clearly linked with Simon's policy concerns.

7. Simon, "David Simon Says."

8. Beilenson and McGuire, *Tapping into "The Wire": The Real Urban Crisis,"* x–xi.

9. Hackworth, *The Neoliberal City: Governance, Ideology, and Development in American Urbanism*, 43.

10. Ibid., 96.

11. Postmodernity is not simply an aesthetic regime. It is a system in which certain styles are redolent of meanings that have implications for all aspects of social and cultural life. Season 3 offers a critique of many of the core assumptions of neoliberal governance and economics. The gist of this political philosophy declares that the public sphere has a very limited economic role and therefore a minimal social function. The complementary economic vision asserts the sanctity of trade without encumbrances, whether those are unions, private or public bureaucracy, or tariffs. The expression of neoliberalism has been to reduce the public sector to its minimum by eliminating and privatizing its services. In a revisiting of the laissez-faire vision of the late nineteenth century, neoliberals believe that the market, if unsullied by the devices of government and other bureaucratic impediments, will provide wealth and social amenities to the most citizens. As David Harvey explains, "The assumption that individual freedoms are guaranteed by freedom of the market is a cardinal feature of neoliberal thinking" (*Brief History of Neoliberalism*, 7). In this vision of economics and governance, the role of the state is reduced to guaranteeing competition and, complementarily, maintaining social order so that disorder does not sully the purity of market forces; see Harvey, *The Condition of Postmodernity*, and Jameson, *Postmodernism*. Jameson asserts that postmodernity ushers in an aesthetic regime that is emblematic of a far more comprehensive cultural and political shift. The razing of the projects not only dispersed the populations of those dismal and dangerous buildings, but also signaled a distinctive change in how one views the state and how one views space.

12. See my discussion of this in *Starring New York: Filming the Grime and Glamour of the Long 1970s*, 103–134.

13. See Waquant, "Crafting the Neoliberal State: Workfare, Prisonfare, and Social Insecurity" and *Punishing the Poor: The Neoliberal Government of Social Insecurity*.

14. That name refers to a nearby railroad cut, but came to refer to the notoriously violent prison itself, which was closed by Governor Martin O'Malley in 2007. See Helderman, "In a Surprise Move, Md. Closes Jessup Prison, Transfers Inmates."

15. See Marx, *Grundrisse*, 538–553; and Harvey, "The Geography of Capitalist Accumulation"; Jessop, "Spatial Fixes, Temporal Fixes, and Spatio-Temporal Fixes," 150.

16. An example of this is the early-nineteenth-century case of Manchester, England, where the looms were located, and rural Alabama, where the cotton was cultivated, largely through slave labor. Faster ships, better roads, and streamlined wagons were devised toward this end. This desire, furthered by technology, as well as by other productive and administrative efficiencies, envisions a more rapid turnover of capital, and the acceleration of turnover is the goal of every capitalist, since circulating capital allows relatively less capital to maximize its effectiveness in the marketplace. Indeed, one of the features of the softball game, a derivation of baseball—which is a relic of the mid-nineteenth century—is that it is of indeterminate duration—unlike, say, American football, in which the clock defines the duration of the game. A baseball game is not over until the last out is recorded: it can theoretically take forever. This introduction of the technology of the timekeeping machine in sports, which occurred later in the nineteenth century, is roughly commensurate with the elaboration of the modern industrial workplace and its fetishization of efficiency. Thus, the game is the game, but each game is distinct.

17. See Adams, *Time*, 136–139.

18. Such a view of regimentation evokes similarities between the space of restriction defined by the penal system and that of the Fordist factory, a situation in which a worker is circumscribed within a system of production and is presumably owned by an employer for the duration of the workday. In such a situation, the worker's disposition to shrink time as a means of dealing with limits of power and, therefore, restrictions of space becomes analogous to Avon's notion of only doing two days. But of course, some workdays feel as if they last forever. And much as the demise of the housing projects did not result in the end of restricted and poor housing—it meant only that housing became more scarce, more expensive, and more precarious—so too the demise of the factory system did not result in free and happy workers; rather, it resulted in casual, nonunionized labor, and a race to the bottom in overall production costs.

CHAPTER 4

1. Simon, "Case Closed."

2. Simon, "The Straight Dope."

3. See, for example, Jackson, "At the Origins of Neoliberalism: The Free Economy and the Strong State, 1930–1947," particularly his discussion regarding the

connection between thinkers such as Hayek and Mises, emphasizing their connection and correction of laissez-faire, and showing that they saw a role for the state in ensuring the inviolability of free markets (130–136). See also Duménil, *Capital Resurgent: Roots of the Neoliberal Revolution*, in particular, part 4, "The Lessons of History" (143–155).

4. Simon, "The Straight Dope."

5. See Hardt and Negri, *Commonwealth*, for a thorough discussion of this idea.

6. In "The Future of the Ghetto," Douglas Massey and Nancy Denton argue that segregation defines a self-contained system of urban poverty and isolation, and that the fact of "American apartheid" need not privilege the explanation of race or class as a primary cause; rather, they point to the synergistic effects of each on the other: "Race and class-based explanations for the underclass are frequently discussed as if they are mutually exclusive. . . . By presenting the case for segregation's present role as a central cause of urban poverty, we seek to end the specious opposition of race and class. We argue that race operates powerfully through urban housing markets and that racial segregation interacts with black class structure to produce a uniquely disadvantaged neighborhood environment for African Americans" (220–221).

7. See, for example, Spencer, "The Social Organism."

8. Catton, "Foundations of Human Ecology," 79; citations in the original have been omitted.

9. See N. Smith, *American Empire: Roosevelt's Geographer and the Prelude to Globalization*. Smith's analysis of the role of geography in the creation of the map of the twentieth century is extraordinary.

10. For a discussion of the role of sociology in devising and affirming the system of racial categories, see Gilroy, *Against Race: Imagining Political Culture Beyond the Color Line*, particularly chapter 1, "The Crisis of Race and Raciology" (39–40), in which he discusses the role of ecology as a concept in codifying race. See also Weikert, *Hitler's Ethic: The Nazi Pursuit of Evolutionary Progress* and *From Darwin to Hitler: Evolutionary Ethics, Eugenics, and Racism in Germany*.

11. For a further gloss on Murray's views, see his home page on the American Enterprise website, an organization funded largely by the far-right coal and dirty-energy baron Koch Brothers, www.aei.org/scholar/charles-murray.

12. Simon, "The Straight Dope."

13. Anderson and Massey, "The Sociology of Race in the United States," 4.

14. Buendía and Ares, *The Production of the East Side, West Side, and Central City School*, 36.

15. Lefebvre, *The Production of Space*, 8–9, 49–57, 285–292.

16. Zhang, "What Is Lived Space?," 221; see also, Elden, *Understanding Lefebvre: Theory and the Possible*.

17. Sassen, *Cities in a World Economy*, 269.

18. Harvey, *Enigma of Capital*, 167.

19. Kunkel, "How Much Is Too Much."

20. Harvey, "Globalization and the Spatial Fix," 26.

CHAPTER 5

1. Simon, "Case Closed."

2. Davis and Brocht, *Subsidizing the Low Road: Economic Development in Baltimore*, 2. The authors assert: "As federal funding to cities declined, Baltimore development officials have had to depend more on other sources, most notably tax expenditures (i.e., targeted reductions in taxes to provide incentives). The city offers a number of tax credits and exemptions and has recently received the go-ahead from the state to use tax increment financing" (16).

3. Project for Excellence in Journalism, *The State of the News Media, 2013*, "Newspapers: By the Numbers."

4. Ibid.

5. Accounts of the doings of such conservative stalwarts of the press—Robert McCormick, Harry Chandler, and Frank Gannett—well contextualize their influence into the 1960s; see, for example, Lichtman, *White Protestant Nation: The Rise of the American Conservative Movement*; Storrs, *The Second Red Scare and the Unmaking of the New Deal Left*; Teel, *The Public Press, 1900–1945*.

6. Deloitte, *Public Sector, Disrupted: How Disruptive Innovation Can Help Government Achieve More for Less*, 41, 3. A section on disruptively innovating higher education offers largely ineffective models as "innovations," including online diploma mills such as DeVry and the University of Phoenix, as models for state institutions (25).

7. Habermas, *The Structural Transformation of the Public Sphere: An Inquiry into a Category of Bourgeois Society*, 18–27.

8. Parsons, "The Professions and Social Structure," 35.

9. Hallin, "Neoliberalism, Social Movements, and Change in Media Systems in the Late Twentieth Century," 46.

10. Alvarez, *The Wire*, 404.

11. Schudson, *Sociology of News*, 110, 169.

12. Lasch, "A Response to Joel Feinberg," 42.

13. As in the case of Christopher Hitchens, Christopher Lasch's critique of US liberalism moved him further and further to the political right as his life went on. It is no accident that the culturally right *New Criterion* offered an appreciation by the culture warrior Roger Kimball a year after Lasch's death, in April 1995. According to Kimball, "Lasch is at his Arnoldian best when he observes that tolerance for diversity does not require a lowering or selective application of standards. 'The latest variation on this familiar theme,' he writes, 'its *reductio ad absurdum*, is that a respect for cultural diversity forbids us to impose the standards of privileged groups on

the victims of oppression.' What this amounts to is 'a recipe for universal incompetence'" ("Christopher Lasch vs. the Elites").

14. Simon, "*The Wire*'s Final Season and the Story Everyone Missed."

15. Scocca, "Deadline U.S.A. '06: Old *Baltimore Sun* Gasps and Leaps."

16. Project for Excellence in Journalism, *The State of the News Media, 2011*. These trends are confirmed in the graphs accompanying the article.

17. Brown, *Edgework: Critical Essays on Knowledge and Politics*, 39–40.

18. Ibid., 43.

19. The broader process of reproduction defined here and often throughout the series is that which Hardt and Negri refer to as "biopolitical," a term derived from Foucault, who employed it to define how bodies became sites of domination in a broad expanse of Western cultural history. Hardt and Negri move this discussion from a consideration of the overarching power of capitalism to reproduce itself, moving from defining the bodily subjectivity of its populations as a site of control, to one showing that it potentially defining a "common," a domain of mutuality that is potentially a bottom-up means of restoring noninstrumental human relations (*Commonwealth*, 172–175).

20. Ibid., 142–149.

21. See Butler, *Precarious Life: The Powers of Mourning and Violence*, particularly 128–152, in which she discusses the salient contemporary definitions and processes of humanization and dehumanization.

22. According to Antonio Tosi, "The homeless in the USA are subject to repression in public spaces on . . . grounds of undesirability. . . . In the US the homeless constitute a general figure of hardship and degradation: the term goes beyond its literal meaning of the lack of a home and assumes the role of a metonym" (Tosi, "Homelessness and the Control of Public Space: Criminalising the Poor?," 231).

CONCLUSION

1. Simon, "Does the News Matter to Anyone Anymore?"

2. See Harvey, *Seventeen Contradictions and the End of Capitalism*, 193 and, more broadly, 182–198.

3. Talbot, "Stealing Life."

4. Simon, "The Straight Dope."

5. For example, the *Washington Post* as a newspaper continues to lose money, while its properties—particularly Kaplan Higher Education—outside the news business continue to profit; see Kirkman, "Washington Post Co.'s Kaplan Bet May Have Cost It the Paper."

6. Simon, interview by Bill Moyers.

7. Lanahan, "Secrets of the City: What *The Wire* Reveals about Urban Journalism"; ellipsis points in the original.

8. Hardt and Negri, *Commonwealth*, 282.

9. Ibid., 282.

10. See Harvey, *Rebel Cities: From the Right to the City to the Urban Revolution* and *Brief History of Neoliberalism*; see also Hardt and Negri, *Commonwealth*, 272–273.

11. See L. Williams, "How *The Wire* Is, and Isn't, 'Dickensian'"; Berlatsky, "*The Wire* Was Really a Victorian Novel"; Colman, "*The Wire* as Great Victorian Novel."

12. See Kelleter, "*The Wire* and its Readers." According to Kelleter: "Many ruling assumptions of the series . . . derive from the [American] naturalism's philosophical investment in scientism, antigentility, and determinism" (137).

13. I am aware that these novels may be viewed as cathartic, since their tragedies may provoke readers' sympathies. But social rebellion failed to occur in light of their illumination of circumstances, and even Upton Sinclair concluded that he had failed to reach readers' hearts, hitting only their stomachs. See Corkin, *Realism and the Birth of the Modern United States: Literature, Cinema, and Culture*; Michaels, *The Gold Standard and the Logic of Naturalism*.

14. Harvey, *Rebel Cities*, 73.

15. Commentators have discussed a kind of commoning of the news as a viable possibility. For example, Ezra Klein writes in support of some kind of public funding, citing the BBC and NPR as examples: "The question, then, is whether we want newspapers (and magazines and so forth) so agonizingly vulnerable to these [market] pressures. The news, after all, is not a market good. Among other things, it is not profitable to sell it. But we think society needs it. Cross-subsidization from advertising and classifieds worked so long as they worked. Those days are over" ("Should Newspapers Be Funded By the Government?").

16. See, for example, Cowan and Westphal, *Public Policy and Funding the News*.

17. Talbot, "Stealing Life."

18. Littlefield, "David Simon, Reality Writing."

19. Talbot, "Stealing Life."

Bibliography

Abell Foundation. *Annual Report*, 2007. www.abell.org/sites/default/files/publications/ar2007.pdf.

Adams, Barbara. *Time*. Cambridge: Polity, 2004.

Agnew, John. "Space and Place." In *The SAGE Handbook of Geographical Knowledge*, edited by John Agnew and David N. Livingstone, 316–330. London: Sage, 2011. Available at www.sscnet.ucla.edu/geog/downloads/856/416.pdf.

Alvarez, Rafael. "Season One: Overview." In *The Wire: Truth Be Told*, 45–51. New York: Grove, 2009.

———. *The Wire: Truth Be Told*. New York: Grove, 2009.

Alterman, Eric. "Think Again: Charles Murray and the Power of Mainstream Media Amnesia." *American Progress*, February 9, 2012. www.americanprogress.org/issues/media/news/2012/02/09/11159/think-again-charles-murray-and-the-power-of-mainstream-media-amnesia.

Anderson, Elijah, and Douglas S. Massey. "The Sociology of Race in the United States." In *Problem of the Century: Racial Stratification in the United States*, edited by Elijah Anderson and Douglas S. Massey, 1–12. New York: Sage, 2004. https://www.russellsage.org/sites/all/files/anderson_massey_chapter1_pdf.pdf.

Appadurai, Arjun. *Fear of Small Numbers: An Essay in the Geography of Anger*. Durham, NC: Duke University Press, 2006.

———. *Modernity at Large: Cultural Dimensions of Globalization*. Minneapolis: University of Minnesota Press, 1996.

Ashkenas, Jeremy, and Haeyoun Park. "The Race Gap in America's Police Departments." *New York Times*, September 4, 2014. www.nytimes.com/interactive/2014/09/03/us/the-race-gap-in-americas-police-departments.html?_r=0.

Baltimore Census Data. Based on 2000 US Census data. AreaConnect.com, http://baltimore.areaconnect.com/statistics.htm.

Beilenson Peter L., and Patrick A. McGuire. *Tapping into "The Wire": The Real Urban Crisis*. Baltimore: Johns Hopkins University Press, 2012.

Bennett, Drake. "This Will Be on the Midterm. You Feel Me? Why So Many Colleges Are Teaching *The Wire*." *Slate*, March 24, 2010. www.slate.com/articles/arts/culturebox/2010/03/this_will_be_on_the_midterm_you_feel_me.single.html.

Berlatsky, Noah. "*The Wire* Was Really a Victorian Novel." *Atlantic*, September 10, 2012. www.theatlantic.com/entertainment/archive/2012/09/the-wire-was-really-a-victorian-novel/261164.

Braudy, Leo. *On the Waterfront*. London: BFI, 2005.

Braziel, Jana. *Diaspora: An Introduction*. Malden, MA: Blackwell, 2008.

Brown, Wendy. *Edgework: Critical Essays on Knowledge and Politics*. Princeton, NJ: Princeton University Press, 2005.

Buendía, Edward, and Nancy Ares. *The Production of the East Side, West Side, and Central City School*. New York: Lang, 2006.

Busfield, Steve, and Paul Owen, eds. *"The Wire" Re-Up: The "Guardian" Guide to the Greatest TV Show Ever Made*. London: Random House UK, 2010.

Butler, Judith. *Precarious Life: The Powers of Mourning and Violence*. New York: Verso, 2004.

Catton, William. "Foundations of Human Ecology." *Sociological Perspectives* 37, no. 1 (Spring 1994): 75–95.

Colman, Dan. "*The Wire* as Great Victorian Novel." *Open Culture*, March 25, 2011. www.openculture.com/2011/03/the_wire_as_great_victorian_novel.html.

Comaroff, Jean, and John L. Comaroff. "Millennial Capitalism: First Thoughts on a Second Coming." In *Millennial Capitalism and the Culture of Neoliberalism*, edited by Jean Comaroff and John L. Comaroff, 10–16. Durham, NC: Duke University Press, 2001.

Corkin, Stanley. *Realism and the Birth of the Modern United States: Literature, Cinema, and Culture*. Athens: University of Georgia Press, 1996.

———. *Starring New York: Filming the Grime and Glamour of the Long 1970s*. New York: Oxford University Press, 2011.

Cowan, Geoffrey, and David Westphal. *Public Policy and Funding the News*. Los Angeles: Annenberg School for Communication and Journalism, University of Southern California, 2010.

Davis, Kate, and Chauna Brocht. *Subsidizing the Low Road: Economic Development in Baltimore*. With Phil Mattera and Greg LeRoy. Washington, DC: Good Jobs First, 2002. www.goodjobsfirst.org/sites/default/files/docs/pdf/balt.pdf.

Deloitte. *Public Sector, Disrupted: How Disruptive Innovation Can Help Government Achieve More for Less*. GovLab Study. www2.deloitte.com/content/dam/Deloitte/global/Documents/Public-Sector/dttl-ps-publicsectordisrupted-08082013.pdf.

Dos Passos, John. *The Big Money*. New York: Modern Library, 1937.

Duménil, Gérard. *Capital Resurgent: Roots of the Neoliberal Revolution*. Translated by Derek Jeffers. Cambridge, MA: Harvard University Press, 2004.

Elden, Stuart. *Understanding Lefebvre: Theory and the Possible*. London: Continuum, 2004.

Friedman, Eric. "Vacant Properties in Baltimore: Strategies for Reuse." Available from the Abell Foundation, www.abell.org/sites/default/files/files/2003%20Friedman.pdf.

Friedman, Lawrence M. "Public Housing and the Poor: An Overview." *California Law Review* 54, no. 2 (May, 1966): 642–669.

Gibb, Jane, and Roger Sabin. "Who Loves Ya, David Simon?" *Dark Matter*, May 29, 2009. www.darkmatter101.org/site/2009/05/29/who-loves-ya-david-simon.

Gilroy, Paul. *Against Race: Imagining Political Culture beyond the Color Line*. Cambridge, MA: Harvard University Press, 2000.

Habermas, Jürgen. *The Structural Transformation of the Public Sphere: An Inquiry into a Category of Bourgeois Society*. Cambridge, MA: MIT Press, 1991.

Hackworth, Jason. *The Neoliberal City: Governance, Ideology, and Development in American Urbanism*. Ithaca, NY: Cornell University Press, 2006.

Haglund, David. "The Visual Style of *The Wire*." *Browbeat* (blog), *Slate*, April 9, 2012. www.slate.com/blogs/browbeat/2012/04/09/the_wire_s_visual_style_watch_a_video_essay_by_erlend_lavik_video_.html.

Hallin, Daniel. "Neoliberalism, Social Movements, and Change in Media Systems in the Late Twentieth Century." In *The Media and Social Theory*, edited by David Hesmondhalgh and Jason Toynbee, 43–58. New York: Routledge, 2008.

Hardt, Michael, and Antonio Negri. *Commonwealth*. Cambridge, MA: Belknap, 2011.

Harvey, David. *A Brief History of Neoliberalism*. New York: Oxford University Press, 2005.

———. *The Condition of Postmodernity: An Enquiry into the Origins of Cultural Change*. New York: Wiley-Blackwell, 1991.

———. *The Enigma of Capital: And the Crises of Capitalism*. New York: Oxford University Press, 2010.

———. "The Geography of Capitalist Accumulation." In *Human Geography: An Essential Anthology*, edited by John A. Agnew, David N. Livingstone, and Alisdair Rogers, 600–622. New York: Wiley-Blackwell, 1996.

———. "Globalization and the Spatial Fix." *Geographische revue* 2 (2001): 23–30.

———. *Justice, Nature, and the Geography of Difference*. Cambridge, MA: Blackwell, 1996.

———. *Rebel Cities: From the Right to the City to the Urban Revolution*. New York: Verso, 2012.

———. *Seventeen Contradictions and the End of Capitalism*. New York: Oxford University Press, 2014.

———. *Spaces of Capital: Towards a Critical Geography*. New York: Routledge 2001.

———. *Spaces of Global Capitalism: A Theory of Uneven Geographical Development*. London: Verso, 2006.

———. *Spaces of Hope*. Berkeley: University of California Press, 2000.

Helderman, Rosalind S. "In a Surprise Move, Md. Closes Jessup Prison, Transfers Inmates." *Washington Post*, March 19, 2007. www.washingtonpost.com/wp-dyn/content/article/2007/03/18/AR2007031800137.html.

Higgs, Robert. *Depression, War, and Cold War: Studies in Political Economy*. Oakland, CA: Independent Institute, 2006.

Hirsch, Joshua. "Film Gris Reconsidered." *Journal of Popular Film and Television* 34, no. 2 (2006): 82–93.

Jackson, Ben. "At the Origins of Neoliberalism: The Free Economy and the Strong State, 1930–47." *Historical Journal* 53, no. 1 (2010): 129–151.

Jakobson, Roman. "On Realism in Art." In *Language in Literature*, edited by Krystyna Pomorska and Stephen Rudy, 19–27. Cambridge, MA: Belknap, 1987.

Jameson, Fredric. *Postmodernism; or, The Cultural Logic of Late Capitalism*. Durham, NC: Duke University Press, 1992.

———. "Realism and Utopia in *The Wire*." *Criticism* 52, no. 3 (Summer–Fall 2010): 359–372.

Jessop, Bob. "Spatial Fixes, Temporal Fixes, and Spatio-Temporal Fixes." In *David Harvey: A Critical Reader*, edited by Noel Castree and Derek Gregory, 142–166. New York: Wiley-Blackwell, 2006.

Jones, Jacqueline. "Southern Diaspora: Origins of the Northern 'Underclass.'" In *The Underclass Debate: Views from History*, edited by Michael B. Katz, 27–54. Princeton, NJ: Princeton University Press, 1993.

Jordan, Gregory. "The Causes of Poverty: Cultural vs. Structural; Can There Be a Synthesis?" *Perspectives in Public Affairs* 1 (Spring 2004): 18–34. www.asu.edu/mpa/Jordan.pdf.

Joseph, Philip. "Soldiers in Baltimore: *The Wire* and the New Global Wars." *New Centennial Review* 13, no. 1 (2013): 209–240.

Katz, Michael B. "The Urban 'Underclass' as a Metaphor of Social Transformation." In *The "Underclass" Debate: Views from History*, edited by Michael B. Katz, 3–26. Princeton, NJ: Princeton University Press, 1992.

Kelleter, Frank. "*The Wire* and Its Readers." In "*The Wire*": *Race, Class, and Genre*, edited by Liam Kennedy and Steven Shapiro, 33–70. Ann Arbor: University of Michigan Press, 2012.

Kennedy, Liam, and Stephen Shapiro, eds. "*The Wire*": *Race, Class, and Genre*. Ann Arbor: University of Michigan Press, 2012.

Kimball, Roger. "Christopher Lasch vs. the Elites." *New Criterion*, April 1995. Review of *The Revolt of the Elites*, by Christopher Lasch. www.newcriterion.com/articles.cfm/Christopher-Lasch-vs-the-elites-5131.

Kinder, Marsha. "Re-Wiring Baltimore: The Emotive Power of Systemics, Seriality, and the City." *Film Quarterly* 62, no. 2: 54–64.

Kirkman, Donald. "Washington Post Co.'s Kaplan Bet May Have Cost It the Paper." *Huffington Post*, August 6, 2013. www.huffingtonpost.com/2013/08/06/washington-post-kaplan_n_3715396.html.

Klein, Ezra. "Should Newspapers Be Funded by the Government?" *Washington*

Post, July 2, 2009. http://voices.washingtonpost.com/ezra-klein/2009/07/should_newspapers_be_funded_by.html.

Kunkel, Benjamin. "How Much Is Too Much." Review of *The Enigma of Capital: And the Crises of Capitalism*, by David Harvey, and *A Companion to Marx's "Capital,"* by David Harvey. *London Review of Books*, February 3, 2011, 9–14. www.lrb.co.uk/v33/no3/benjamin-kunkel/how-much-is-too-much.

Lanahan, Lawrence. "Secrets of the City: What *The Wire* Reveals about Urban Journalism." *Columbia Journalism Review*, January 10, 2008. www.cjr.org/cover_story/secrets_of_the_city.php?page=all#sthash.5JMK9m4n.dpuf.

Langdon, Jennifer. *Caught in the Crossfire: Adrian Scott and the Politics of Americanism in 1940s Hollywood*. New York: Columbia University Press, 200.

Lasch, Christopher. "A Response to Joel Feinberg." *Tikkun* 3 (May 1988): 41–42.

Leadership Conference on Civil and Human Rights. www.civilrights.org/publications/reports/fairhousing/historical.html.

Lefebvre, Henri. *The Production of Space*. Translated by Donald Nicholson-Smith. Malden, MA: Blackwell, 1992.

Lemann, Nicholas. "Evening the Odds: Is There a Politics of Inequality?" *New Yorker*, April 23, 2012. www.newyorker.com/arts/critics/atlarge/2012/04/23/120423crat_atlarge_lemann.

———. *The Promised Land: The Great Black Migration and How It Changed America*. New York: Vintage, 1992.

Lichtman, Alan. *White Protestant Nation: The Rise of the American Conservative Movement*. New York: Grove, 2009.

Lipsitz, George. *How Racism Takes Place*. Philadelphia: Temple University Press, 2011.

Littlefield, Kinney. "David Simon, Reality Writing." *Writer*, November 13, 2012. www.writermag.com/2012/11/13/david-simon-reality-writing.

Lucasi, Stephen. "Networks of Affiliation: Familialism and Anticorporatism in Black and White." In *"The Wire": Urban Decay and American Television*, edited by Tiffany Potter and C. W. Marshall, 135–148. New York: Continuum, 2009.

Maland, Charles. "Crime, Critique, and Cold War Culture, 1951." *Film Criticism* 26, no. 3 (2002): 1–30.

Martin, Brett. *Difficult Men: Behind the Scenes of a Creative Revolution; From "The Sopranos" and "The Wire" to "Mad Men" and "Breaking Bad."* New York: Penguin, 2013.

Marx, Karl. *Grundrisse*. Translated by Martin Nicolaus. London: Penguin, 1973.

Massey, Douglas, and Nancy Denton. "The Future of the Ghetto." In *Race and Ethnicity in the United States: Issues and Debates*, edited by Stephen Steinberg, 114–126. Oxford: Blackwell, 2000.

Michaels, Walter Benn. *The Gold Standard and the Logic of Naturalism*. Berkeley: University of California Press, 1988.

Mittell, Jason. "Teaching *The Wire*." *JustTV* (blog), February 6, 2009. http://justtv.wordpress.com/2009/02/06/teaching-the-wire.

Murray, Charles. *Coming Apart: The State of White America, 1969–2010*. New York: Crown, 2012.

———. *Losing Ground: American Social Policy, 1950–1980*. New York: Basic Books, 1984.

Murray, Charles, and Richard Herrnstein. *The Bell Curve: Intelligence and Class Structure in American Life*. New York: Free Press, 1994.

Navasky, Victor. *Naming Names*. New York: Viking, 1980.

Orr, Marion. *The Politics of School Reform in Baltimore, 1986–1998*. Lawrence: University Press of Kansas, 1999.

Orser, Edward. "Flight to the Suburbs: Suburbanization and Racial Change on Baltimore's West Side." In *The Baltimore Book: New Views of Local History*, edited by Elizabeth Fee and Linda Shopes, 203–226. Philadelphia: Temple University Press, 1992.

Parsons, Talcott. "The Professions and Social Structure." *Social Forces* 17, no. 4 (May 1939): 458–461.

Potter, Tiffany, and C. W. Marshall, eds. *"The Wire": Urban Decay and American Television*. New York: Continuum, 2009.

Project for Excellence in Journalism. *The State of the News Media, 2011*. Washington, DC: Pew Research Center, 2011. www.stateofthemedia.org/files/2011/07/sotm_final_2011.pdf.

———. *The State of the News Media, 2012*. Washington, DC: Pew Research Center, 2012. www.stateofthemedia.org/overview-2012.

———. *The State of the News Media, 2013*. Washington, DC: Pew Research Center, 2013. www.stateofthemedia.org/2013.

Rae, Douglas W. *City: Urbanism and Its End*. New Haven, CT: Yale University Press, 2003.

Rapf, Joanna, ed. *On the Waterfront*. Cambridge Film Handbooks. New York: Cambridge University Press, 2003.

Rothbard, Murray. *A History of Money and Banking in the United States*. Auburn, AL: Ludwig Von Mies Institute, 2002.

Rothkerch, Ian. "What Drugs Have Not Destroyed, the War on Them Has." *Salon*, June 29, 2002. www.salon.com/2002/06/29/simon_5.

Salam, Reihan. "*The Wire* as High Art." *American Scene*, October 16, 2007. http://theamericanscene.com/2007/10/16/the-wire-as-high-art.

Sassen, Saskia. *Cities in a World Economy*. 4th ed. New York: Sage, 2011.

———. *The Global City: New York, London, Tokyo*. 2nd ed. Princeton, NJ: Princeton University Press, 2001.

Scandalum Magnatum [blog]. "Balzac of Baltimore." January 13, 2008. http://scandalum.wordpress.com/2008/01/13/balzac-of-baltimore.

Schmoke, Kurt. "The Wire and the Real Baltimore." *Guardian*, January 11, 2008. www.theguardian.com/commentisfree/2008/jan/11/thewireandtherealbaltimor.

Schudson, Michael. *The Sociology of News*. New York: Norton, 2003.

Scocca, Tom. "Deadline U.S.A. '06: Old *Baltimore Sun* Gasps and Leaps." *New York Observer*, August 21, 2006.

Service Employees International Union. *Putting Baltimore's People First*. Baltimore: SEIU, 2004.

Sheehan, Helena, and Seamus Sweeney. "*The Wire* and the World: Narrative and Metanarrative." *Jump Cut* 51, Spring 2009. http://ejumpcut.org/archive/jc51.2009/Wire/index.html.

Siegel, Eric. "White Flight Shows Signs of Declining." *Baltimore Sun*, October 16, 2003. http://articles.baltimoresun.com/2003-10-16/news/0310160065_1_white-flight-white-population-north-baltimore.

Simon, David. "Case Closed." Interview by Bret McCabe. *City Paper*, March 12, 2008. www.citypaper.com/news/thewire/bcpnews-case-closed-20150520-story.html#nt=oft09a-7gp1.

———. "David Simon Says." Interview by Jesse Walker. *Reason*, October 2004. http://reason.com/archives/2004/10/01/david-simon-says.

———. "Does the News Matter to Anyone Anymore?" *Washington Post*, January 20, 2008. www.washingtonpost.com/wp-dyn/content/article/2008/01/18/AR2008011802874.html.

———. "Down to the Wire." *Baltimore Magazine*, February 2008. www.baltimoremagazine.net/old-site/arts/2008/02/down-to-the-wire.

———. Interview by Bob Andelman. Mr. Media Radio, May 9, 2007. http://andelman.com/2007/05/by-bob-andelman-david-simonthe-wire.html.

———. Interview by Nick Hornby. *Believer*, August 2007. www.believermag.com/issues/200708/?read=interview_simon.

———. Interview by Bill Moyers. *Bill Moyers Journal*, April 17, 2009. www.pbs.org/moyers/journal/04172009/transcript1.html.

———. "The Straight Dope." Interview by Bill Moyers. *Guernica*, April 1, 2011. https://www.guernicamag.com/interviews/simon_4_1_11.

———. "Under the Wire." Interview by Bret McCabe. *City Paper*, May 28, 2003. www.citypaper.com/news/thewire/bcpnews-under-the-wire-20150520-story.html.

———. "*The Wire*'s Final Season and the Story Everyone Missed," *Huffington Post*, March 17, 2008. www.huffingtonpost.com/david-simon/the-wires-final-season-an_b_91926.html.

Simon, David, and Edward Burns. *The Corner: A Year in the Life of an Inner-City Neighborhood*. New York: Broadway, 1998.

Smith, Michael Peter. *City, State, and Market*. New York: Blackwell, 1988.

Smith, Neil. *American Empire: Roosevelt's Geographer and the Prelude to Globalization*. Berkeley: University of California Press, 2004.

———. *The New Urban Frontier: Gentrification and the Revanchist City*. London: Routledge, 1996.

———. *Uneven Development: Nature, Capital, and the Production of Space*. Oxford: Blackwell, 1986.

Soja, Edward. *Seeking Spatial Justice*. Minneapolis: University of Minnesota Press, 2010.

Spencer, Herbert. "The Social Organism." *Westminster Review*, January 1860. Reprinted in *Spencer's Essays: Scientific, Political, and Speculative*, 3 vols. London: Williams and Norgate, 1891. Available from the Library of Economics and Liberty, www.econlib.org/library/LFBooks/Spencer/spnMvS9.html.

Storrs, Landon R. Y. *The Second Red Scare and the Unmaking of the New Deal Left*. Princeton: Princeton University Press, 2012.

Talbot, Margaret. "Stealing Life: The Crusader behind *The Wire*." *New Yorker*, October 22, 2007. www.newyorker.com/reporting/2007/10/22/071022fa_fact_talbot?currentPage=all.

Teel, Leonard Ray. *The Public Press, 1900–1945*. Westport, CT: Praeger, 2006.

Telegraph. "*The Wire*: Arguably the Greatest Television Programme Ever Made." April 2, 2009. www.telegraph.co.uk/news/uknews/5095500/The-Wire-arguably-the-greatest-television-programme-ever-made.html.

Toscano, Alberto, and Jeff Kinkle. "Baltimore as World and Representation: Cognitive Mapping and Capitalism in 'The Wire.'" *Dossier*, April 8, 2009.

Tosi, Antonio. "Homelessness and the Control of Public Space: Criminalising the Poor?" *European Journal of Homelessness* 1 (December 2007): 221–238.

University of Maryland. "What Is Compstat?" www.compstat.umd.edu/what_is_cs.php.

US Attorneys. District of New Jersey and Eastern District of New York. "Genovese Organized Crime Family Soldier and Associates Indicted on Racketeering Charges, Including Extortion of International Longshoremen's Association Members." Press release, January 20, 2011. http://media.nj.com/ledgerupdates_impact/other/Depiro,%20Stephen%20et%20al.%20Arrest,%20Indictment%20PR.pdf.

US Census. "Quick Facts, Baltimore, Maryland." http://quickfacts.census.gov/qfd/states/24/24510.html.

US Department of Transportation. Research and Innovative Technology Administration. Bureau of Transportation Statistics. *America's Container Ports: Linking Markets at Home and Abroad*. Washington, DC: Government Printing Office, 2011. https://www.rita.dot.gov/bts/sites/rita.dot.gov.bts/files/publications/americas_container_ports/2011/pdf/entire.pdf.

Vint, Sheryl. *The Wire*. Detroit: Wayne State University Press, 2013.

Walters, Ben. "*The Wire* for Tourists?" *Film Quarterly* 62, no. 2 (Winter 2008–2009). www.filmquarterly.org/2008/12/the-wire-for-tourists.

Waquant, Loïc. "Crafting the Neoliberal State: Workfare, Prisonfare, and Social Insecurity." *Sociological Forum* 25, no. 2 (June 2010): 197–220.

———. *Punishing the Poor: The Neoliberal Government of Social Insecurity*. Durham, NC: Duke University Press, 2009.

Waterfront Commission of New York Harbor. "Division of Criminal Justice and Waterfront Commission Arrest Top Union Official in Alleged Shake-Down of

Dock Workers." Press release, April 22, 2010. www.waterfrontcommission.org/newspage31.html.

Weikert, Richard. *From Darwin to Hitler: Evolutionary Ethics, Eugenics, and Racism in Germany*. London: Palgrave MacMillan, 2004.

———. *Hitler's Ethic: The Nazi Pursuit of Evolutionary Progress*. London: Palgrave MacMillan, 2009.

Weisberg, Jacob. "*The Wire* on Fire: Analyzing the Best Show Every Broadcast on Television." *Slate*, September 13, 2006. www.slate.com/articles/news_and_politics/the_big_idea/2006/09/the_wire_on_fire.html.

Welsh, Irvine, Michael Connelly, John Williams, John Harvey, Dreda Say Mitchell, and Mark Billingham. "Is This the Best TV Series Ever Made?" *Observer*, July 19, 2008. www.guardian.co.uk/media/2008/jul/20/television.irvinewelsh.

Wikrent, Tony. "Yes, Poverty Is Worse than They Ever Admitted." *Economic Populist* (blog), October 21, 2009. www.economicpopulist.org/content/yes-poverty-worse-they-ever-admitted.

Wilde, Joe. "*The Wire* Named No. 1 TV Show of All Time by Entertainment Weekly." *Contact Music*, June 30, 2013. www.contactmusic.com/in-depth/the-wire-entertainment-weekly-top-ten-shows-albums-movies_3741091.

Williams, Linda. "How The Wire Is, and Isn't, 'Dickensian.'" *Huffington Post*, July 2, 2014. www.huffingtonpost.com/linda-williams/the-wire-dickens_b_5549385.html.

———. *On "The Wire."* Durham, NC: Duke University Press, 2015.

Williams, Rhonda Y. *The Politics of Public Housing: Black Women's Struggles against Urban Inequality*. New York: Oxford University Press, 2005.

Wilson, William Julius. *When Work Disappears: The World of the New Urban Poor*. New York: Vintage, 1997.

Zhang, Zhongyuan. "What Is Lived Space?" *Ephemera* 6, no. 2 (2006): 219–223.

Index

Page numbers followed by the letter f denote stills from the series.